T0333192

ÉDITION FRANÇAISE
ENGLISH
FOR EVERYONE

MANUEL D'APPRENTISSAGE
NIVEAU ❹ AVANCÉ

AUDIO OFFERT
Site Internet et appli
www.dkefe.com

L'auteur

Victoria Boobyer est auteur indépendant, conférencière et formatrice d'enseignants avec de l'expérience en matière d'enseignement de l'anglais et de la gestion des enseignants. Elle s'intéresse vivement à l'utilisation des lectures graduelles et à celle, judicieuse, de la technologie dans l'enseignement.

Les consultants pédagogiques

Tim Bowen a enseigné l'anglais et formé des enseignants dans plus de trente pays. Il est le coauteur d'ouvrages sur l'enseignement de la prononciation et sur la méthodologie de l'enseignement des langues, et est l'auteur de nombreux ouvrages pour les enseignants d'anglais. Il travaille actuellement comme auteur indépendant de matériels pédagogique, éditeur et traducteur. Il est membre du Chartered Institute of Linguists.

Kate O'Donovan, irlandaise, est titulaire d'un PDGE, et d'une licence d'histoire et d'anglais. Elle a travaillé en Suisse, à Oman et au Bahreïn. Depuis 2014 à Paris, elle enseigne l'anglais au British Council où elle est aussi coordinatrice.

La consultante linguistique

Susan Barduhn est professeur d'anglais et formatrice expérimentée d'enseignants. Elle a, en tant qu'auteur, contribué à de nombreuses publications. Elle donne non seulement des cours d'anglais dans le monde entier, mais est également présidente de l'Association internationale des professeurs d'anglais langue étrangère et conseillère auprès du Conseil britannique et du département d'État américain. Elle est actuellement professeur à la School for International Training dans le Vermont, aux États-Unis.

ÉDITION FRANÇAISE
ENGLISH
FOR EVERYONE

MANUEL D'APPRENTISSAGE
NIVEAU ❹ AVANCÉ

Penguin Random House

Rédacteurs Lili Bryant, Ben Ffrancon Davies
Éditeurs artistiques Daniela Boraschi, Clare Joyce,
Clare Shedden, Michelle Staples
Assistants d'édition Jessica Cawthra, Sarah Edwards
Illustrateurs Edwood Burn, Denise Joos, Clare Joyce,
Michael Parkin, Jemma Westing
Producteur audio Liz Hammond
Rédacteur en chef Daniel Mills
Éditeur artistique en chef Anna Hall
Gestionnaire de projet Christine Stroyan
Concepteur couverture Natalie Godwin
Éditeur couverture Claire Gell
Responsable conception couverture
Sophia MTT
Production, préproduction Luca Frassinetti
Production Mary Slater
Éditeur Andrew Macintyre
Directeur artistique Karen Self
Directeur de publication Jonathan Metcalf

DK Inde
Concepteur couverture Surabhi Wadhwa
Éditeur couvertures en chef Saloni Singh
Concepteur PAO en chef Harish Aggarwal

Publié en Grande-Bretagne en 2016
par Dorling Kindersley Limited
80 Strand, London, WC2R 0RL

Titre original : *English for Everyone. Course Book.
Level 4. Advanced.*

Copyright © 2016 Dorling Kindersley Limited
Une société faisant partie du groupe Penguin Random House

Pour la version française
© 2017 Dorling Kindersley Limited

Adaptation et réalisation : Édiclic
Révision pédagogique : Kate O'Donovan
Traduction : Estelle Demontrond-Box pour Édiclic
Lecture-correction : Paul Cléonie

ISBN: 978-0-2413-0362-7
Imprimé et relié en Chine

UN MONDE D'IDÉES
www.dk.com

Sommaire

Fonctionnement du cours

English for everyone est un ouvrage conçu pour toutes les personnes désireuses d'apprendre l'anglais par elles-mêmes. Comme tout cours de langue, il porte sur les compétences de base : grammaire, vocabulaire, prononciation, compréhension orale, expression orale, compréhension écrite et expression écrite. Ici, les compétences sont enseignées de façon visuelle, à l'aide d'images et de schémas pour vous aider à comprendre et à bien mémoriser. Pour être plus efficace, suivez la progression du livre en veillant à utiliser les enregistrements à votre disposition sur le site Internet et sur l'application. À la fin de chaque unité, vous pouvez effectuer les exercices supplémentaires dans le cahier d'exercices afin de renforcer votre apprentissage.

LIVRE D'EXERCICES

MANUEL D'APPRENTISSAGE

Numéro de chapitre Il vous aide à suivre votre progression.

Les points d'apprentissage Chaque chapitre débute par un résumé des points d'apprentissage clés.

Modules Chaque chapitre est divisé en modules, qui doivent être réalisés dans l'ordre. Vous pouvez faire une pause à la fin de chaque module.

Apprentissage linguistique Les modules avec un fond coloré vous enseignent un nouveau vocabulaire et une nouvelle grammaire. Étudiez-les attentivement avant de faire les exercices.

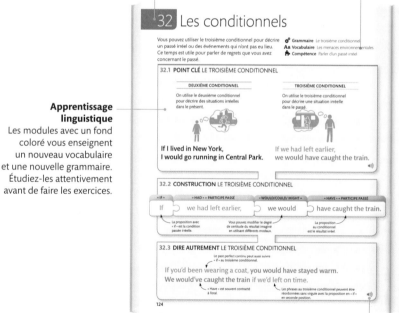

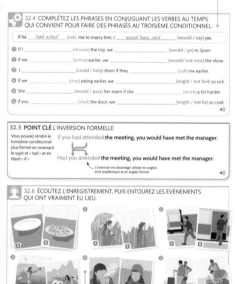

Support audio La plupart des modules sont accompagnés d'enregistrements sonores de locuteurs anglophones pour vous aider à améliorer vos compétences en matière de compréhension et d'expression orales.

Exercices Les modules sur fond blanc vous proposent des exercices destinés à renforcer vos connaissances.

Modules linguistiques

Les nouveaux points sont enseignés de manière progressive : d'abord une explication simple de leur emploi, puis des exemples supplémentaires de leur emploi courant et une explication détaillée de leurs constructions clés.

Numéro de module Chaque module est identifié par un numéro unique qui vous permet d'évaluer votre progression et de trouver facilement les enregistrements associés.

Titre de module Le point enseigné apparaît ici avec une introduction courte.

15.1 POINT CLÉ LE DOUBLE COMPARATIF

Vous pouvez faire des comparaisons pour décrire la cause et l'effet en utilisant deux comparatifs dans la même phrase.

The harder I train, the stronger I get.

Laisse entendre que faire de l'exercice vous rend plus fort.

Exemples linguistiques Les exemples sont contextualisés. La couleur permet de repérer facilement les nouvelles constructions expliquées par des annotations.

15.2 AUTRES EXEMPLES LE DOUBLE COMPARATIF

The worse the children behave, the angrier the teacher gets.

The louder the cat meows, the louder the dog barks.

Guide graphique Des images ou pictogrammes clairs et simples facilitent également l'apprentissage et la mémorisation.

Enregistrements associés Ce symbole indique que les phrases modèles sont disponibles en enregistrements audio.

15.3 CONSTRUCTION LE DOUBLE COMPARATIF

« THE »	EXPRESSION COMPARATIVE	SUJET	VERBE	« THE »	EXPRESSION COMPARATIVE	SUJET	VERBE
The	harder	I	train,	the	stronger	I	get.

Guide de construction Ces aides visuelles permettent de décomposer la grammaire anglaise en éléments simples pour repérer et recréer des constructions, même complexes.

Vocabulaire Tout au long du manuel, vous trouverez des modules de vocabulaire avec des expressions et mots anglais courants et utiles, accompagnés d'images pour vous aider à les mémoriser.

Espace pour écrire Il est recommandé que vous écriviez vous-même les traductions pour conserver une trace à titre de référence.

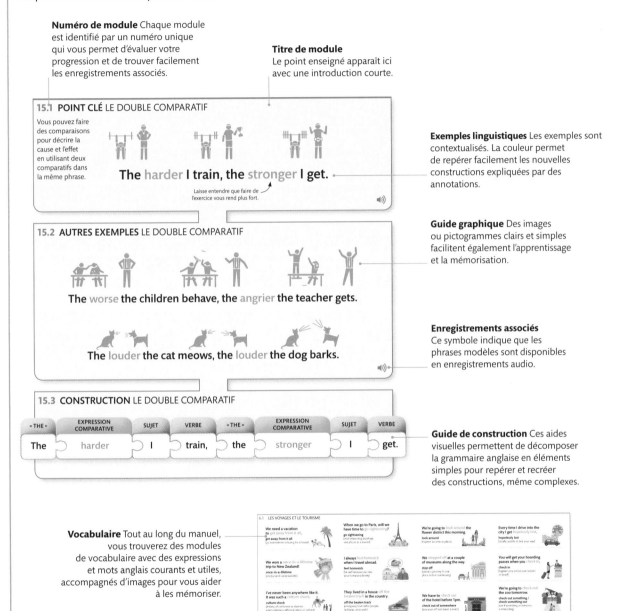

Modules d'exercices

Chaque exercice est soigneusement conçu pour mettre en pratique et tester les nouveaux points linguistiques enseignés dans les chapitres correspondants du manuel d'apprentissage. Les exercices accompagnant le manuel vous aideront à mieux mémoriser ce que vous avez appris et donc à mieux maîtriser la langue anglaise. Chaque exercice est introduit par un symbole indiquant la compétence travaillée.

 GRAMMAIRE
Appliquez les nouvelles règles grammaticales dans différents contextes.

 COMPRÉHENSION ÉCRITE
Étudiez la langue cible dans des contextes anglophones authentiques.

 COMPRÉHENSION ORALE
Évaluez votre niveau de compréhension de l'anglais oral.

 VOCABULAIRE
Consolidez votre compréhension du vocabulaire clé.

 EXPRESSION ÉCRITE
Entraînez-vous à rédiger des textes en anglais.

 EXPRESSION ORALE
Comparez votre anglais oral aux enregistrements audio types.

Numéro de module
Chaque module est identifié par un numéro unique qui vous permet de trouver facilement les réponses et les enregistrements associés.

Consignes des exercices Chaque exercice est introduit par une consigne courte qui vous explique ce que vous devez faire.

57.4 COMPLÉTEZ LES PHRASES AVEC « COULD », « WOULD » OU « WOULDN'T ».

The safari I want to go on lasts four weeks. I wish I _could_ get more time off work.

❶ I wish you _____ criticize my clothes. I think I look fabulous!

❷ My neighbor plays the trumpet all the time. I wish he _____ be a little quieter.

❸ Mike's car always breaks down. He wishes he _____ afford a new one.

❹ We work far too hard. I wish we _____ do this more often!

Exemple de réponse La réponse des premières questions de chaque exercice vous est donnée pour vous aider à mieux comprendre la consigne.

Supports audio Ce symbole indique que les réponses de l'exercice sont disponibles sous forme d'enregistrements audio. Écoutez-les une fois l'exercice terminé.

Supports graphiques
Des images ou pictogrammes sont fournis afin de vous aider à comprendre les exercices.

Espace pour écrire
Il est recommandé que vous écriviez vos réponses dans le livre, à titre de référence pour la suite.

Exercice de compréhension orale Ce symbole indique que vous devez écouter un enregistrement audio afin de répondre aux questions de l'exercice.

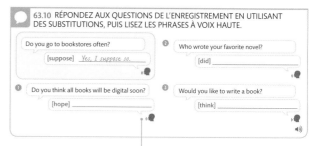

63.10 RÉPONDEZ AUX QUESTIONS DE L'ENREGISTREMENT EN UTILISANT DES SUBSTITUTIONS, PUIS LISEZ LES PHRASES À VOIX HAUTE.

Do you go to bookstores often?
[suppose] _Yes, I suppose so._

❷ Who wrote your favorite novel?
[did] _____

❶ Do you think all books will be digital soon?
[hope] _____

❸ Would you like to write a book?
[think] _____

Exercice d'expression orale
Ce symbole indique que vous devez donner les réponses à voix haute, puis les comparer aux enregistrements fournis dans les fichiers audio.

60.7 ÉCOUTEZ L'ENREGISTREMENT, PUIS INDIQUEZ CE QUI S'EST RÉELLEMENT PASSÉ.

Audio

English for everyone contient de nombreux documents audio. Il vous est recommandé de les utiliser autant que possible, afin d'améliorer votre compréhension de l'anglais parlé et d'acquérir un accent et une prononciation plus naturels. Chaque dossier peut être lu, mis en pause ou répété aussi souvent que vous le désirez, jusqu'à ce que vous soyez sûr d'avoir parfaitement compris ce qui a été dit.

EXERCICES DE COMPRÉHENSION ORALE
Ce symbole indique que vous devez écouter un enregistrement afin de pouvoir répondre aux questions d'un exercice.

AUDIO ASSOCIÉ
Ce symbole indique qu'un enregistrement supplémentaire est à votre disposition une fois le module terminé.

AUDIO OFFERT
Site Internet et appli
www.dkefe.com

Suivez votre progression

La méthode est conçue pour vous permettre de suivre votre progression grâce à des modules d'analyses et des récapitulatifs réguliers. Les réponses aux exercices sont fournies et vous pouvez ainsi vérifier votre compréhension de chaque élément pédagogique.

Check-lists Chaque chapitre se termine par une check-list afin de vérifier les nouvelles compétences apprises.

Modules bilan À la fin de chaque unité, vous trouverez un module bilan plus détaillé résumant les points linguistiques appris.

Cases à cocher Utilisez ces cases pour indiquer les compétences que vous pensez avoir assimilées. Revenez en arrière et retravaillez tout point que vous ne pensez pas encore maîtriser.

Réponses
Trouvez les réponses de chaque exercice à la fin du manuel.

Enregistrements
Ce symbole indique qu'il vous est possible d'écouter les réponses.

Numéros des exercices
Faites-les correspondre avec l'identifiant unique situé au coin supérieur gauche de chaque exercice.

01 Converser

Les verbes ont plusieurs formes au présent, y compris la forme continue et la forme parfaite (perfect). Vous devez comprendre ces différences pour formuler des question tags.

⚙ **Grammaire** Les temps du présent
Aa Vocabulaire Faire de nouvelles rencontres
🧩 **Compétence** Utiliser les question tags

1.1 POINT CLÉ LE PRÉSENT SIMPLE ET LE PRÉSENT CONTINU

PRÉSENT SIMPLE

On utilise le présent simple pour parler de quelque chose qui se produit en général, ou qui fait partie d'une routine quotidienne.

PRÉSENT CONTINU

On utilise le présent continu pour parler de quelque chose qui se produit maintenant et qui va continuer pendant un certain temps.

I usually cycle to work, but today I'm walking instead.

🔊

1.2 RÉCRIVEZ LA NOTE EN CORRIGEANT LES ERREURS SURLIGNÉES.

Hi José,

Today is being my first day in my new job, so I leave the house early. I'm being a bit nervous, but I'm also being very excited! Anyway, I already run late, and I'm needing to leave to catch the bus. Don't be forgetting to pick up some milk on your way home from work tonight!

See you later!

Hi José,

Today is my first day...

1.3 POINT CLÉ LE PRESENT PERFECT ET LE PRESENT PERFECT CONTINU

PRESENT PERFECT	PRESENT PERFECT CONTINU
On utilise le present perfect pour parler du passé proche ou d'expériences générales commencées dans le passé et qui se poursuivent au moment où l'on parle.	On utilise le present perfect continu pour parler d'une action commencée dans le passé mais qui se poursuit maintenant ou qui a des conséquences présentes.

I've **just** started **a new job.** I've been meeting **new people all week.**

🔊

 ## 1.4 COMPLÉTEZ LES PHRASES EN CONJUGUANT LES VERBES AU PRESENT PERFECT OU AU PRESENT PERFECT CONTINU.

I _have been waiting_ (wait) for a bus all morning, but I still _haven't seen_ (not see) one!

1 I _____ (read) for hours. My eyes _____ (start) hurting.

2 Has the mail _____ (arrive) yet? I _____ (expect) a letter all week.

3 My leg _____ (hurt) all day, but I _____ (not see) a doctor yet.

4 Have you _____ (see) my keys? I _____ (look) for them for ages.

5 Have you _____ (hear) about Carl? He _____ (decide) to move.

6 I _____ (finish)! I _____ (write) this essay for ages.

7 Have you ever _____ (visit) France? We _____ (look) at brochures.

8 I _____ (try) to reach Tao all day, but he _____ (not answer) yet.

🔊

13

1.5 POINT CLÉ LES QUESTION TAGS

Si la proposition principale est affirmative, le question tag est à la forme négative, et vice versa. Dans la plupart des cas, le question tag se forme avec « do ».

Les question tags sont de courtes questions ajoutées à la fin d'un énoncé dans une conversation informelle.

You like **meeting new people,** don't you?

You don't like **meeting new people,** do you?

Si le verbe principal est « be », on utilise aussi « be » dans le question tag.

La forme négative interrogative de « I am » est « aren't I ».

I am **working tomorrow,** aren't I?

George isn't **working today,** is he?

Si la proposition principale comprend un auxiliaire ou un modal, le question tag utilise ce même verbe.

You have **met the new boss,** haven't you?

We shouldn't **interrupt him,** should we?

1.6 RELIEZ CHAQUE ÉNONCÉ AU QUESTION TAG CORRESPONDANT.

Nina's always late for work,

1. They aren't very welcoming,
2. He should try harder to be friendly,
3. She hasn't made many friends here,
4. He doesn't like going to new places,
5. They're so happy to be here,
6. They would be here if they could,

are they?

does he?

has she?

isn't she?

wouldn't they?

aren't they?

shouldn't he?

1.7 POINT CLÉ L'INTONATION AVEC LES QUESTION TAGS

Si l'intonation est montante à la fin d'un question tag, cela signifie que la question requiert une réponse.

You'd like to move offices, wouldn't you?

[I am asking whether or not you would like to move offices.]

Si l'intonation est descendante à la fin d'un question tag, cela signifie que le locuteur invite simplement l'auditeur à marquer son accord.

You've already met Evelyn, haven't you?

[I already know you've met Evelyn.]

1.8 ÉCOUTEZ LES QUESTIONS, PUIS INDIQUEZ SI UNE RÉPONSE EST REQUISE OU PAS.

You came here last year, didn't you?
Answer required ☑ **Answer not required** ☐

1 You moved to the other side of town, didn't you?
Answer required ☐ **Answer not required** ☐

2 They haven't treated you very well, have they?
Answer required ☐ **Answer not required** ☐

3 You're staying with your dad tonight, aren't you?
Answer required ☐ **Answer not required** ☐

4 You bought something for dinner, didn't you?
Answer required ☐ **Answer not required** ☐

5 You don't have any money for a taxi, do you?
Answer required ☐ **Answer not required** ☐

6 Maria doesn't seem to like Sue, does she?
Answer required ☐ **Answer not required** ☐

1.9 AJOUTEZ DES QUESTION TAGS AUX PHRASES, PUIS LISEZ-LES AVEC LES DEUX TYPES D'INTONATION.

Clara doesn't still work for the same company, _____*does she*_____ ?

1 People don't have their own office space here, _____ ?

2 You have been introduced to Mr. Thomas, _____ ?

3 You'd like to come to dinner with us all tonight, _____ ?

4 Oscar and Kate aren't here yet, _____ ?

---

02 Les verbes d'action et d'état

On appelle « verbes d'action » ou « verbes dynamiques », les verbes qui décrivent des actions ou des événements ; on appelle « verbes d'état » ou « verbes statifs », ceux qui décrivent des états.

⚙ **Grammaire** Les verbes d'état aux formes continues
Aa Vocabulaire Les verbes d'action et les verbes d'état
🧩 **Compétence** Décrire les états

2.1 POINT CLÉ LES VERBES D'ACTION ET D'ÉTAT

Les verbes d'action peuvent être utilisés aux formes simples et continues.
Les verbes d'état ne sont généralement pas utilisés à la forme continue.

ACTION	ÉTAT

 I read **every day.** ✅

I am reading **right now.** ✅

 I own **two cars.** ✅

I am owning **two cars.** ❌

2.2 POINT CLÉ UTILISER LES VERBES D'ÉTAT AVEC LES FORMES CONTINUES

Certains verbes peuvent être à la fois d'action et d'état.
Lorsque ces verbes décrivent une action, ils peuvent être utilisés à la forme continue.

ACTION	ÉTAT

 I am thinking about taking up fencing.
[Right now, I'm considering taking up fencing.]

 I think **fencing is a great sport.**
[In my opinion, fencing is a great sport.]

 The chef is tasting his soup.
[The chef is testing the soup's flavor.]

 This soup tastes **disgusting!**
[The soup has a disgusting flavor.]

D'autres verbes d'état peuvent être utilisés à la forme continue. Ils conservent leur sens statif, mais accentuent un changement, une évolution ou le caractère temporaire d'une situation.

FORME CONTINUE	FORME SIMPLE

 Are you feeling **better today?**
You seemed sick yesterday.

 How do you feel
about Modern art?

16

2.3 COCHEZ LES PHRASES CORRECTES.

He's wanting to buy a house. ☐
He wants to buy a house. ☑

1 She has long, wavy hair. ☐
She's having long, wavy hair. ☐

2 Sorry, I'm not believing you. ☐
Sorry, I don't believe you. ☐

3 That jacket fits you very well. ☐
That jacket is fitting you very well. ☐

4 I rarely think about the past. ☐
I'm rarely thinking about the past. ☐

5 Jess is having a great time at the party. ☐
Jess has a great time at the party. ☐

6 That milk is smelling dreadful. ☐
That milk smells dreadful. ☐

7 I'm thinking about going home soon. ☐
I think about going home soon. ☐

8 I'm slowly realizing the problem here. ☐
I slowly realize the problem here. ☐

9 You seem unhappy. Can I help? ☐
You're seeming unhappy. Can I help? ☐

🔊

2.4 COMPLÉTEZ LES PHRASES AVEC LES MOTS DE LA LISTE.

Hi Sara,

I'm writing about Gavin. I _____think_____ there's something wrong. I'm not

_____ that it's anything serious, but he doesn't _____

to be his usual happy self. Maybe he's not _____ in well in his new

job. I was going to _____ that the three of us go out for a drink, or

perhaps you would _____ a meal. Let me know what you think.

Tina

| seem | suggest | ~~think~~ | suggesting | prefer | fitting |

---

03 Utiliser les collocations

Les collocations sont généralement composées de deux mots, parfois plus. Votre anglais sera plus fluide si vous les utilisez.

⚙ **Grammaire** Les collocations
Aa Vocabulaire Les opinions et les croyances
🧩 **Compétence** Parler de votre vie

3.1 POINT CLÉ LES COLLOCATIONS

Une collocation est un groupe de mots qui vont naturellement ensemble et dont l'association semble évidente pour les locuteurs expérimentés d'une langue.

He has a low opinion of the film. ✓
He has a light opinion of the film. ✗

— « Light » peut avoir un sens similaire à « low » (« not much »), mais ne semble pas évident à côté de « opinion ».

There was light rain forecast today. ✓
There was low rain forecast today. ✗

— « Low » peut avoir un sens similaire à « light », mais ne peut pas être en collocation avec « rain ».

🔊

Aa 3.2 COMPLÉTEZ LES PHRASES AVEC LES MOTS DE LA LISTE AFIN DE CRÉER DE NOUVELLES COLLOCATIONS.

It is [extremely *unlikely*] that there will be a happy ending.

1. She doesn't have any [family] left, only an uncle.
2. Sometimes the only solution is to [your best] and hope.
3. All their lives they appeared to be [married] .
4. Unfortunately, the financial crisis [ruined his] .
5. He first [into business] when he was only 17.
6. Looking at old photographs can [stir up] .
7. I can [distinctly] meeting him 20 years ago.
8. Looking at them, the difference in age is [visible] .

close
career
went
do
happily
~~unlikely~~
memories
clearly
remember

🔊

3.3 LISEZ L'ARTICLE, PUIS COCHEZ LES BONNES RÉPONSES.

Lara Estelle has recently died.
True ☐ **False** ☑

❶ Lara was a famous fashion designer.
True ☐ **False** ☐

❷ The author's mother does not like Lara Estelle's music.
True ☐ **False** ☐

❸ The author's father was a soccer fan.
True ☐ **False** ☐

❹ Lara became famous in the 1980s.
True ☐ **False** ☐

❺ Steven was Lara's second husband.
True ☐ **False** ☐

❻ Lara and Steven are no longer married.
True ☐ **False** ☐

❼ The author's father has forgiven Lara now.
True ☐ **False** ☐

LIFE, LOVE, AND LARA

Lara Estelle celebrates her 70th birthday today

It's difficult to imagine now, but in her younger days Lara "The Shades" Estelle was always in the news. How did she create such a sensation? Opinions are divided. Some people say that she was a brilliant musician with an iconic fashion sense. Others believe she was the cause of one of the country's most dramatic sporting upsets.

My parents' views on Lara Estelle are poles apart and, therefore, typical of many of their generation. My mother still loves Lara's music and used to have the same platinum white hair and dark sunglasses as her idol. My father, however, remembers 1980 and his favorite soccer team losing in the final game of the season. He still firmly believes that Lara caused Dun City to lose. But how could a singer cause such drama?

The quality of her music is a matter of opinion, but in 1979 Lara was a top-selling artist. She met her first husband Steven Jones, Dun City's star player, backstage at one of her concerts. Within weeks they were engaged. Lara told Steven that, to prove his love for her, their wedding must be on the same day as the league final that season. He agreed, and there is still a popular belief among City fans that their team lost because Jones did not play. The couple divorced a year later and City never won any trophies again. To this day, my father dislikes Lara's music.

Steven and Lara were married in a glamorous ceremony in 1979.

Aa 3.4 RELIEZ CHAQUE DÉFINITION À LA COLLOCATION CORRESPONDANTE.

a subject on which people hold different views —————— a matter of opinion

opinions are divided

❶ completely opposed — a popular belief

❷ an opinion held by a lot of people — a matter of opinion

❸ people hold differing points of view — firmly believe

❹ to hold a strong opinion that something is true — poles apart

🔊

19

3.5 LISEZ LE BLOG DE MARIAM, PUIS RÉPONDEZ AUX QUESTIONS.

Mariam Davies
• WILDLIFE PHOTOGRAPHER •

 ABOUT ME

I was born in a small town in northern France and went to college in Scotland to study architecture. While at college, I joined the photography club. We used to go on field trips to amazing places and I met my husband, the landscape photographer Julian Davies, while photographing dolphins from a boat. During my last year in college, a wildlife magazine published a number of my photos of birds. This was a major turning point for me and, after we graduated, Julian and I became freelance photographers. We were based in Europe while our twin boys were growing up, but since they both graduated last year, we have started exploring and photographing further afield. We spent some time in Africa this year, and want to take photographs in Japan and Korea next year.

What is Mariam's profession?

Mariam is a wildlife photographer.

1 Where is Mariam from?

_____

2 What subject did she study in college?

_____

3 How did she meet her husband?

_____

4 What important turning point in her life does she mention?

_____

5 Do Mariam and Julian have children?

_____

6 Where are they planning to travel next year?

_____

 3.6 ÉCOUTEZ L'ENREGISTREMENT, PUIS RELIEZ CHAQUE ÉVÉNEMENT AU MOMENT OÙ IL S'EST PRODUIT.

| 23 years ago | This morning | One month ago | 25 years ago | 3 years ago |

3.7 BARREZ LES MOTS INCORRECTS DANS CHAQUE PHRASE.

Lisa ~~was receiving~~ / received an email from her friend ~~every morning~~ / this morning.

1. Lisa was going / went to Thailand 25 years since / ago.

2. Bill had taught / was teaching when Lisa arrived in Thailand.

3. Lisa and Bill were getting married / got married 23 years ago, on / in March

4. Lisa had been traveling / has traveled for 25 years before she returned.

5. Barbara has graduated / graduated from college previous / last month.

3.8 COMPLÉTEZ AVEC « WHEN » OU « WHILE » POUR DÉCRIRE LES ÉVÉNEMENTS DE LA LIGNE CHRONOLOGIQUE, PUIS LISEZ LES PHRASES À VOIX HAUTE.

CONSEIL
Utilisez « when » pour les actions achevées et « while » pour les actions en cours.

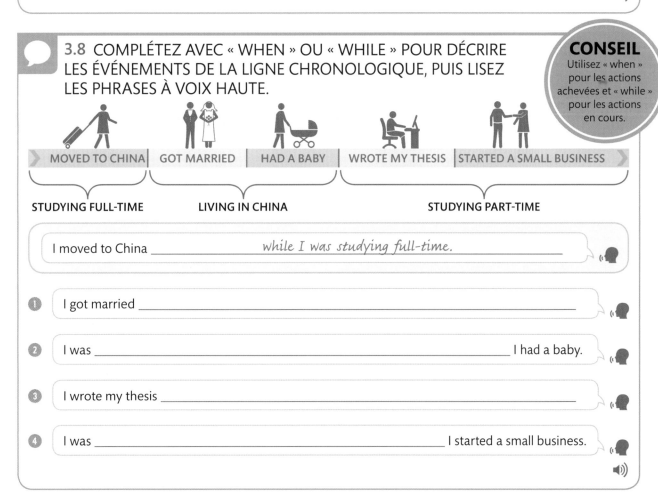

MOVED TO CHINA GOT MARRIED HAD A BABY WROTE MY THESIS STARTED A SMALL BUSINESS

STUDYING FULL-TIME   LIVING IN CHINA   STUDYING PART-TIME

I moved to China _____ *while I was studying full-time.* _____

1. I got married _____

2. I was _____ I had a baby.

3. I wrote my thesis _____

4. I was _____ I started a small business.

03 ✓ CHECK-LIST

⚙ Les collocations ☐   **Aa** Les opinions et les croyances ☐   🧩 Parler de votre vie ☐

04 Les descriptions complexes

Lorsque vous décrivez quelque chose avec plusieurs adjectifs, ces derniers doivent suivre un ordre précis. Il y a plusieurs catégories d'adjectifs.

⚙ **Grammaire** Les adjectifs d'ordre général et spécifique
Aa Vocabulaire Les personnalités
🧩 **Compétence** L'ordre des adjectifs

4.1 POINT CLÉ L'ORDRE DES ADJECTIFS

Les adjectifs d'opinion se placent avant les adjectifs factuels. Les adjectifs d'opinion d'ordre général viennent toujours avant es adjectifs d'opinion spécifiques.

ADJECTIFS D'OPINION   ADJECTIF FACTUEL

What a **nice, friendly little cat!**

« Nice » est un adjectif d'opinion d'ordre général. « Nice » peut servir à décrire beaucoup de choses.

« Friendly » est un adjectif d'opinion spécifique. On l'utilise exclusivement pour décrire des personnes ou des animaux.

🔊

4.2 AUTRES EXEMPLES L'ORDRE DES ADJECTIFS

 It's a **fantastic, exciting new movie.**

 He's a **wonderful, kind old man.**

 What a **horrible, ugly plastic table.**

 That's a **lovely, stylish cotton shirt.**

🔊

4.3 CONSTRUCTION L'ORDRE DES ADJECTIFS

Les adjectifs factuels suivent également un ordre particulier.

ADJECTIFS D'OPINION   ADJECTIFS FACTUELS

	GÉNÉRAL	SPÉCIFIQUE	TAILLE	FORME	ÂGE	COULEUR	MATÉRIAU	
What a	nice,	friendly	little					cat!
He's a	wonderful,	kind			old			man.
That's a	lovely,	stylish					cotton	shirt.

4.4 ÉCRIVEZ LES ADJECTIFS DE LA LISTE DANS L'ENCADRÉ CORRESPONDANT.

GÉNÉRAL	SPÉCIFIQUE	TAILLE	FORME	ÂGE	COULEUR	MATÉRIAU
awful						

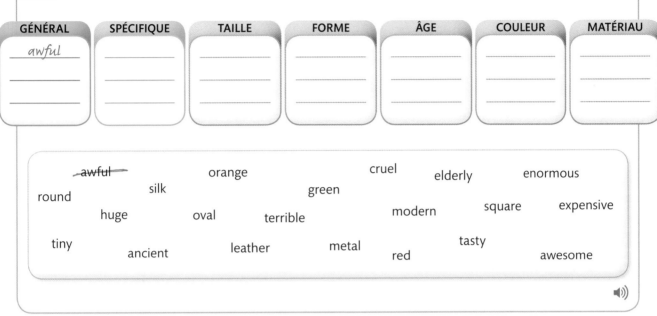

~~awful~~   orange   cruel   elderly   enormous

round   silk   green   square   expensive

huge   oval   terrible   modern

tiny   ancient   leather   metal   tasty   awesome

red

🔊

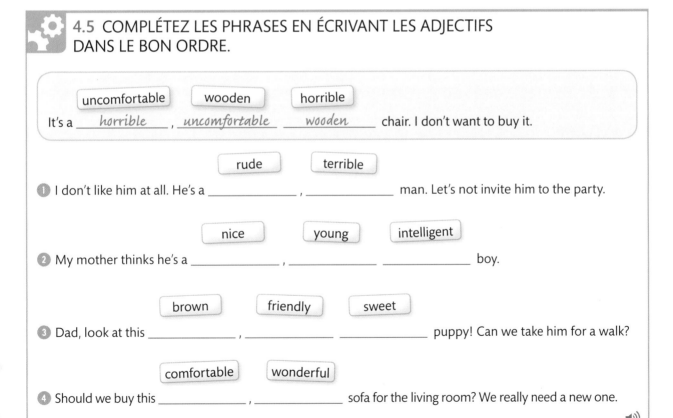

4.5 COMPLÉTEZ LES PHRASES EN ÉCRIVANT LES ADJECTIFS DANS LE BON ORDRE.

| uncomfortable | wooden | horrible |

It's a ___*horrible*___ , ___*uncomfortable*___ ___*wooden*___ chair. I don't want to buy it.

| rude | terrible |

1 I don't like him at all. He's a _____ , _____ man. Let's not invite him to the party.

| nice | young | intelligent |

2 My mother thinks he's a _____ , _____ _____ boy.

| brown | friendly | sweet |

3 Dad, look at this _____ , _____ _____ puppy! Can we take him for a walk?

| comfortable | wonderful |

4 Should we buy this _____ , _____ sofa for the living room? We really need a new one.

🔊

4.6 LISEZ L'ÉVALUATION DES COMPÉTENCES, PUIS COCHEZ LES BONNES RÉPONSES.

Performance Review: Jorge Perez

Jorge is very hard-working and his confidence has grown considerably since he joined the company last summer. He often looks beyond the immediate issues and is proactive in dealing with any potential problems before they arise. He has shown himself to be fair-minded, and he often helps others in his team. In fact, he has proved that he has a natural flair for communication and leadership. We are delighted that Jorge has recently started a leadership skills course, and we will look to promote him when it is completed.

Performance Review: Maria Moran

Given that Maria works in the HR department, we were hoping that her communication skills would have developed more. Calling one of her colleagues "bone-idle" during an appraisal is typical of her blunt approach. Fortunately, the colleague in question is broad-minded and accepted an apology. Despite taking part in several training opportunities, Maria continues to take a narrow-minded approach to her work. Her refusal to acknowledge other people's opinions can make her seem big-headed and arrogant.

Jorge has worked for the same company for several years.
True ☐ **False** ☐ **Not given** ☑

❶ The author is pleased that Jorge is taking a leadership course.
True ☐ **False** ☐ **Not given** ☐

❷ Jorge is going to be promoted next month.
True ☐ **False** ☐ **Not given** ☐

❸ Maria works in the Sales department.
True ☐ **False** ☐ **Not given** ☐

❹ Maria has taken part in a number of training courses.
True ☐ **False** ☐ **Not given** ☐

❺ Maria is fairly broad-minded in terms of her approach to work.
True ☐ **False** ☐ **Not given** ☐

4.7 ÉCOUTEZ L'ENREGISTREMENT, PUIS COCHEZ LE BON RÉSUMÉ.

Un responsable parle à son employé, Paul, de son efficacité au travail cette année.

❶ On the whole, Paul hasn't really settled in very well in his new role. He is hard-working, but needs to work on his team-building and communication skills. ☐

❷ On the whole, Paul has settled in really well in his new role. He is a hard-working and popular member of the team, but he needs to work on his communication skills. ☐

❸ On the whole, Paul has settled in really well in his new role. He is hard-working, but needs to try to become more popular and improve his communication skills. ☐

4.8 COMPLÉTEZ LES PHRASES AVEC LES PRÉFIXES NÉGATIFS DE LA LISTE.

They were really rude and __un__ friendly.

1. His last employer said he was ____ trustworthy.

2. She doesn't realize how ____ sensitive she is.

3. He's 25 now, but he's rather ____ mature at work.

4. I'm afraid she's quite an ____ efficient worker.

5. He gossips and is ____ kind to his co-workers.

6. Her office desk and her work are ____ organized.

7. He makes mistakes because he's ____ patient.

8. She's ____ loyal to the company.

im	dis	un	in

🔊

Aa 4.9 ENTOUREZ 10 ADJECTIFS DANS LA GRILLE, PUIS CLASSEZ-LES.

```
G E X C E L L E N T O N S
N E B N L L N R T Q E P V
N D E F J P O P U L A R D
R I N R E R T I U T C O I
Q U V U E P C A M D C A I
E D I S L O Y A L A E C D
H Z L T S L O Z C O U T Z
E A V R T S V V J S N I D
L C M A T U R E G J K V I
P H I T P A I L I E I E S
F W C I M P A T I E N T D
U B C N A F G E I J D L M
L N Q G A R R O G A N T D
```

POSITIVE ADJECTIVES

1. _helpful_

2. _____

3. _____

4. _____

5. _____

NEGATIVE ADJECTIVES

6. _disloyal_

7. _____

8. _____

9. _____

10. _____

🔊

Il est très utile de savoir comment commencer une phrase avec le mot « it » en anglais. Vous pouvez utiliser « it is » en début de phrase pour faire une déclaration d'ordre général.

⚙ Grammaire Le « it » introductif
Aa Vocabulaire Les talents et les aptitudes
🧩 Compétence Exprimer des vérités générales

5.1 POINT CLÉ LE « IT » INTRODUCTIF

Certaines locutions types commençant par « it is » peuvent être utilisées en début de phrase. « It » est le sujet de la phrase et peut être employé pour parler de vérité ou de croyance générale.

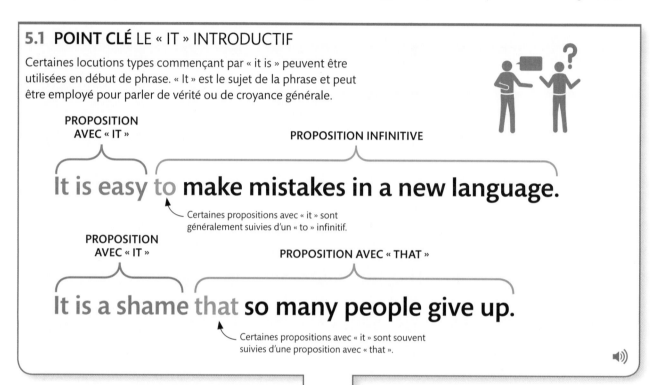

PROPOSITION AVEC « IT »

PROPOSITION INFINITIVE

It is easy to **make mistakes in a new language.**

Certaines propositions avec « it » sont généralement suivies d'un « to » infinitif.

PROPOSITION AVEC « IT »

PROPOSITION AVEC « THAT »

It is a shame that **so many people give up.**

Certaines propositions avec « it » sont souvent suivies d'une proposition avec « that ».

5.2 AUTRES EXEMPLES LE « IT » INTRODUCTIF

 It is important to **be relaxed about making mistakes.**

 It is essential to **give yourself time to study regularly.**

 It's true that **being able to speak a second language is useful.**

 It's unlikely that **you will be comfortable speaking aloud at first.**

 It is difficult to **remember new words if you don't write them down.**

5.3 COMPLÉTEZ LES PHRASES AVEC LES MOTS DE LA LISTE.

It's _____*important to*_____ have the skills to communicate globally.

1 With busy work and social lives, it's _____ most people have little time to study.

2 Languages are so useful. It is _____ so few people learn a second language.

3 Learning doesn't have to be expensive. It is not _____ spend a lot of money.

4 Try internet study groups. It is _____ meet other language learners online.

5 Don't worry if you need time. It's _____ you'll be able to speak fluently quickly.

easy to   a shame that   unlikely that   essential to   ~~important to~~   true that

◀))

5.4 POINT CLÉ COMMENCEZ PAR UNE PROPOSITION INFINITIVE.

Vous pouvez placer la proposition infinitive en début de phrase si vous désirez mettre l'accent sur son contenu.

La construction avec « it » en début de phrase est néanmoins plus courante.

It is easy to begin learning.

To begin learning is easy! Keeping it going is harder.

Placer la proposition infinitive en début de phrase fonctionne très bien avec les phrases courtes.

5.5 BARREZ LES MOTS INCORRECTS DANS CHAQUE PHRASE.

It is worth working hard. To / ~~That~~ / ~~It~~ give up now would be a shame.

1 Remember, it's important to / that / it be relaxed about making mistakes.

2 With so many options, it's no longer difficult to / that / it find language courses online.

3 To / That / It take the exam now would be a waste of time. She hasn't studied at all.

4 To / That / It is unlikely that he will finish the class before the end of the year.

5 Don't give up! It's true to / that / it the more you study, the better you will become.

◀))

📖 **5.6 LISEZ LES MESSAGES DU FORUM DE DISCUSSION, PUIS COCHEZ LES BONNES RÉPONSES.**

Who is learning a language which involves clicking?
Alice ☐   Dave ☐   Mei ☐   Sam ☑

① Who finds their language lessons a little boring?
Alice ☐   Dave ☐   Mei ☐   Sam ☐

② Who can speak a number of different languages very well?
Alice ☐   Dave ☐   Mei ☐   Sam ☐

③ Who was encouraged to learn a language by someone else?
Alice ☐   Dave ☐   Mei ☐   Sam ☐

④ Who thinks they have a natural ability for learning languages?
Alice ☐   Dave ☐   Mei ☐   Sam ☐

⑤ Who is conducting research about learning languages?
Alice ☐   Dave ☐   Mei ☐   Sam ☐

Lingo-net

ABOUT | NEWS | FORUM | CONTACT

ARE YOU A LANGUAGE LEARNER?

Alice: I'm working on a TV program and am looking for people to share language learning experiences. Do you have a hidden talent or even a complete inability to learn languages? Get in touch!

Dave: I'm trying to learn Native American Pawnee. I don't have any natural ability and most words have at least 10 syllables! The lessons drag on a bit but I'll keep on doing them until I'm fluent.

Mei: I think I have an aptitude for language-learning. I'm fluent in four languages. I'd love to learn Sentinelese but it's impossible because no-one knows what it sounds like!

Sam: I've only ever spoken English, but one of my professors has a remarkable capacity for languages and speaks Xhosa (a South African language with click sounds). He asked if I'd like to learn it, and I took him up on the offer. It's very difficult, but he's shown me some online videos to help.

Aa   **5.7 COMPLÉTEZ LES PHRASES POUR CRÉER DES COLLOCATIONS EN UTILISANT LES PHRASES DE L'EXERCICE 5.6.**

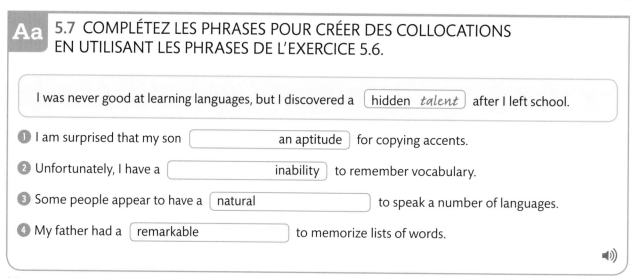

I was never good at learning languages, but I discovered a (hidden *talent*) after I left school.

① I am surprised that my son (an aptitude) for copying accents.

② Unfortunately, I have a (inability) to remember vocabulary.

③ Some people appear to have a (natural   ) to speak a number of languages.

④ My father had a (remarkable   ) to memorize lists of words.

🔊

5.8 RÉPONDEZ AUX QUESTIONS DE L'ENREGISTREMENT, PUIS LISEZ LES RÉPONSES À VOIX HAUTE.

Do you like learning new languages?

It isn't easy to *learn a new language, but I find it a lot of fun.*

1 Why do you think learning languages is important?

It is important to _____

2 What advice would you give to new learners?

It's best to _____

3 What is the hardest thing about learning languages?

It is difficult to _____

---

05 ✓ **CHECK-LIST**

⚙ Le « it » introductif ☐   **Aa** Les talents et les aptitudes ☐   🧩 Exprimer des vérités générales ☐

↻ **BILAN** L'ANGLAIS QUE VOUS AVEZ APPRIS DANS LES CHAPITRES 1-5

NOUVEAU POINT LINGUISTIQUE	EXEMPLE TYPE	☑	CHAPITRE
LES TEMPS DU PRÉSENT	I usually cycle. Today I'm walking instead. I've just started a job. I've been meeting people.	☐	1.1, 1.3
LES VERBES D'ACTION ET D'ÉTAT	The chef is tasting his soup. This soup tastes disgusting!	☐	2.1, 2.2
LES COLLOCATIONS	He has a low opinion of the film. There was light rain forecast today.	☐	3.1
L'ORDRE DES ADJECTIFS	What a nice, friendly little cat!	☐	4.1, 4.3
LE « IT » INTRODUCTIF	It is easy to make mistakes in a new language.	☐	5.1

Vocabulaire

6.1 LES VOYAGES ET LE TOURISME

We need a vacation to get away from it all.

get away from it all
[go somewhere relaxing for a break]

When we go to Paris, will we have time to go sightseeing?

go sightseeing
[visit interesting buildings and places as a tourist]

We won a once-in-a-lifetime trip to New Zealand!

once-in-a-lifetime
[unique and unrepeatable]

I always feel homesick when I travel abroad.

feel homesick
[be sad because you miss your home and family]

I've never been anywhere like it. It was such a culture shock.

culture shock
[feeling of confusion or distress when visiting a different place or culture]

They lived in a house off the beaten track in the country.

off the beaten track
[a long way from other people, buildings, and roads]

The hotels in this area all look a little bit run-down.

run-down
[in a bad condition through lack of care or repair]

There are so many birds in this unspoiled countryside.

unspoiled
[something or somewhere that has not been changed or altered]

I'll never settle down. I get itchy feet every few years.

itchy feet
[a desire to travel or move]

My son's thirst for adventure worries me sometimes.

thirst for adventure
[a desire for exciting experiences]

We're going to look around the flower district this morning.

look around
[explore an area or place]

We stopped off at a couple of museums along the way.

stop off
[pause a journey in one place before continuing]

We have to check out of the hotel before 1pm.

check out of somewhere
[pay your bill and leave a hotel]

The first leg of the journey is a long flight to Singapore.

leg of a journey
[a stage in a journey from one place to another]

I'm really looking forward to seeing the pyramids.

look forward to something
[feel excited about something that is going to happen]

Every time I drive into the city I get hopelessly lost.

hopelessly lost
[totally unable to find your way]

You will get your boarding passes when you check in.

check in
[register your arrival at an airport or hotel]

We're going to check out the zoo tomorrow.

check out something / check something out
[see if something or someone is interesting]

It's only a weekend getaway, so we won't need much luggage.

getaway
[a vacation, particularly a short one]

My parents came to the airport to see me off.

see off somebody / see somebody off
[go to the station or airport to say goodbye to someone]

07 Les verbes à particule

Les verbes à particule se présentent sous différentes formes. Ils sont composés de 2 ou 3 éléments qui sont parfois séparables. Ils sont très communs, surtout en anglais parlé.

⚙ **Grammaire** Vue d'ensemble des verbes à particule
Aa **Vocabulaire** Le voyage
🧩 **Compétence** Utiliser des verbes à particule complexes

7.1 POINT CLÉ LES VERBES À PARTICULE

Les verbes à particule se composent d'un verbe et d'une ou de plusieurs particules. Un verbe peut utiliser différentes particules pour former différents verbes à particule.

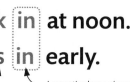

We must check **in** at noon.
She always checks **in** early.

Le verbe s'accorde avec le sujet. ⟶   ⟵ La particule ne s'accorde pas.

7.2 RÉCRIVEZ LES PHRASES EN CORRIGEANT LES ERREURS DES VERBES À PARTICULE.

He **work outs** at least twice a week.
He works out at least twice a week.

① Be careful, it's absolutely **pour downing** with rain.

_____

② He's behind on his work, so he needs to **catch-up**.

_____

③ They are **take downing** the offensive posters today.

_____

④ She'll have a backup. She always **backs ups** her files.

_____

⑤ They **split ups** every time they have an argument.

_____

7.3 POINT CLÉ LES VERBES À PARTICULE

Si un verbe à particule séparable a un objet direct, cet objet direct peut parfois se placer entre le verbe et la particule.

Si l'objet direct est un pronom, ce dernier doit se placer entre le verbe et la particule.

He filled in the customs form.

He filled the customs form in.

He filled it in.   He filled in it.

32

7.4 RÉCRIVEZ LES PHRASES EN PLAÇANT LA PARTICULE DU VERBE AU BON ENDROIT.

> The school is putting on a show.
> *The school is putting a show on.*

1 I'll pick up your shopping for you.

_____

2 They're putting up posters outside again.

_____

3 Have you checked out the restaurant menu?

_____

4 He hasn't set up the computer yet.

_____

🔊

7.5 RÉCRIVEZ LES PHRASES EN UTILISANT DES PRONOMS.

> She is looking up the location.
> *She is looking it up.*

1 He should ask Mary out if he wants to.

_____

2 Remember to take out the recycling later.

_____

3 You should send the phone back if it's broken.

_____

4 Could you turn off the lights when you leave?

_____

🔊

7.6 POINT CLÉ LES VERBES À PARTICULE DE 3 MOTS

Certains verbes à particule contiennent plus de deux mots. Dans ce cas, l'accentuation orale se fait sur le deuxième mot.

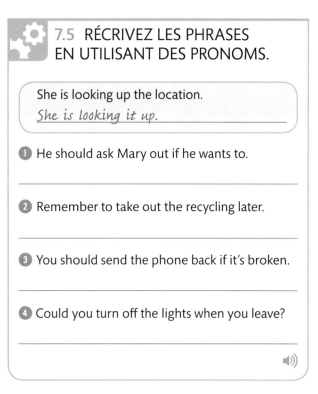

VERBE + PARTICULE + PRÉPOSITION

She always comes up with exciting travel plans.

L'accentuation se fait ici sur « up ».

🔊

7.7 COMPLÉTEZ LES PHRASES AVEC LES VERBES DE LA LISTE, PUIS LISEZ-LES À VOIX HAUTE.

> My sister's always _coming up with_ ways to save money. 🗣

1 My big brother is a CEO. I have a lot to _____. 🗣

2 Slow down! I can't _____ you any more, I'm tired. 🗣

3 His parents aren't very strict. He _____ everything! 🗣

keep up with
get away with
live up to
~~come up with~~

🔊

33

7.8 LISEZ L'ARTICLE, PUIS NUMÉROTEZ LES IMAGES DANS LE BON ORDRE.

(A) ☐

(B) 1

(C) ☐

(D) ☐

(E) ☐

(F) ☐

YOUR LIFE STORY

My year off turned into a career

When I was a teenager, I decided to take a gap year before going to university. I had already done loads of research online and decided to go to a Greek island to pick olives. I had calculated that I could earn enough money to travel cheaply to Asia. Although the people were wonderful, by the end of the olive harvest I felt I was a bit cut off on such a small island, so I bought a plane ticket and set off to Malaysia.

While I was in Malaysia, I decided to become an English teacher. I knew right away that teaching was what I wanted to do for the rest of my life. A short while later, I graduated with a degree in teaching. After just 10 years, I opened my very first English-language school.

7.9 ÉCOUTEZ L'ENREGISTREMENT, PUIS COCHEZ LES BONNES RÉPONSES.

Maria Soames, auteur célèbre de récits de voyage, explique la raison pour laquelle elle a commencé à écrire.

Which country did Maria first travel to?
Vietnam ☐
Indonesia ☑
Cambodia ☐

❶ Which animals did Maria want to see?
Chameleons ☐
Kangaroos ☐
Komodo dragons ☐

❷ What job does Maria do, besides writing?
Tour guide ☐
Travel rep ☐
Magazine editor ☐

❸ Where did Maria record her experiences?
Diary ☐
Notebook ☐
Blog ☐

❹ Which of the following hasn't Maria written?
Travel guides ☐
Newspaper articles ☐
Travel blog ☐

❺ What reason does Maria not give for liking her job?
Meeting people ☐
Material for writing ☐
Good pay ☐

Aa 7.10 RELIEZ CHAQUE DÉFINITION AU VERBE À PARTICULE CORRESPONDANT.

go to a place of departure with someone to say goodbye → take off

see somebody off

1. stop someone from going somewhere and isolate them → see somebody off

2. pause a journey in one place before continuing — stop off

3. start flying — set off

4. start a trip — cut off

Aa 7.11 OBSERVEZ LES IMAGES, PUIS COMPLÉTEZ LES PHRASES AVEC LES VERBES À PARTICULE DE L'EXERCICE 7.10.

I like to _stop off_ for coffee on my way to work.

1. Our plane was due to _____ an hour ago.

2. We have to _____ really early for our vacation.

3. He went with her to the train station to _____ .

4. They missed the ferry, so they were _____ from the mainland.

Les temps narratifs

Lorsque vous racontez une histoire (même s'il ne s'agit que de ce qui vous est arrivé récemment), vous devez utiliser plusieurs temps pour être bien compris.

⚙️ **Grammaire** Le past perfect continu

Aa Vocabulaire Les adjectifs et les idiomes du voyage

🧩 **Compétence** Parler de plusieurs actions passées

8.1 POINT CLÉ LES TEMPS NARRATIFS

Vous pouvez utiliser différents temps du passé pour indiquer que des actions ou des états passés se chevauchent, ou pour préciser quelle action ou quel état a eu lieu en premier.

PRÉTÉRIT

Le prétérit décrit des actions ou des états qui ont eu lieu lors d'une période spécifique achevée.

Une période spécifique achevée (« l'été dernier ») est précisée ; le prétérit est par conséquent utilisé.

Last summer, we flew to London. There's so much to do there!

PRÉTÉRIT CONTINU

Le prétérit continu décrit une action qui a commencé avant, et peut-être même après, une autre action passée.

While we were walking around the city, we took some photos in front of Big Ben.

On utilise souvent le prétérit et le prétérit continu conjointement pour dire qu'une action a interrompu une autre action plus longue.

PAST PERFECT

Le past perfect décrit des actions ou des états qui sont survenus avant autre chose dans le passé.

Cette action est survenue avant autre chose dans le passé (le voyage à l'étranger) ; le past perfect est par conséquent utilisé.

Fortunately, we had looked up all the best places to go beforehand.

NOW

8.2 COMPLÉTEZ LES PHRASES EN CONJUGUANT LES VERBES AU PRÉTÉRIT OU AU PRÉTÉRIT CONTINU.

We __were flying__ (fly) over France when we _____ *saw* _____ (see) the Alps for the first time.

1 I _____ (walk) down the road when someone _____ (ask) me to take their photo.

2 Someone _____ (talk) during the tour until we _____ (tell) them to be quiet.

3 I _____ (stop) twice to take photos while I _____ (drive) through the country.

4 We _____ (decide) to order some champagne while we _____ (eat) lunch.

5 We were lost and our feet _____ (ache) before we finally_____ (find) a map shop.

🔊

8.3 COMPLÉTEZ LES PHRASES EN UTILISANT LE PAST PERFECT, PUIS LISEZ-LES À VOIX HAUTE.

Our friend **told** us the city tour was great, so we went on it.

We went on the city tour because ___ *our friend had told us it was great.* ___

1 We **walked** all around the city and my feet really ached by the end of the day.

My feet really ached by the end of the day because _____

2 We **spent** a long time planning the trip and it was perfect.

The trip was perfect because _____

3 We **crossed** over the wrong bridge and got completely lost.

We got completely lost because _____

4 Our tour guide **recommended** a great show, so we went to see it.

We went to see a great show because _____

🔊

8.4 **POINT CLÉ** LE PAST PERFECT CONTINU

On utilise le past perfect continu pour décrire une action ou une activité qui avait lieu avant un autre moment du passé.

He had been learning **English for two years before he** went **to London.**

TWO YEARS BEFORE   **PAST**   **NOW**

8.5 **CONSTRUCTION** LE PAST PERFECT CONTINU

SUJET	« HAD »	« BEEN »	PARTICIPE PRÉSENT	RESTE DE LA PHRASE
He	had	been	learning	**English for two years.**

 8.6 COMPLÉTEZ LES PHRASES EN CONJUGUANT LES VERBES AU PAST PERFECT CONTINU.

They _____*had been flying*_____ (fly) for ages, so she decided to walk around the aisles.

❶ We _____ (wait) for at least an hour when the taxi finally arrived.

❷ I eventually went to the pharmacy because I _____ (not feel) well for days.

❸ We went to see the movie because they _____ (promote) it for months.

❹ The streets were beautiful and white because it _____ (snow) all night.

8.7 LISEZ L'ARTICLE, PUIS COCHEZ LES BONNES RÉPONSES.

Travel Underground is on TV on Fridays.
True ☐ **False** ☐ **Not given** ☑

1 Travel Underground is a one-off documentary.
True ☐ **False** ☐ **Not given** ☐

2 The city was rediscovered by accident.
True ☐ **False** ☐ **Not given** ☐

3 Derinkuyu is Turkey's deepest underground city.
True ☐ **False** ☐ **Not given** ☐

4 People used the city as a place to stay safe.
True ☐ **False** ☐ **Not given** ☐

TV GUIDE

What's on TV tonight?
Tonight, 9pm

This week, the Travel Underground series visits Turkey and tells the remarkable story of Derinkuyu in Cappadocia. Back in 1963, a resident had been knocking a wall down in his house, but stopped when something caught his eye. He decided to keep on digging, and it was soon obvious that he had discovered something incredible. This documentary charts the fascinating history of Derinkuyu, the deepest underground city in Turkey. Far below the surface, Derinkuyu had been a place of safety for many peoples for hundreds of years.

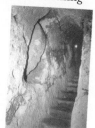

8.8 ÉCOUTEZ L'ENREGISTREMENT, PUIS COCHEZ LE RÉSUMÉ CORRECT.

1 The Underground Cities tour lasts for one day. You need to pack your own lunch, and you can't take too much luggage with you. ☐

2 The tour lasts for two days, so you need to take lots of luggage with you and an overnight bag. There is a traditional lunch included. ☐

3 The tour takes place over two days. You get a chance to explore by yourself, but you shouldn't take a lot of luggage. ☐

4 The tour starts in the underground city, with a lunch on the second day. It's just a short tour, so there's no need for an overnight bag. ☐

Aa 8.9 RELIEZ LES EXPRESSIONS DE L'EXERCICE 8.8 À LEUR DÉFINITION.

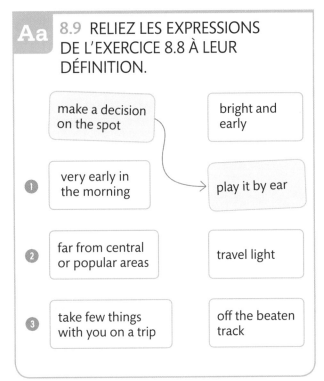

make a decision on the spot	bright and early
1 very early in the morning	play it by ear
2 far from central or popular areas	travel light
3 take few things with you on a trip	off the beaten track

08 ✔ CHECK-LIST

⚙ Le past perfect continu ☐ **Aa** Les adjectifs et les idiomes du voyage ☐ 🧩 Parler de plusieurs actions passées ☐

Lorsque vous voulez donner un conseil ou faire une recommandation, vous pouvez utiliser plusieurs modaux. Vous pouvez moduler l'intensité de votre conseil en employant différents modaux.

⚙ **Grammaire** Les modaux pour le conseil et l'opinion
Aa Vocabulaire Les recommandations
🧩 **Compétence** Donner des conseils et votre opinion

9.1 POINT CLÉ FAIRE DES RECOMMANDATIONS

L'une des façons les plus courantes de faire une recommandation ou une suggestion est d'utiliser des verbes modaux. Lorsque vous donnez des conseils, vous exprimez généralement aussi votre opinion sur un sujet.

CONSEIL
Vous pouvez ajouter de l'emphase en utilisant « really » devant « should », « ought to » et « must ».

Suggestion d'ordre général.

You { could / might } visit the park. It's nice.

Suggestion plus forte.

You { should / ought to } visit the castle. It's great.

Suggestion très forte.

You must visit the palace. It is beautiful!

9.2 COCHEZ LES BULLES QUI CONTIENNENT DES RECOMMANDATIONS.

My son is going to Paris next week. You went last year, didn't you?

Yes, I did! He should visit the Tuileries Garden; it's beautiful. ✓

2
You really must try the new Italian restaurant on Main Street.

I'm going there at lunch time! Why don't you come with me?

1
It's such a sunny day! You could go to the park later if you have time.

I have to go shopping. I'll definitely try to go if I finish early.

3
What should I do for my birthday this year? I can't believe I'll be 30!

You ought to have a big party with all your friends. It would be great!

9.3 COMPLÉTEZ LES PHRASES AVEC LES RECOMMANDATIONS DE LA LISTE.

> The food in the restaurant is fresh and homemade. The selection at breakfast was just awesome. _____ *You should definitely eat there.* _____

1. Everything about this hotel, from the dark interior to the hard stares of the grumpy staff, was unwelcoming. _____

2. The hotel's employees are wonderful. They did everything to make our honeymoon perfect. _____

3. Not bad, although the furniture in the hotel was falling apart. The walls were very thin and it was quite noisy. _____

4. I paid for a room with a view of the ski slopes, but all I could see was the wall of the building across from us. _____

5. Outstanding! I can understand the rave reviews for this great place. Our balcony overlooked the ocean. _____

> You should tell them if it's a special occasion.　　You could ask to change rooms if this happens.
>
> 　　You might want to bring earplugs.　　~~You should definitely eat there.~~
>
> You must ask for a room with an ocean view!　　They ought to hire a new receptionist!

🔊

9.4 ÉCOUTEZ L'ENREGISTREMENT, PUIS COCHEZ SI JEFF A AIMÉ OU PAS L'ACTIVITÉ.

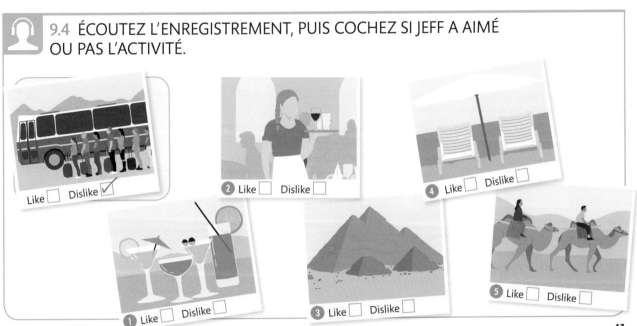

Like ☐　Dislike ☑

2 Like ☐　Dislike ☐

4 Like ☐　Dislike ☐

1 Like ☐　Dislike ☐

3 Like ☐　Dislike ☐

5 Like ☐　Dislike ☐

9.5 POINT CLÉ DONNER DES CONSEILS

Vous pouvez également utiliser les modaux pour donner des conseils fondés sur des faits.
Ces derniers peuvent mettre en évidence les conséquences négatives si ces conseils sont ignorés.

You { should / ought to } wear a hat. It's very sunny.

Conseil d'ordre général.

You must wear a hat or you'll get sunburned.

Fort conseil : ne pas prendre en compte ce
conseil entraînera des conséquences négatives.

9.6 DIRE AUTREMENT DONNER DES CONSEILS

Vous pouvez également
donner des conseils en
utilisant les locutions :
« If I were you... »
et « You had better... »
(expression généralement
contractée en « You'd
better »).

Vous pouvez utiliser cette formule figée pour donner
des conseils en vous mettant à la place de votre auditeur.

If I were you, I would wear a hat.

You'd better wear a hat.

Cette formule est utilisée pour donner des conseils
très forts, peut-être même pour menacer.

CONSEIL
Vous entendrez
peut-être « If I was you... »,
mais cette formule est
incorrecte en anglais
formel.

9.7 BARREZ LES VERBES INCORRECTS, PUIS LISEZ LES PHRASES À VOIX HAUTE.

The open air concert hall is amazing. You really ought to / ~~might~~ see it.

① That snake is poisonous. You must / could go to the doctor about that bite or it'll get worse.

② We might / had better go back to the boat. It's leaving soon and we don't want to miss it.

③ Perhaps you must / could go to France this summer. That would be nice.

④ Everyone says the castle is stunning and that we must / could see the view from the tower.

9.8 LISEZ LA CARTE POSTALE D'ANNE, PUIS INDIQUEZ SES PRÉFÉRENCES.

The airline	Like ☐	Dislike ☑

1. The beach resort — Like ☐ — Dislike ☐
2. The hotel staff — Like ☐ — Dislike ☐
3. The food — Like ☐ — Dislike ☐
4. The pyramids — Like ☐ — Dislike ☐
5. The camel ride — Like ☐ — Dislike ☐
6. The weather — Like ☐ — Dislike ☐

Hi Sara,

I'm writing from the airport. If I were you, I'd avoid flying with CheapAir. There were so many delays! The resort was nice, and the staff were wonderful, but the trip itself seemed to really drag on. The food wasn't very good either. The highlights for me were the excursions. The pyramids were amazing and then yesterday I had a great time riding camels. It was much too hot though. You really must try to visit one day, though I'm not sure I'd go again! You should have dinner with us once we're back. I have loads of photos to show you.

Lots of love, Anne

9.9 COMPLÉTEZ LA CARTE POSTALE EN RECOMMANDANT UN VOYAGE.

Hi _____
I'm traveling back tonight. I can't believe my trip is over already!
I really enjoyed _____
_____
The town was _____
_____
You really should _____
_____
Lots of love,
_____

10 Faire des prédictions

Lorsque vous parlez d'un événement futur, vous pouvez être amené à évaluer le degré de probabilité qu'il a de se produire. Il y a plusieurs méthodes pour y parvenir.

⚙ **Grammaire** Les degrés de probabilité
Aa Vocabulaire Les idiomes temporels
🧩 **Compétence** Parler de possibilité

10.1 POINT CLÉ LES DEGRÉS DE PROBABILITÉ

De nombreuses constructions s'offrent à vous pour exprimer les degrés de probabilité qu'un événement a de se produire. Ceux-ci vont de la certitude que cet événement ne se produira pas à la certitude qu'il se produira.

> **Will the hotel be ready next month?**

No, the hotel definitely won't be ready by then.
No, the hotel won't be ready by then.

The hotel probably won't be ready by then.
The hotel is unlikely to be ready by then.

The hotel might be ready by then.

It's likely that the hotel will be ready by then.
The hotel will probably be ready by then.

Yes, the hotel will be ready by then.
Yes, the hotel will definitely be ready by then.

🔊

10.2 RELIEZ CHAQUE ÉNONCÉ À LA PRÉDICTION QUI LUI CORRESPOND.

There are lots of delays today.

We probably won't get tickets.

1 I don't have much money.

He'll pass them all, no problem.

2 He's worked so hard for his exams.

She'll probably go to Australia one day.

3 She's a talented young pianist.

Our train will definitely be delayed too.

4 Look at the line outside the stadium.

She might be famous one day.

5 You don't have a very good voice.

He might be running a marathon soon.

6 My sister loves to travel.

I definitely won't go on vacation this year.

7 Joe goes running every day.

You definitely won't ever be in an opera.

10.3 ÉCOUTEZ L'ENREGISTREMENT, PUIS RELIEZ CHAQUE IMAGE À L'EXPRESSION QUI CONVIENT.

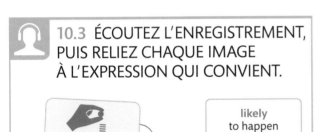

likely to happen

might happen

probably won't happen

2

unlikely to happen

3

definitely will happen

4

10.4 ÉCOUTEZ L'ENREGISTREMENT, PUIS SOULIGNEZ LES SYLLABES ACCENTUÉES.

u n s u r p r i s i n g l y

1 f u n d a m e n t a l l y

2 e s s e n t i a l l y

3 s u r p r i s i n g l y

4 p r e d i c t a b l y

5 f o r t u n a t e l y

6 i n t e r e s t i n g l y

7 l u c k i l y

8 u n f o r t u n a t e l y

PROPERTY

HOUSE PRICES ON THE RISE

A normal goal for many young people is to fly the nest and move into a house of their own. In many tourist areas, however, this is becoming a very unlikely goal for young local people. In resorts around the world, tourists are buying properties either as short-term investments or to live in part-time. As people from the cities (or wealthy countries) compete to buy the properties, it is only a matter of time until the prices rise. These prices are unlikely to be affordable for young local people. This makes it more difficult for them to remain in their own towns if they want to live independently.

In the long run, there is a cost to society and communities. Marisa Cali lives in a picturesque village on a Greek island. "Many of the houses in the village are now empty most of the year. There are fewer people around. It's not like it used to be, but I guess it's the shape of things to come for many island villages."

Some local governments are insisting that a percentage of all new homes built in such areas must be affordable for locals. Other governments are charging higher fees for overseas buyers. So far, these policies have had little impact on the situation.

What does "flying the nest" mean?

"Flying the nest" means leaving your parents' home.

---

❶ What two reasons are mentioned for buying second homes?

_____

❷ What problem are many local young people facing in tourist areas?

_____

❸ How has Marisa Cali's village changed?

_____

❹ What two things are some local governments doing to counter this problem?

_____

He's broken his arm, but, thankfully, there's no [*long-term*] injury.

① This is only a [ ] solution. We'll have to fix the fence properly soon.

② OK, we'll order pizza tonight, but [ ] we need to sort out a meal plan.

③ I don't understand this new digital system, but I know it's [ ].

④ It was [ ] before the company hit its targets.

| the shape of things to come | ~~long-term~~ | only a matter of time | in the long run | short-term |

---

10 ✓ **CHECK-LIST**

⚙ Les degrés de probabilité ☐   **Aa** Les idiomes temporels ☐   Parler de possibilité ☐

🔄 **BILAN** L'ANGLAIS QUE VOUS AVEZ APPRIS DANS LES CHAPITRES 7-10

NOUVEAU POINT LINGUISTIQUE	EXEMPLE TYPE	☑	CHAPITRE
LES VERBES À PARTICULE	He filled the customs form in. She always comes up with exciting plans.	☐	7.1, 7.3, 7.6
LES TEMPS NARRATIFS	As we were walking home, we saw a juggler. We had already exchanged our money.	☐	8.1
LE PAST PERFECT CONTINU	He had been learning English for two years before he went to London.	☐	8.4
FAIRE DES RECOMMANDATIONS	You must visit the palace. It is beautiful!	☐	9.1
DONNER DES CONSEILS	You should wear a hat. It's very sunny. If I were you, I would wear a hat.	☐	9.5 9.6
LES DEGRÉS DE PROBABILITÉ	The hotel's unlikely to be ready by next month. It will definitely be ready by then.	☐	10.1

11.1 LA FAMILLE ET LES RELATIONS

I look up to my older brother.

look up to somebody
[have respect and admiration for someone]

You're lucky that you take after your intelligent mother.

take after somebody
[have characteristics of a parent or relative]

They brought up their children to be polite and respectful.

bring up somebody / bring somebody up
[care for a child and teach them how to behave]

It is important to grow up in a caring environment.

grow up
[develop from a child to an adult]

She got along with her colleagues.

get along with somebody / get on with somebody
[have a positive relationship with somebody]

My siblings fell out with each other for a few years.

fall out with somebody
[stop being friends with somebody, often after an argument]

We fell in love while we were traveling across Europe together.

fall in love with somebody
[begin to love somebody]

I broke up with him after a big argument.

break up with somebody
[end a romantic relationship]

They drifted apart after they stopped working for the same company.

drift apart
[slowly become less friendly or close to somebody]

I made friends with her a long time ago.

make friends with somebody
[become friendly with a person]

We've been close friends for more than 20 years.

close friend
[a friend who you know very well]

I am really surprised by how much we have in common.

have something in common
[share an interest or opinion]

My sister gave birth to a baby girl a few months ago.

give birth to somebody
[have a child]

Curly hair runs in the family.

run in the family
[be a common feature of a family]

We used to fight a lot, but we see eye to eye nowadays.

see eye to eye with somebody
[agree with or have similar opinions to somebody]

As soon as I met Tom, we just clicked.

click with somebody
[like somebody quickly and easily]

We bumped into her teacher in the supermarket.

bump into somebody
[meet someone unexpectedly]

My dad is putting his foot down about doing chores.

put your foot down
[be strict about something]

Our parents taught us to stick up for each other at school.

stick up for somebody
[speak out in support of somebody]

I think the world of my first grandchild.

think the world of somebody
[have a very high opinion of somebody]

Les marqueurs rhétoriques peuvent être utilisés pour indiquer une relation entre deux phrases, ou segments de phrase. Cette relation peut être une relation de cause, effet, emphase, contraste ou comparaison.

⚙ **Grammaire** Lier l'information
Aa **Vocabulaire** L'histoire familiale
🧩 **Compétence** Parler de relations

12.1 POINT CLÉ LES MARQUEURS RHÉTORIQUES DE RELATION INFORMELS

Certains marqueurs rhétoriques sont essentiellement utilisés dans le discours informel.

CONSEIL
Pour souligner le lien entre les mots à l'oral, vous pouvez accentuer le marqueur rhétorique.

Indique un contraste.

I like listening to music, { but / though } my mother hates it.

Indique une comparaison.

He's a talented swimmer, { like / just as } his great-grandfather was.

Indique un résultat.

Staying in touch is easy, { because / since / as } we all have smartphones.

Indique un effet.

We grew up together, so we tell each other everything.
We are very close. As a result, we know everything about each other.

Indique une emphase.

All my siblings are tall, { especially / particularly } my older sister.

12.2 RELIEZ LES PHRASES EN UTILISANT DES MARQUEURS RHÉTORIQUES.

> Julie likes her older brother. She doesn't see him very often. [but]
> *Julie likes her older brother, but she doesn't see him very often.*

1 All my siblings love playing football. My brother loves it the most. [especially]

_____

2 We are all quite interested in our family history. We've made a family tree. [so]

_____

3 I love talking to my aunt. She has lots of interesting stories from her travels abroad. [because]

_____

4 My grandmother thinks I should get married. I am not as traditional as she is. [but]

_____

5 We don't have big family gatherings very often. My grandparents live abroad. [since]

_____

 ## 12.3 ÉCOUTEZ L'ENREGISTREMENT, PUIS RELIEZ LES PAIRES D'IMAGES.

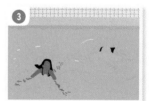

12.4 POINT CLÉ LES MARQUEURS RHÉTORIQUES DE RELATION FORMELS

Certains marqueurs rhétoriques sont essentiellement utilisés dans le discours formel.

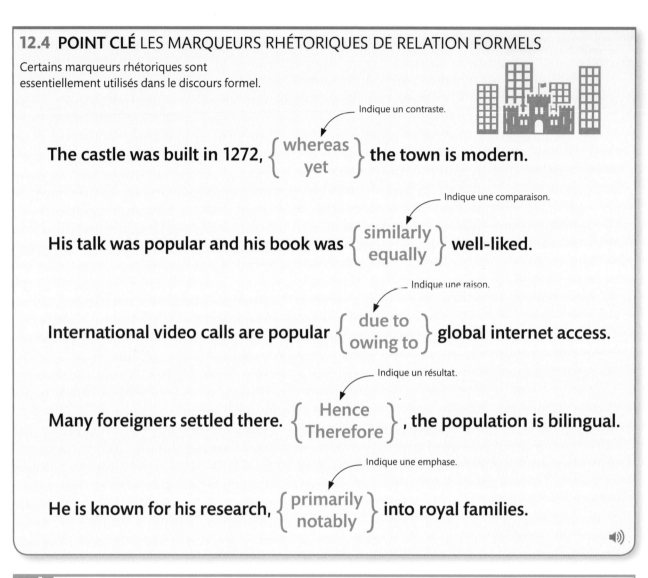

Indique un contraste.

The castle was built in 1272, { whereas / yet } the town is modern.

Indique une comparaison.

His talk was popular and his book was { similarly / equally } well-liked.

Indique une raison.

International video calls are popular { due to / owing to } global internet access.

Indique un résultat.

Many foreigners settled there. { Hence / Therefore }, the population is bilingual.

Indique une emphase.

He is known for his research, { primarily / notably } into royal families.

12.5 COMPLÉTEZ LES PHRASES AVEC DES MARQUEURS RHÉTORIQUES FORMELS.

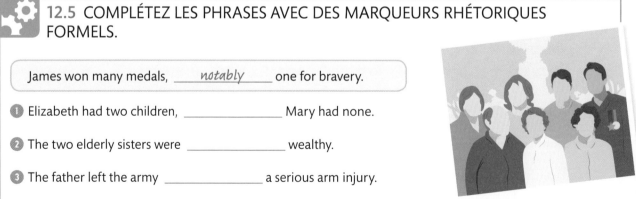

James won many medals, ___*notably*___ one for bravery.

1 Elizabeth had two children, _____ Mary had none.

2 The two elderly sisters were _____ wealthy.

3 The father left the army _____ a serious arm injury.

4 James and Tom were identical twins. _____ , they looked alike.

12.6 CHOISISSEZ LE MARQUEUR RHÉTORIQUE QUI CONVIENT LE MIEUX.

I like sandwiches, ~~whereas~~ / but the rest of my family are big pizza fans.

1. You have failed to respond to our messages. So / Hence , your subscription has been canceled.

2. My friends say I take after my dad, owing to / because we both like mountain biking.

3. After a successful book tour, the professor's lectures were equally / like well-received.

4. I love my aunts, notably / especially Meera, because she's so funny.

12.7 LISEZ L'ANNONCE, PUIS COCHEZ LES BONNES RÉPONSES.

It is less difficult to explore your family history than it used to be.
True ✓ False ☐

1. You have to go to the library to use the service.
True ☐ False ☐

2. J.W.'s great-grandfather died in battle.
True ☐ False ☐

3. N.H. enjoys socializing more than her parents.
True ☐ False ☐

4. The service has an annual $20 fee.
True ☐ False ☐

GENEALOGY OK

It has never been easier to research your family's history. Millions of family records, including births, deaths, marriages, as well as military and emigration records, are now available online. As a result, you can now find your ancestors from the comfort of your home. All of this and more can be discovered if you join our Genealogy OK club for only $20 a month.

Here are two of our members' stories:

"I thought that all my family were pacifists, like me. It turns out that my great-grandmother was a spy, and her young husband was a heroic soldier who died in combat." - J.W.

"I've always wondered where I get my party animal personality, since my mother and father are quite quiet. I've discovered that my great-grandmother and her sister were well-known socialites in years gone by." - N.H.

---

13 Les habitudes et les états passés

Pour parler d'habitudes ou d'états du passé, vous pouvez utiliser « used to » ou « would ». L'anglais emploie souvent ces formes pour contraster le passé avec le présent.

⚙ **Grammaire** « Used to » et « would »
Aa Vocabulaire Les valeurs familiales
🧩 **Compétence** Contraster le passé avec le présent

13.1 POINT CLÉ « USED TO »

Vous pouvez utiliser « used to » avec un infinitif pour parler d'habitudes passées.

Fait référence à une habitude passée.

We used to play tennis every day, but now we prefer golf.

PAST — NOW

Vous pouvez également l'utiliser pour parler d'états fixes à un moment indéfini du passé.

Fait référence à un état passé.

We used to live in London before we moved to Sydney.

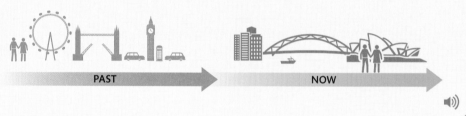

PAST — NOW

13.2 AUTRES EXEMPLES « USED TO »

« Used » devient « use » avec les formes négatives et interrogatives.

 Did you use to ride a scooter when you were a student?

 **I didn't use to believe in ghosts until I visited a haunted house.**

13.3 DIRE AUTREMENT « USED TO » ET LES HABITUDES

Vous pouvez aussi utiliser « would » pour parler d'habitudes passées de façon un peu plus formelle.

 When I was little, we would go for a picnic every Saturday.

 Whenever there was soccer on TV, we just wouldn't do our homework.

13.4 ⚠ ERREURS COURANTES « USED TO »

Il est incorrect d'utiliser « used to » conjointement à des moments précis
du passé, ou si vous dites avoir fait quelque chose plusieurs fois.

We used to play lots of board games when I was young. ✓

We used to play lots of
board games yesterday. ✗

We used to play board
games twenty times. ✗

13.5 COMPLÉTEZ LES PHRASES AVEC LES MOTS ENTRE PARENTHÈSES.

Whenever my uncle visited, he _____*would bring*_____ (would / bring) presents for us all.

1 My mother _____ (use to / walk) five miles to school and back.

2 I _____ (not / use to / like) using the internet, but now I think it's great!

3 _____ (do) you _____ (use to / eat) your lunch at school?

4 My grandmother's house _____ (not / use to / have) electricity.

5 Whenever I had a toothache, my dad _____ (would / take) me to a scary dentist.

13.6 RÉCRIVEZ LES PASSAGES SURLIGNÉS EN CORRIGEANT LES ERREURS.

used to be

1 _____

2 _____

3 _____

4 _____

5 _____

6 _____

When my grandmother tells me about how things did used to be, I realize how lucky I was as a child. I use to complain about having to walk to school in the rain, whereas she would to walk five miles to school in all types of weather, including snow! I used to got upset when a teacher told me off in class. I had usually done something really bad, but my grandmother didn't used to do anything bad. She used to wrote with her left hand, but back then, teachers will be punish you just for that!

13.7 ÉCOUTEZ L'ENREGISTREMENT, PUIS COCHEZ LES BONNES RÉPONSES.

  Rui et Livia ont un débat sur les valeurs familiales qui changent.

What does Rui say about young people?
They don't watch movies any more ☐
They watch movies on their own ☑
They don't go to the movies any more ☐

① What does Livia say about families?
They don't watch movies together ☐
They still watch movies on the TV ☐
They go to the movies together ☐

② What beneficial internet content does Livia mention?
Documentaries and old movies ☐
Documentaries and news archives ☐
Documentaries and new movies ☐

③ Where does Rui think young people used to get their values from?
Older family members ☐
Movies ☐
The Internet ☐

④ What does Livia say young people think about honesty?
It's very important to them ☐
It's not that important any more ☐
It's important for adults to be honest ☐

⑤ What does Livia say is important in today's world?
Understanding historical values ☐
Communicating with other people ☐
Understanding other people's values ☐

Aa 13.8 EN VOUS AIDANT DES INDICES, ÉCRIVEZ LES MOTS DE LA LISTE AU BON ENDROIT DANS LA GRILLE.

❶ Agreeing with or tolerating something

❷ Telling the truth

❸ What a person believes is right or wrong

❹ Wanting more things than you really need

❺ The qualities of someone's personality

❻ To say or do something that stops another person's actions

| values | ~~acceptance~~ | interrupt |
| character | greedy | honesty |

1 across: a c c e p t a n c e

13.9 LISEZ LE BLOG, PUIS RÉPONDEZ AUX QUESTIONS.

Researching my roots

HOME | ENTRIES | ABOUT | CONTACT

A long lost brother

A few years ago, my grandfather told me about a brother who he hadn't seen in a very long time. They lost touch over 50 years ago while they were both serving in the army overseas. I decided that I would try to find my great-uncle, the brother who my grandfather used to talk about so fondly.

I was in the library when I met a man called Robert who was also researching his family history. His grandfather also had a brother he hadn't seen for 50 years. The more we talked, the more similarities we had. Our grandfathers had both become teachers after they left the army. We realized after talking for an hour that our grandfathers were brothers. Astonishingly, they lived less than 20 miles apart from each other, and even used to live on the very same street! Last week my grandfather and my great-uncle met again for the first time in half a century.

When did the author's grandfather and great-uncle lose touch?

They lost touch over 50 years ago while they were both serving in the army overseas.

❶ Why did the author and Robert start talking?

_____

❷ What similarities did the author's grandfather and Robert's grandfather have?

_____

❸ Why was it surprising that the author's grandfather and great-uncle hadn't met in 50 years?

_____

❹ What happened last week?

_____

13 ✓ CHECK-LIST

⚙ « Used to » et « would » ☐   **Aa** Les valeurs familiales ☐   🧩 Contraster le passé avec le présent ☐

14 Comparer et contraster

Employer « as... as » est une manière facile de faire des comparaisons. Vous pouvez l'utiliser pour comparer et contraster des quantités ou des qualités de personnes, d'objets, de situations et d'idées.

⚙ **Grammaire** Les comparaisons avec « as... as »
Aa Vocabulaire Les collocations adjectif-nom
🧩 **Compétence** Comparer et contraster

14.1 POINT CLÉ LES COMPARAISONS AVEC « AS... AS »

Vous pouvez utiliser « as... as » avec un adjectif pour comparer des choses similaires et « not as... as » ou « not so... as » pour contraster des choses différentes.

Lisa is as tall as Marc.

Penny is not { as / so } tall as Marc.

14.2 AUTRES EXEMPLES LES COMPARAISONS AVEC « AS... AS »

Vous pouvez modifier la structure « as... as » pour plus de détails ou d'emphase.

Accentue l'égalité.

Bottled water is just as expensive as coffee.

Compare la similarité.

The girls were almost as loud as the boys.

Cette expression est très similaire à « almost as » mais accentue la différence plutôt que les points communs.

The movie is not quite as good as the book.

Degré de différence spécifique.

The bike is half as long as the car.

Souligne la différence.

The mouse is nowhere near as big as the bird.

14.3 OBSERVEZ LES IMAGES, COMPLÉTEZ LES PHRASES AVEC « AS... AS », PUIS LISEZ-LES À VOIX HAUTE.

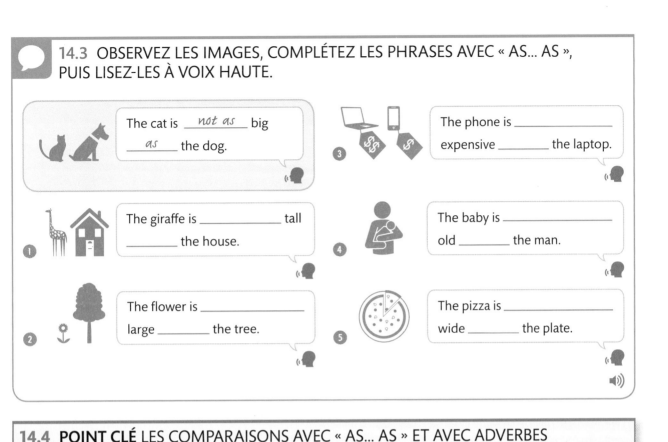

The cat is *not as* big *as* the dog.

The phone is _____ expensive _____ the laptop.

The giraffe is _____ tall _____ the house.

The baby is _____ old _____ the man.

The flower is _____ large _____ the tree.

The pizza is _____ wide _____ the plate.

14.4 POINT CLÉ LES COMPARAISONS AVEC « AS... AS » ET AVEC ADVERBES

Vous pouvez aussi utiliser la structure « as... as » avec des adverbes,
souvent suivis d'expressions de capacité ou de possibilité.

I don't visit as often as my sister.

We sang as loudly as possible.

He arrived as early as he could.

The boys study as hard as the girls.

14.5 ÉCOUTEZ L'ENREGISTREMENT, PUIS COCHEZ LES BONNES RÉPONSES.

Which is more expensive?
The soup ☐ **The steak** ☑

1 Which is funnier?
The old video ☐ **The new video** ☐

2 Which is faster?
The motorcycle ☐ **The car** ☐

3 Which is bigger?
The old house ☐ **The new house** ☐

4 Who is smarter?
Simon ☐ **Andrew** ☐

5 How frequently does Akiko visit now?
More often ☐ **Less often** ☐

14.6 LISEZ L'ARTICLE, PUIS COCHEZ LES BONNES RÉPONSES.

The young baby's father is called...
Sam ☐ Zach ☐ Jon ☑

1 The mother of the baby is...
a teacher ☐ a lawyer ☐ unemployed ☐

2 The person on parental leave from work is...
Sam ☐ Zach ☐ Jon ☐

3 When Samantha walks to work it takes...
35 mins ☐ 40 mins ☐ 45 mins ☐

4 Samantha does not walk to work if the weather is...
cold ☐ windy ☐ rainy ☐

5 Most days Samantha walks to work...
alone ☐ with a friend ☐ with her family ☐

6 Her friends and family think her decision is...
stupid ☐ good ☐ bad ☐

A different approach

The surprise benefits of shared parental leave
by Samantha Pope

The new "shared parental leave" law is great for my family. As a lawyer I earn twice as much as my husband, Jon, who is a teacher. This meant that we were going to pay a high price for me taking a career break at this time. I returned to work quite soon after our baby, Zach, was born, and Jon has taken parental leave from his work to be at home.

Of course, I still share lots of time with Zach. Because Jon is a heavy sleeper, I wake up to do nighttime duties. This does make me a bit tired, but a strong coffee in the morning and a quick walk to work (unless there's heavy rain) normally wakes me up. In the morning, Jon and Zach usually walk with me through the park. We were surprised to discover that this 40-minute walk is actually almost as quick as me driving the car in heavy traffic at rush hour.

I was worried that my friends and family would have a low opinion of me going back to work as soon as I did, but in the end everyone agreed with us.

Aa 14.7 COMPLÉTEZ LES PHRASES AVEC LES MOTS DE LA LISTE AFIN DE CRÉER DES COLLOCATIONS.

Every time I walk to work I get caught in [*heavy* rain] .

1 Thankfully, our baby is a [sleeper] and only wakes once a night.

2 The commute to work takes ages, even when there is [traffic] .

3 Feeling sick every day is a [price] to pay for going on a cruise.

4 I only really wake up in the morning after a [coffee] .

5 My mother has a [opinion] of anyone who doesn't work hard.

| ~~heavy~~ | strong | high | low | heavy | light |

CONSEIL
Les mots qui sont cooccurrents avec un adjectif sont souvent cooccurrents avec leur contraire. Par exemple, « heavy rain » et « light rain ».

14.8 COMPLÉTEZ LES PHRASES AVEC LES MOTS DE LA LISTE.

Alex and Sue are both chefs. Sue owns a café and Alex works in a famous restaurant. Sue's cooking is ___*just as*___ good _____ Alex's, maybe even better, although his cooking is mostly savory and she has a sweet tooth. Unfortunately, just because her food costs _____ much _____ his, some people do not have as _____ an opinion of her skills. Her café is seen as somewhere with _____ prices to grab a bite to eat, not somewhere to wine and dine people. Sue says this is a small price to pay for owning her own business. Some people just like to go out of their way to pay _____ much _____ they should for a three-course meal in Alex's restaurant, rather than enjoy a delicious piece of cake or pastry in Sue's café.

as	half as	high	as	twice as	low	as	~~just as~~

Aa 14.9 RELIEZ LES SYNTAGMES À LEUR DÉFINITION.

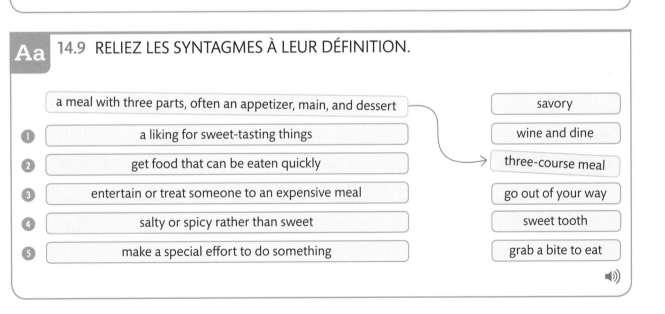

a meal with three parts, often an appetizer, main, and dessert — savory

1. a liking for sweet-tasting things — wine and dine
2. get food that can be eaten quickly — three-course meal
3. entertain or treat someone to an expensive meal — go out of your way
4. salty or spicy rather than sweet — sweet tooth
5. make a special effort to do something — grab a bite to eat

14 ✅ CHECK-LIST

⚙️ Les comparaisons avec « as... as » ☐   **Aa** Les collocations adjectif-nom ☐   🧩 Comparer et contraster ☐

15 Le double comparatif

Vous pouvez utiliser deux comparatifs dans une phrase pour montrer l'effet d'une action. Vous pouvez aussi les employer pour montrer que quelque chose est en train de changer.

🔧 **Grammaire** Le double comparatif
Aa **Vocabulaire** L'âge et la population
🧩 **Compétence** Exprimer la cause et l'effet

15.1 POINT CLÉ LE DOUBLE COMPARATIF

Vous pouvez faire des comparaisons pour décrire la cause et l'effet en utilisant deux comparatifs dans la même phrase.

The harder I train, the stronger I get.

Laisse entendre que faire de l'exercice vous rend plus fort.

15.2 AUTRES EXEMPLES LE DOUBLE COMPARATIF

The worse the children behave, the angrier the teacher gets.

The louder the cat meows, the louder the dog barks.

15.3 CONSTRUCTION LE DOUBLE COMPARATIF

« THE »	EXPRESSION COMPARATIVE	SUJET	VERBE	« THE »	EXPRESSION COMPARATIVE	SUJET	VERBE
The	harder	I	train,	the	stronger	I	get.

15.4 ÉCRIVEZ LES MOTS SUIVANTS DANS LE BON ORDRE AFIN DE RECONSTITUER LES PHRASES.

| The | terrified | he | more | drives | become. | faster | the | I |

The faster he drives, the more terrified I become.

1. | longer | went | the | more | The | the | film | on | bored | I | became. |

_____

2. | quicker | it | more | the | rained | The | the | vegetables | grew. |

_____

3. | me | more | not | The | she | the | to | laugh | told | more | I | laughed. |

_____

4. | a | it | dessert | The | contains | is | for | sugar | more | the | worse | you. |

_____

◀))

 15.5 RÉCRIVEZ LES PHRASES EN CORRIGEANT LES ERREURS.

I've noticed that the less I sleep, grumpier I am.
I've noticed that the less I sleep, the grumpier I am.

1. The louder my music is, the more angrier my mother gets.

_____

2. The young the skier is, the less frightened of falling they are.

_____

3. The annoyed my teacher gets, more I giggle nervously.

_____

4. Faster the car went, louder the passengers screamed.

_____

◀))

15.6 DIRE AUTREMENT LE DOUBLE COMPARATIF

Un double comparatif utilisant « the better » peut être raccourci en supprimant le sujet et le verbe.

How do you like your tea?

The stronger the better.

Can I bring my brother along?

Sure! The more the merrier.

Cette expression signifie que les personnes sont les bienvenues.

15.7 RELIEZ CHAQUE QUESTION À LA RÉPONSE CORRESPONDANTE.

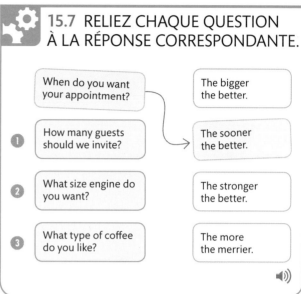

When do you want your appointment?

The bigger the better.

1 How many guests should we invite?

The sooner the better.

2 What size engine do you want?

The stronger the better.

3 What type of coffee do you like?

The more the merrier.

15.8 POINT CLÉ LE DOUBLE COMPARATIF

Un comparatif peut être répété pour montrer que quelque chose est en train de changer.

The weather is getting colder and colder.

La répétition accentue le fait que le changement est continu.

15.9 LISEZ L'ARTICLE, PUIS COCHEZ LES BONNES RÉPONSES.

People are living longer than they used to.
True ✓ **False** ☐ **Not given** ☐

1 There are fewer babies being born these days.
True ☐ **False** ☐ **Not given** ☐

2 Pensions and social care will cost nations more.
True ☐ **False** ☐ **Not given** ☐

3 A younger workforce is more experienced.
True ☐ **False** ☐ **Not given** ☐

4 Retired people have more time to do charity work.
True ☐ **False** ☐ **Not given** ☐

YOUR HEALTH

We're all living longer and longer

Life expectancy has risen around the world and older people make up a larger and larger proportion of the population in many countries.

An aging population can cause challenges such as increasing pension and social care costs.

However, there are also potential benefits. The older a workforce is, the more skills and experience it has. Also, as people live longer after retirement, they can offer more time to good causes such as volunteering for charity.

15.10 ÉCOUTEZ L'ENREGISTREMENT, PUIS COCHEZ LES BONNES RÉPONSES.

 Une station de radio diffuse un reportage
sur les populations vieillissantes.

> What two reasons are mentioned for people living longer?
> *The news report mentions improved healthcare and improved standards of living.*

1 What economic issue do aging populations lead to?

_____

2 In the first suggested solution, who is responsible for people's care in old age?

_____

3 In the second suggested solution, who is responsible for people's care in old age?

_____

4 What is the third suggested solution?

_____

---

15 ✓ CHECK-LIST

⚙ Le double comparatif ☐   **Aa** L'âge et la population ☐   🧩 Exprimer la cause et l'effet ☐

↻ BILAN L'ANGLAIS QUE VOUS AVEZ APPRIS DANS LES CHAPITRES 12-15

NOUVEAU POINT LINGUISTIQUE	EXEMPLE TYPE	☑	CHAPITRE
LES MARQUEURS RHÉTORIQUES DE RELATION INFORMELS	I like listening to music, but my mother hates it.	☐	12.1
LES MARQUEURS RHÉTORIQUES DE RELATION FORMELS	The castle is ancient, whereas the town is modern.	☐	12.4
« USED TO » ET « WOULD »	We used to live in London before we moved to Sydney. Whenever my uncle visited, he would bring us presents.	☐	13.1, 13.3
LES COMPARAISONS AVEC « AS... AS »	Lisa is as tall as Marc.	☐	14.1
LE DOUBLE COMPARATIF	The harder I train, the better I get. The weather is getting colder and colder.	☐	15.1, 15.6, 15.8

16.1 LES ÉTUDES

My daughter took a year off **before starting university.**

take a year off (US) / take a year out (UK)
[have a year away from education or work]

My brother enrolled in **an accounting course this week.**

enrol in (US) / enrol on (UK)
[register to start something]

The college provides housing for undergraduates.

undergraduate
[someone studying for a first degree at college or university]

She is a graduate **student of biochemistry.**

graduate (US) / postgraduate (UK)
[study carried out following graduation from a first degree]

When I was a freshman, **everything seemed so exciting.**

freshman (US) / fresher (UK)
[a student in their first year at college or university]

Make sure you plan ahead. You have to write four essays this semester.

semester (US) / term (UK)
[a period of time in an academic calendar, during which classes are held]

I will be the first person in my family to get a degree.

get a degree
[be awarded a qualification after college or university]

It is very important to attend classes **regularly and keep notes.**

attend classes
[go to lessons or lectures]

I was so nervous before I took my driving test, **but I passed!**

take a test / take an exam
[answer questions or perform actions to show how much you know about something]

My tutors give me regular feedback on **my projects.**

give someone feedback on something
[provide comments and advice on how somebody is doing something]

I worked late last night to meet the deadline for this report.

meet a deadline
[finish something within a given time]

He's so unreliable! He's always missing deadlines for projects.

miss a deadline
[fail to finish something within a given time]

We have continuous assessment, not final exams.

continuous assessment
[grading based on work done over a long period]

You can't draw a comparison between then and now.

draw a comparison between
[point out similarities between things]

The essay asked us to compare the similarities between the countries.

compare similarities
[consider and describe how things are alike]

We looked at two pictures and contrasted the differences.

contrast differences
[consider and describe how things differ from each other]

Their views on this subject are polar opposites.

polar opposite
[completely different]

There is a clear distinction between these projects.

clear distinction
[an obvious difference]

For twins, their interests are strikingly different.

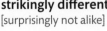

strikingly different
[surprisingly not alike]

Your hard work has made a world of difference this year.

a world of difference
[a significant level of difference]

17 Prendre des notes

Les marqueurs rhétoriques peuvent aider l'auditeur ou le lecteur à mieux comprendre votre message. Ils sont très utiles lorsque l'on prend des notes.

⚙ **Grammaire** Organiser l'information
Aa Vocabulaire La vie universitaire
🧩 **Compétence** Prendre des notes

17.1 POINT CLÉ LES MARQUEURS RHÉTORIQUES D'ORGANISATION FORMELS

Certains marqueurs rhétoriques précisent ce qui suit. Ils facilitent l'organisation de paragraphes et de passages plus longs de texte formel.

> **CONSEIL**
> Les marqueurs rhétoriques sont généralement placés en début de phrase ou de proposition.

Les marqueurs de séquence peuvent vous être utiles pour ordonner l'information.

First, it is important to consider which courses you want to study.

Certains marqueurs introduisent des points nouveaux ou supplémentaires.

Moreover, you should bear in mind where you want to study.

D'autres mettent l'accent sur des exemples.

For instance, you should consider if you want to study abroad.

On utilise les marqueurs de conclusion pour résumer.

In conclusion, several factors will affect your choice of college.

🔊

Aa 17.2 LISEZ LE PROSPECTUS, PUIS CLASSEZ LES MARQUEURS RHÉTORIQUES DANS LE BON ENCADRÉ.

INTERNATIONAL OPTIONS

WHY STUDY ABROAD?

First, it is easier to learn a foreign language abroad. You can enjoy other aspects of the country's culture such as the food and music. Second, you can get a global perspective on your subject. Additionally, universities abroad may specialize in different subjects. Furthermore, your university base may act as a springboard for further travel in the region. For example, a Korean base could lead to more Asian travel. Overall, there are many cultural and educational reasons to study abroad. To sum up, study abroad opens doors.

SEQUENCING
first
_____

EXAMPLES
such as
_____

ADDING
additionally
_____

CONCLUDING
overall
_____

🔊

17.3 BARREZ LE MOT INCORRECT DANS CHAQUE PHRASE.

> Some universities are known globally, for example / ~~secondly~~ Yale and Oxford.

1 Others, additionally / such as Sydney University and Toronto, are renowned for their stunning historical buildings.

2 Moreover / To sum up, there are newer universities like Moscow and Xiamen that have equally impressive buildings.

3 For instance / Next, Moscow State University is incredibly impressive at night.

4 Third / Additionally, a number of modern university buildings in Australia are spectacular.

5 Such as / Overall, there are some amazing educational buildings around the world.

6 To sum up / First, it can be worth your time to look at educational buildings, even if you are visiting as a tourist.

🔊

17.4 ÉCOUTEZ L'ENREGISTREMENT, PUIS COCHEZ LES BONNES RÉPONSES.

Une discussion a lieu au sujet de la Semaine de bienvenue, la première semaine des étudiants.

> Classes start on Monday in two weeks.
> True ☐   False ☐   Not given ✓

1 Clubs are free to join during Welcome Week.
True ☐   False ☐   Not given ☐

2 You will need your ID to register.
True ☐   False ☐   Not given ☐

3 You can find all the books on your book list in the library.
True ☐   False ☐   Not given ☐

4 Your library card can be used in the cafeteria.
True ☐   False ☐   Not given ☐

5 You should tell your academic department about accommodation problems.
True ☐   False ☐   Not given ☐

17.5 POINT CLÉ LES MARQUEURS RHÉTORIQUES D'ORGANISATION INFORMELS

Vous pouvez utiliser un certain nombre de marqueurs rhétoriques généraux pour passer d'un sujet à l'autre en anglais parlé.

Ici, « Right » permet d'attirer l'attention avant de dire quelque chose d'important.

Right, let's get started...

Ici, « OK » permet de montrer à votre interlocuteur que vous l'avez bien entendu.

... **OK,** and are you happy with your choice?

Ici, « So » indique que vous arrivez à une conclusion.

... **So,** I think we agree overall.

🔊

69

17.6 POINT CLÉ LE CONDITIONNEL ZÉRO

Vous pouvez utiliser le conditionnel zéro pour parler de choses qui sont généralement ou toujours vraies.

If you study every day, you learn more quickly.

On peut parfois utiliser « when » au lieu de « if ».

When you sign up for a club, you meet new people.

« Unless » signifie « if... not. » (If you don't have a lot of money, don't join every club.)

Unless you have a lot of money, don't join every club.

17.7 RELIEZ LE DÉBUT DE CHAQUE PHRASE À LA FIN QUI LUI CORRESPOND.

When you join the photography club → you can exhibit your own work.

you can join the historical society.

❶ You must pay to play tennis

unless you need more time to think.

❷ If you are a history student,

unless you join the club.

❸ If you join the water sports club,

❹ You can join today

you can learn how to sail.

17.8 COMPLÉTEZ LES PHRASES AVEC LES MOTS DE LA LISTE.

If you try to write every word, you ____*get*____ lost very quickly.

❶ If you hear _____ markers, use them to help organize your notes.

❷ When you take notes, _____ a simple shorthand with symbols and abbreviations.

❸ If your handwriting is messy, try to _____ sure it is readable.

❹ Unless you record every lecture, try to _____ your notes soon after.

discourse

review

make

~~get~~

use

17.9 ÉCOUTEZ LE COURS UNIVERSITAIRE, PUIS CHOISISSEZ LES MEILLEURES NOTES DE SYNTHÈSE.

Before start the course... more information on taking notes at university. Spoken already about tips and advice but a little about passive and active note-taking differences. If have handout and listen to lecture and underline something = not actively engaging in the lecture. Recording lecture/ borrowing friend's notes = not engaging in the lecture. Trying to write every word from lecture = passively note-taking.

Passive and active note-taking: June 17

Passive note-taking examples:
1. Underlining
2. Recording
3. Borrowing notes
4. Writing down everything

Doesn't save time in the end because can't remember what said.

Lecture notes from June 17

- Passive note-taking is "not actively engaging in the lecture"

- If you "sit and record the lecture or borrow your friend's notes then you are not fully engaging"

- It is still passive note-taking "even if you try to write down every word from the lecture".

1 ☐   **2** ☐   **3** ☐

 17.10 ÉCOUTEZ LE RESTE DU COURS, PUIS PRENNEZ DES NOTES SUR CE QUE VOUS ENTENDEZ.

Active note-taking examples:

_____

_____

_____

_____

_____

17 ✔ **CHECK-LIST**

⚙ Organiser l'information ☐   **Aa** La vie universitaire ☐   🧩 Prendre des notes ☐

18 Exprimer l'approximation

La langue anglaise possède de nombreuses expressions utiles pour décrire des quantités et montants approximatifs. Vous pouvez les utiliser lorsqu'un chiffre n'est pas connu ou est approximatif.

⚙ **Grammaire** La généralisation
Aa Vocabulaire Les expressions de quantités approximatives
🧩 **Compétence** Parler de nombres

18.1 POINT CLÉ LES QUANTITÉS APPROXIMATIVES

Si vous avez des chiffres précis, il peut être utile de les communiquer. Toutefois, vous devrez peut-être utiliser des termes plus généraux si vous n'avez pas de chiffres ou si vous voulez éviter des répétitions.

3 out of 15 students live off campus.

In some cases, **students live off campus.**

« Some » est un terme très vague. Les seuls chiffres qui ne sont pas concernés dans cet exemple sont 0, 1 ou 15 (élèves).

🔊

18.2 AUTRES EXEMPLES LES QUANTITÉS APPROXIMATIVES

> **CONSEIL**
> Les termes « minority » et « majorité » sont souvent qualifiés : par exemple « small minority » ou « vast majority ».

Une minorité est moins de la moitié, mais évoque souvent beaucoup moins de la moitié.

In a minority of cases, }
In a few cases, } **employers provide funding for education.**

« Most » et « majority » veulent dire plus de la moitié.

In most cases, }
In the majority of cases, } **students can contact their professors online.**

Les références vagues peuvent signifier une majorité ou une minorité de cas.

In some cases, }
In a number of cases, } **students can live in dorms on campus.**

🔊

18.3 ÉCOUTEZ L'ENREGISTREMENT, PUIS NUMÉROTEZ LES IMAGES DANS LE BON ORDRE.

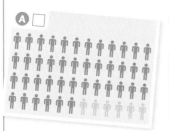 Ⓐ ☐

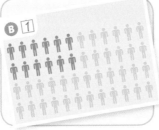 Ⓑ ①

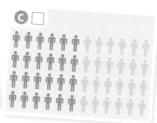 Ⓒ ☐

 Ⓓ ☐

18.4 POINT CLÉ LES STATISTIQUES APPROXIMATIVES

Vous pouvez généraliser des statistiques en les modifiant avec des termes
tels que « approximately », « well » ou « just ».

 Approximately **half of the students are from Europe.**

 Just under **a third of the assessment consists of coursework.**

 Well over **50 percent of the course is online.**

 18.5 BARREZ LE MOT INCORRECT DANS CHAQUE PHRASE.

> **52%** Approximately / ~~well over~~ half of the students are male.

❶ **97%** The vast majority / minority of the lecture halls have wireless internet access.

❷ **27%** Just / well over a quarter of classes are recorded for students to listen to online.

❸ **85%** After one week, most / some people know their way around campus.

❹ **4%** Only a huge / tiny minority of our students do not have smartphones.

❺ **72%** Well over / under half of our students eat a hot meal on campus.

❻ **67%** Just over / under two-thirds of our professors can speak two languages.

18.6 POINT CLÉ DES NOMBRES SURPRENANTS

Certaines expressions sont utilisées pour indiquer qu'un nombre ou une quantité en particulier sont surprenants.

Ceci indique que la somme de 100 € est étonnamment importante.

Other universities charge as much as **€100 for this service.**

Ceci indique que cette somme d'argent est étonnamment modeste.

For as little as **$5 per semester, you can join the club.**

Ceci indique que ce nombre d'événements est étonnamment important.

There are as many as **25 free student events each month.**

Ceci indique que ce nombre de jours est étonnamment faible.

The library is generally closed for as few as **2 days a month.**

📖 18.7 LISEZ LE PROSPECTUS, PUIS COCHEZ LES BONNES RÉPONSES.

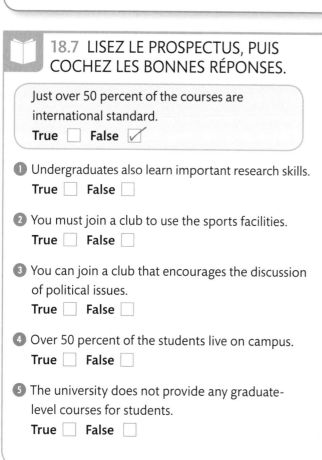

Just over 50 percent of the courses are international standard.
True ☐ False ☑

① Undergraduates also learn important research skills.
True ☐ False ☐

② You must join a club to use the sports facilities.
True ☐ False ☐

③ You can join a club that encourages the discussion of political issues.
True ☐ False ☐

④ Over 50 percent of the students live on campus.
True ☐ False ☐

⑤ The university does not provide any graduate-level courses for students.
True ☐ False ☐

Why study with us?

Academic Excellence We are one of the top 20 colleges in the country in terms of teaching quality, with the vast majority of our courses rated as international standard. Our undergraduates come from all over the world, attracted by our outstanding teaching and research guidance.

Superb Facilities We strive to ensure that you have a first-class student experience. Our excellent sports facilities are open to all and include an Olympic-size swimming pool. For those interested in the arts, we have a successful drama department, an art gallery, and a multiscreen cinema. We have as many as 40 different sport, cultural, political, and volunteering clubs to choose from.

Accommodation In most cases, our students prefer to live on campus. In other cases, however, students may wish to live off campus. Our friendly accommodation team can also help with this.

Careers Our Career Development Center can help with your present and future career choices. Approximately half our students continue to pursue a graduate-level course with us. Our dedicated team can help you make the best choice for your future.

18.8 POINT CLÉ REMETTRE EN QUESTION DES GÉNÉRALISATIONS

Une façon polie d'indiquer que vous n'êtes pas d'accord avec une généralisation est de la remettre en question. Utilisez des questions telles que « Is that so? », « Really? », « Is that right?" et « Are you sure? » avant de contester une généralisation.

I've been told that the campus is very unwelcoming and quiet.

Is that so? **My experience has not been like that at all.**

Vous pouvez ne pas être d'accord avec le commentaire après votre question.

18.9 RÉPONDEZ AUX QUESTIONS EN REMETTANT EN QUESTION LES GÉNÉRALISATIONS DES FAITS DU PROSPECTUS DE L'EXERCICE 18.7, PUIS LISEZ LES PHRASES À VOIX HAUTE.

All the students come from the same country.

Is that right? *I read that there were students from all over the world there.*

① There isn't much to do there.

Really? _____

② The accommodation is really poor.

Is that so? _____

③ They don't offer you any advice for after you have graduated.

Are you sure? _____

---

19 Changer l'emphase

Il y a de nombreuses manières de changer l'emphase en anglais : vous pouvez par exemple avoir recours à une construction grammaticale moins courante, comme la voix passive.

🔧 **Grammaire** La voix passive
Aa **Vocabulaire** L'apprentissage en ligne
🧩 **Compétence** Changer l'emphase de la phrase

19.1 POINT CLÉ LA VOIX PASSIVE

Dans une phrase à la voix passive, l'emphase passe de l'agent (personne ou chose effectuant l'action) à l'action (personne ou objet la recevant).

Le focus est sur le fait qu'il y a de nombreuses personnes.

Many people studied the book.

Le sujet du verbe à la voix active est « Many people ».

The book was studied by many people.

Le focus est sur le livre.

Le sujet du verbe à la voix passive est « the book ».

19.2 QUAND UTILISER LA VOIX PASSIVE

On utilise le passif lorsque l'agent est évident, inconnu ou sans importance. Il est également utile pour décrire un processus dont le résultat de l'action est important.

L'agent n'est pas précisé puisque le verbe fait manifestement référence à la police.

Hopefully, the thief will be arrested soon.

L'agent n'est pas précisé car il est inconnu.

Sarah's laptop was stolen from the library.

L'agent n'est pas précisé puisque le processus est ce qui est important ici, et non pas la personne qui l'a réalisé.

The posters are printed on good quality paper.

19.3 CONSTRUCTION LA VOIX PASSIVE

Pour former le passif, utilisez « be » avec le participe passé. Employez « by » pour introduire l'agent.

Utilisez les différentes formes de « be » pour les formes passées, continues, futures et parfaites (perfect) du passif.

SUJET	« BE »	PARTICIPE PASSÉ	« BY »
The book	was was being will be had been	studied	**by many people.**

19.4 LISEZ LE TEXTE, PUIS CHOISISSEZ LE BON RÉSUMÉ.

The rise of online learning

Massive Open Online Courses (MOOCs) are open to anyone, anywhere, and often have subscriptions in the thousands. Millions of people around the world are currently taking part in MOOCs and studying everything from digital photography through to engineering and science. The courses are free, though you may have to pay for a certificate to prove that you have taken the course.

1️⃣ Millions of people are being enrolled onto each MOOC. ☐

2️⃣ MOOCs are being taken online by millions of people. ☐

3️⃣ MOOCs will be being taken by thousands of people. ☐

 19.5 BARREZ LE MOT INCORRECT DANS CHAQUE PHRASE.

Many of the students could ~~affect~~ / be affected by the changes.

1️⃣ English is spoken / speaks by millions of people across the world.

2️⃣ Online courses are studying / are being studied by a variety of students.

3️⃣ The courses are paying for / are being paid for by a number of universities.

4️⃣ Certificates can be printed out / can print out at home by participants.

5️⃣ Some exams can be taken / take in several different languages.

🔊

 19.6 RÉCRIVEZ LES PHRASES EN UTILISANT LA VOIX PASSIVE.

CONSEIL
N'oubliez pas que vous pouvez ne pas utiliser d'agent si le message est clair.

More than 400 universities across the world offer MOOCs.

MOOCs   _are offered by more than 400 universities across the world._

1️⃣ People write 80 percent of the courses in English.

Eighty percent _____

2️⃣ Some universities offer credits for MOOC courses.

Credits _____

3️⃣ Some people provide technical help for the participants.

Technical help _____

4️⃣ Millions of students will take MOOCs next year.

Next year, MOOCs _____

🔊

19.7 POINT CLÉ LES NOMS FORMÉS À PARTIR DE VERBES À PARTICULE

Certains noms sont formés à partir de verbes à particule, souvent en joignant le verbe et la particule.
À l'oral, l'accentuation est généralement placée sur le verbe.

The teacher asked me to hand out the exam papers.

Verbe ⟋   Particule ⟍

The teacher gave us a handout containing homework tasks.

Nom ⟍

Le nom est parfois formé en plaçant la particule devant le verbe.
Dans ce cas, à l'oral, l'accentuation se place généralement sur la particule.

Oh no! It was sunny and now it's pouring down.

On forme le pluriel en ajoutant un « s »
au nom nouvellement formé. ⟍

We have a rainy season with daily downpours.

🔊

Aa 19.8 RELIEZ CHAQUE DÉFINITION AU MOT QUI LUI CORRESPOND.

people who watch something happening without taking part	crackdown
❶ failure, or a sudden decline in reputation or rank	outset
❷ severe action taken by an authority to stop a certain activity	backup
❸ extra support or help / a copy of computer data	onlookers
❹ the act of signing in to a computer program or system	downfall
❺ time or knowledge that has been put into a project	leftovers
❻ what remains at the end of eating a meal	input
❼ the act of registering your arrival at a hotel or airport	login
❽ the beginning or start of something	check-in

🔊

19.9 LISEZ L'ARTICLE, PUIS COCHEZ LES BONNES RÉPONSES.

A very narrow range of courses is provided online nowadays.
True ☐ **False** ☐ **Not given** ☑

1 Business management is being studied more than any other subject online.
True ☐ **False** ☐ **Not given** ☐

2 With online courses, contributions can be posted at any time.
True ☐ **False** ☐ **Not given** ☐

3 Blended learning courses are written by university professors.
True ☐ **False** ☐ **Not given** ☐

Education Nation

HOME   ENTRIES   ABOUT   CONTACT

Online or face-to-face?

You can take a multitude of courses online nowadays: everything from online yoga through to a Master's degree in business management. But what are the pros and cons of online learning and how does it compare with the face-to-face experience? Of course one major advantage of learning online is that it is often more flexible. You can read and write whenever and wherever you like. Another bonus is that these courses are often cheaper or even free. However, because you are not in the same place as your peers, or even online at the same time, you may miss out on the camaraderie and peer support. Sometimes online learning can be a lonely experience. So, what is the solution? Well, maybe you can have the best of both worlds. With blended learning, you can have some face-to-face lessons while other course content is delivered online.

19.10 COMPLÉTEZ LES PHRASES AVEC LES MOTS DE LA LISTE, EN UTILISANT LES VOIX ET FORME CORRECTES.

My Italian class ___is delivered___ online, with classes on Fridays.

1 The things we learn are _____ in a weekly online exam.

2 The face-to-face lessons expand on the online course _____ .

3 From the _____ , I knew this course would be successful.

4 Lack of motivation has always been my _____ in online learning.

5 The course is _____ by language-learning experts.

6 They have made changes to make it easier to _____ to your account.

7 There has also been a _____ on security to prevent cheating.

outset
~~deliver~~
downfall
write
crackdown
log in
test
input

19 ✓ CHECK-LIST

⚙️ La voix passive ☐   **Aa** L'apprentissage en ligne ☐   🧩 Changer l'emphase de la phrase ☐

20 Cela pourrait arriver

Il y a plusieurs façons de parler de situations futures hypothétiques. Vous pouvez utiliser différentes constructions pour indiquer si vous pensez qu'une hypothèse est probable ou improbable.

⚙ **Grammaire** « What if », « suppose » et « in case »
Aa Vocabulaire Les examens et les évaluations
🧩 **Compétence** Parler de situations hypothétiques

20.1 POINT CLÉ LES ÉVÉNEMENTS SUSCEPTIBLES DE SE PRODUIRE

Si un résultat est susceptible de se produire dans le futur, vous pouvez utiliser « what if », « suppose » et « in case » avec le présent pour l'exprimer.

« What if » signifie « Que se passerait-il si une situation hypothétique avait lieu ? »

L'utilisation du présent indique que le locuteur pense que ceci est susceptible de se produire.

What if I fail my exams?
I won't be able to go to college.

20.2 AUTRES EXEMPLES LES ÉVÉNEMENTS SUSCEPTIBLES DE SE PRODUIRE

« Suppose » fait référence aux conséquences d'une situation hypothétique.

**Suppose they assess our coursework.
We will have to keep a portfolio.**

We should start organizing our project work in case they want to see it.

« In case » signifie que l'on se prépare pour la situation hypothétique.

20.3 RELIEZ LES SITUATIONS AUX CONSÉQUENCES PROBABLES.

What if we don't pass our exams?	Maybe you could apply for funding.
❶ I'm going to take a water bottle	in case the exam room is hot.
❷ Suppose you cannot afford to study.	Maybe we'll have to take them again.
❸ I am studying really hard tonight	Maybe they will have spares.
❹ What if I forget to bring a calculator?	in case we have a test tomorrow.

20.4 POINT CLÉ LES ÉVÉNEMENTS PEU SUSCEPTIBLES DE SE PRODUIRE

Lorsqu'un résultat est possible, mais peu susceptible de se réaliser dans le futur, vous pouvez utiliser « what if » et « suppose » avec le passé pour l'exprimer. Vous pouvez également employer « just in case » avec le présent.

L'emploi du passé indique que le locuteur pense qu'il est peu probable que cet événement se réalise.

Just imagine! What if we all passed our exams with perfect scores?

20.5 AUTRES EXEMPLES LES ÉVÉNEMENTS PEU SUSCEPTIBLES DE SE PRODUIRE

« Suppose » et « supposing » sont interchangeables dans ce contexte.

Suppose I got caught cheating. My parents would be furious.

« Just » est ajouté à « in case » pour parer à l'éventualité d'une situation qui pourrait se produire.

You should apply for a job just in case you fail your exams.

Le verbe reste au présent après « just in case ».

20.6 INDIQUEZ SI LE RÉSULTAT EST PROBABLE OU PEU PROBABLE.

> I've studied hard. I'm buying champagne in case I pass all my exams. **Likely** ☑ **Unlikely** ☐

① What if she notices that I've copied the essay from the internet? **Likely** ☐ **Unlikely** ☐

② Suppose I won the lottery. I could afford to study abroad. **Likely** ☐ **Unlikely** ☐

③ Suppose I write three good essays. That will be enough. **Likely** ☐ **Unlikely** ☐

④ What if I studied for 14 hours every day from now on? **Likely** ☐ **Unlikely** ☐

⑤ Suppose the examiner asks my name in French. What should I say? **Likely** ☐ **Unlikely** ☐

⑥ I'm taking 10 pencils to the exam just in case nine break. **Likely** ☐ **Unlikely** ☐

⑦ It's supposed to stop raining, but I'll bring an umbrella in case it doesn't. **Likely** ☐ **Unlikely** ☐

⑧ What if I misunderstood all the questions? That would be a disaster. **Likely** ☐ **Unlikely** ☐

20.7 POINT CLÉ LE PREMIER ET LE DEUXIÈME CONDITIONNEL

PREMIER CONDITIONNEL

Vous pouvez utiliser le premier conditionnel pour parler de résultats futurs réalistes, si une condition réaliste est remplie.

« If » + présent simple.

If you study really hard this year, you'll pass your university exams.

« Will » + infinitif.

DEUXIÈME CONDITIONNEL

Vous pouvez utiliser le deuxième conditionnel pour prédire des résultats dans le futur, si une condition peu probable est remplie.

« If » + prétérit.

If you went to fewer parties, you would get better results.

« Would » + infinitif.

20.8 LISEZ LE TEXTE, PUIS COCHEZ LES BONNES RÉPONSES.

Students do not need to remember information for exams.
True ☐ **False** ☑

1 Students take three exams at the end of the year.
True ☐ **False** ☐

2 The students currently have continuous assessment.
True ☐ **False** ☐

3 The author thinks exams are a fair way to assess students.
True ☐ **False** ☐

4 Students are told that they can encourage change.
True ☐ **False** ☐

Memorizing is not learning!

W hy are you trying to remember dozens of facts, figures, and quotations? The only reason is so that you can use them in the 12 terrifyingly stressful 3-hour exams that will be the only "proof" of how much you have learned over the academic year. Suppose it didn't have to be this way? What if you had continuous assessment throughout the year that showed what you can do with the knowledge, rather than how much you can cram into your memory? This can happen if you write to the head of your academic departments and urge them to consider 21st-century modes of assessment. Make time and write today.

20.9 ÉCOUTEZ L'ENREGISTREMENT, PUIS INDIQUEZ SI LES RÉSULTATS SONT PROBABLES OU PEU PROBABLES.

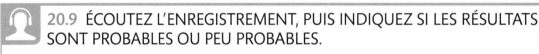

Likely ☐ Unlikely ☑

1 Likely ☐ Unlikely ☐

2 Likely ☐ Unlikely ☐

3 Likely ☐ Unlikely ☐

4 Likely ☐ Unlikely ☐

20.10 RÉPONDEZ AUX QUESTIONS DE L'ENREGISTREMENT, PUIS LISEZ LES RÉPONSES À VOIX HAUTE.

Suppose you could live anywhere. Where would you choose?

I'd live in my hometown to be near my family.

1 If you could meet any historical leader, who would it be?

2 Supposing you were ruler of the world, what would you do?

3 What will you do next if you pass the exam?

---

20 ✓ CHECK-LIST

⚙ « What if », « suppose » et « in case » ☐   **Aa** Les examens et les évaluations ☐   🧩 Parler de situations hypothétiques ☐

↻ BILAN L'ANGLAIS QUE VOUS AVEZ APPRIS DANS LES CHAPITRES 17-20

NOUVEAU POINT LINGUISTIQUE	EXEMPLE TYPE	☑	CHAPITRE
LES MARQUEURS RHÉTORIQUES D'ORGANISATION	First, it is important to consider which courses you want to study.	☐	17.1
FAIRE DES GÉNÉRALISATIONS	In some cases, students live off campus.	☐	18.1
LA VOIX PASSIVE	The book was studied by many people.	☐	19.1
LES NOMS FORMÉS À PARTIR DE VERBES À PARTICULE	The teacher gave us a handout.	☐	19.7
SITUATIONS PROBABLES ET IMPROBABLES	What if I fail my exams? What if we all passed with top grades?	☐	20.1, 20.4

21.1 LE TRAVAIL

It is difficult to work a nine-to-five job when you have young children.

nine-to-five
[a job with regular hours]

We've built a positive working environment for our staff.

working environment
[the conditions in which you work]

Our employees are qualified and also have hands-on experience.

hands-on experience
[the knowledge and skill gained through doing something yourself]

Have you ever held a position in management?

hold a position
[have a job]

My career really took off after I got that first big deal.

take off
[suddenly begin to have more success]

Her chosen career path meant she worked abroad a lot.

career path
[progression within a profession, in a job or through a series of jobs]

I worked my way up from the bottom of the career ladder.

bottom of the career ladder
[a position with the lowest level of responsibility or compensation]

I'm going to college so I don't have to get a dead-end job.

dead-end job
[a position without many prospects]

He was fired for stealing goods from the warehouse.

be fired
[be forced to leave your job for doing something wrong]

Many people were laid off from the factory.

laid off / made redundant (UK)
[made to leave a job because there is not enough work available]

I'm stepping down to let another person do the job.

step down
[stop doing a job voluntarily]

We had to tackle this problem head-on before it got worse.

tackle something head-on
[deal with something directly]

We've set our sights on being number one in our industry.

set your sights on something
[aim to achieve a particular goal]

You need to work hard to get ahead in this industry.

get ahead
[make more progress than others]

We took on three new members of staff this year.

take somebody on / take on somebody
[employ somebody]

I'm sorry I didn't answer your email. I was snowed under.

be snowed under
[have too much work to do]

She must have her hands full with those four children.

have your hands full
[be busy with a task or many tasks]

I can't come out because I'm up to my eyes with work.

be up to your eyes / ears
[be so busy that you can't take on anything else]

He always goes the extra mile to ensure deliveries are on time.

go the extra mile
[do more than you are required to do]

The deal involved give and take on both sides.

give and take
[compromise]

22 Les demandes d'emploi

En anglais, les prépositions ne peuvent être suivies que d'un groupe nominal ou d'un gérondif. Cela est particulièrement important lorsque vous parlez de l'ordre dans lequel les événements ont eu lieu.

🔧 **Grammaire** Les prépositions et le gérondif
Aa Vocabulaire Les demandes d'emploi
🧩 **Compétence** Écrire un CV et une lettre de candidature

22.1 POINT CLÉ LES PRÉPOSITIONS ET LE GÉRONDIF

Si vous voulez utiliser un verbe après une préposition, ce verbe doit être au gérondif, ce qui est la forme en « -ing » du verbe.

After graduating, I worked in a hospital.

Préposition　　　Gérondif

22.2 AUTRES EXEMPLES LES PRÉPOSITIONS ET LE GÉRONDIF

Instead of applying for a job, I went to college.

After seeing the job listing, I wrote a cover letter.

22.3 COMPLÉTEZ LES PHRASES AVEC LES MOTS DE LA LISTE.

Since ___*attending*___ some training sessions, I feel more confident about my work.

❶ _____ seeing that job listing, I thought I would never find my perfect job.

❷ After _____ as an engineer, I volunteered in Cambodia.

❸ _____ working in a low-paid job, I decided to train as an accountant.

❹ Without _____ my exams, it would be difficult to have a decent career.

qualifying	~~attending~~	Instead of	passing	Before

22.4 LISEZ LA LETTRE DE CANDIDATURE, PUIS COCHEZ LES BONNES RÉPONSES.

The job was advertised in the local job center.
True ☐ False ☐ Not given ✓

1 Alice's degree was in Social Media Marketing in the 21st Century.
True ☐ False ☐ Not given ☐

2 Her degree was a mixture of theory and practical training.
True ☐ False ☐ Not given ☐

3 Alice did some voluntary work while studying.
True ☐ False ☐ Not given ☐

4 A project Alice did was similar to this job.
True ☐ False ☐ Not given ☐

5 Alice is very creative, but less interested in details.
True ☐ False ☐ Not given ☐

6 Alice would be happy to start on a low salary.
True ☐ False ☐ Not given ☐

Dear Mrs. Evans,

I'm writing to apply for the Social Media Marketing Assistant post advertised in Social Journal. Please find attached a copy of my résumé for your consideration.

I have recently completed a degree in Digital Marketing, which has prepared me well for this position and has made me very enthusiastic about working in this area. As well as providing a strong theoretical grounding, it required a great deal of practical research and initiative. One of the courses, Social Media Marketing in the 21st Century, was particularly relevant to this position. As part of a project for this course, I developed and managed a social media campaign for a soft drinks company.

I have a keen interest in following developments in digital marketing, and am very creative as well as having a good eye for detail and accuracy.

I would be able to take the position immediately. Thank you for taking the time to consider my application, and I look forward to hearing from you in the near future.

Yours sincerely,

A Williams

Alice Williams

22.5 RELIEZ CHAQUE EXPRESSION À SA DÉFINITION.

has a very close connection	take the position
1 sharp and enthusiastic	post
2 be good at noticing small things	is particularly relevant
3 job	keen
4 soon	have an eye for detail
5 start the job	in the near future

George Brandani

275 Main Street
Minneapolis, MN 55401
george@brandani.com
612-555-1746

I am an award-winning, experienced head barista who has managed teams of up to five colleagues. I have in-depth knowledge of the coffee industry and am certified in current hygiene and health and safety regulations.

EMPLOYMENT HISTORY

Coffee Galore
HEAD BARISTA • June 2013–Present
Coffee Galore is an independent, but very highly rated and vibrant coffee shop. I was part of the initial team that established the inviting, friendly, coffee-drinking experience.

Duties:
• Train and manage one full-time and three part-time baristas
• Order and control stock of foods and beverages
• Ensure maximum sales by devising promotions
• Ensure compliance with hygiene and safety regulations

Coffee Time Out
BARISTA • July 2011–June 2013
Part of a large team of baristas in a well-known chain with strict customer service and hygiene standards.

Duties:
• Make and serve up to 250 coffee drinks per day
• Provide a clean and welcoming environment for the customers

Awards
Creative Barista Champion

Qualifications
I hold current certificates in food hygiene and first aid, as well as being a trained fire warden.

Education
Elmwood High School • 2007–2011
High school diploma

Interests
I am passionate about coffee and like to spend my free time visiting places where it is grown, such as Costa Rica and Colombia. I am also a quiz master for the local quiz league.

George helped set up the Coffee Galore coffee shop.
True ☑   False ☐   Not given ☐

❶ George has worked in coffee shops since he left high school.
True ☐   False ☐   Not given ☐

❷ George does not like his boss in his current job.
True ☐   False ☐   Not given ☐

❸ George has only ever worked for small coffee shops.
True ☐   False ☐   Not given ☐

❹ George is trained to deal with medical emergencies.
True ☐   False ☐   Not given ☐

❺ All of George's hobbies are related to coffee.
True ☐   False ☐   Not given ☐

22.7 ÉCOUTEZ L'ENREGISTREMENT, PUIS COCHEZ LES BONNES RÉPONSES.

Janice Streatham, directrice des ressources humaines, donne des conseils pour écrire un bon CV.

What does Janice say is the most important thing to get right on your résumé?

School qualifications ☐
Employment record ☐
Contact details ☑

1 If you left school early and did unpaid work, what should you emphasize on your résumé?

School qualifications ☐
Work experience and skills ☐
Interests and hobbies ☐

2 What should you do if you spent a year abroad before starting work or college?

Leave a gap in your résumé ☐
Say what you were doing ☐
Say you were doing something else ☐

3 How long should your résumé be?

About four sides of paper ☐
At least two sides of paper ☐
Less than two sides of paper ☐

22.8 COCHEZ LA PHRASE LA PLUS FORMELLE DES DEUX.

I spent ages working in retail even though I didn't really like it. ☐
I worked in retail for many years, then looked for a career change. ☑

1 The job was quite challenging in terms of improving the consumer experience. ☐
The shop floor was a real nightmare and my boss wasn't very nice at all. ☐

2 I went with my mates on holiday to Vietnam and we did some volunteer stuff. ☐
I traveled to Vietnam where I volunteered for a number of educational projects. ☐

3 I did loads of courses about what to do in a fire and how to write risk assessments. ☐
I am a qualified fire warden and am trained in writing risk assessments. ☐

4 I have an in-depth knowledge of real estate due to having eight years' experience. ☐
I know lots of things about selling houses because I've been doing it for ages. ☐

---

22 ✓ CHECK-LIST

⚙ Les prépositions et le gérondif ☐   **Aa** Les demandes d'emploi ☐   🧩 Écrire un CV et une lettre de candidature ☐

23 Poser des questions polies

En anglais, poser des questions directement peut être perçu comme impoli. Les anglophones posent donc couramment des questions de façon plus indirecte.

⚙ **Grammaire** Les questions directes et indirectes
Aa Vocabulaire Les entretiens d'embauche
Compétence Poser des questions poliment

23.1 POINT CLÉ LES QUESTIONS OUVERTES POLIES

Si une question indirecte contient « to be », ce verbe vient après le sujet.

What are your career goals?

⬇

Could you tell me what your career goals are?

Les questions polies commencent généralement par l'une de ces phrases.

L'auxiliaire « to have » vient aussi après le sujet dans les questions indirectes.

What have you designed before?

⬇

I was wondering what you have designed before.

L'auxiliaire « to do » n'apparait pas dans les questions indirectes.

Why do you enjoy working in fashion?

⬇

I'd like to know why you enjoy working in fashion.

🔊

 ## 23.2 RÉCRIVEZ LES QUESTIONS DIRECTES EN QUESTIONS INDIRECTES.

| What are your strengths? | = | Could you tell me _what your strengths are?_ |

1. When are you available? = I was wondering _____

2. Why have you applied for this job? = I'd like to know _____

3. What is our best-selling product? = Do you have any idea _____

4. Who was your last manager? = I'm curious to know _____

🔊

23.3 POINT CLÉ LES QUESTIONS « OUI/NON » POLIES

Une façon indirecte, plus polie, de poser des questions « oui/non » est d'utiliser « if » ou « whether ».

Have you worked in a café before?

⬇

Could you tell me if you have worked in a café before?

« If » peut être remplacé par « whether » pour une question plus formelle.

🔊

23.4 RÉCRIVEZ LES QUESTIONS DIRECTES EN QUESTIONS INDIRECTES AVEC « IF » OU « WHETHER ».

Have you ever led a team? = Could you tell us _if you have ever led a team?_

1 Do you like working with animals? = We were wondering _____

2 Have you applied for other jobs? = Would you mind telling us _____

3 Do you have any computer skills? = Could you tell me _____

4 Do you have relevant experience? = We'd like to know _____

🔊

23.5 ÉCRIVEZ LES MOTS SUIVANTS DANS LE BON ORDRE AFIN DE RECONSTITUER LES QUESTIONS INDIRECTES.

| you | us | tell | your | Could | more | skills? | leadership | about |

Could you tell us more about your leadership skills?

1 | wondering | were | you | last | left | We | why | your | job. |

_____

2 | your | you | future | Could | tell | about | us | career | ambitions? |

_____

3 | like | to | know | you | taking | whether | I'd | like | risks. |

_____

🔊

91

23.6 LISEZ L'ARTICLE, PUIS COCHEZ LES BONNES RÉPONSES.

Wear whatever you want to the interview.
True ☐   **False** ✓

1 You shouldn't wear your interview outfit before the interview.
True ☐   **False** ☐

2 You will probably be asked questions about the company.
True ☐   **False** ☐

3 You should learn detailed answers by heart.
True ☐   **False** ☐

4 You should think of questions to ask the interviewer.
True ☐   **False** ☐

Top Tips for Job Interviews

1 Dress well for the interview. Try on your interview outfit so that you feel comfortable wearing it.

2 Know the company and the job. You will be expected to talk about both of them.

3 Think of potential questions and your answers. Don't learn answers by heart, but think about possible points you could make.

4 Think of questions to ask the interviewer. It's a great opportunity to make yourself look interesting and interested.

5 Be calm and confident. You've got something they like to get this far!

23.7 POINT CLÉ LES EXPRESSIONS DILATOIRES

Si vous avez besoin de gagner du temps pour réfléchir à une question difficile avant d'y répondre, vous pouvez commencer votre réponse par une expression dilatoire qui indique que vous examinez la question.

Would you be happy to work on weekends?

Well, I do have two children.

What are your strengths?

Good question. I have excellent computer skills.

Why should we hire you?

Let's see... I think my experience would be very useful.

23.8 ÉCOUTEZ L'ENREGISTREMENT, PUIS COCHEZ LES BONNES RÉPONSES.

Sunaina interroge Rhodri pour un poste dans sa société.

What does Rhodri say about Alphomega?

Its reputation is not that good	☐
Its reputation is growing	☐
It's a well-respected company	☑

1 Why does Rhodri say that, as a new graduate, he would benefit the company?

He is clever and so learns things easily	☐
He has learned new techniques and skills	☐
He will not have developed bad habits	☐

2 Why didn't Sunaina ask about Rhodri's strengths?

She had already read about them	☐
She thought he might not tell the truth	☐
She thought it might be boring	☐

3 What did Rhodri say was his greatest weakness?

He used to be very critical of himself	☐
He gets bored easily because he's so smart	☐
He is honest when he shouldn't be	☐

4 Why had Rhodri researched Alphomega Marketing so thoroughly?

He knew he was coming for an interview	☐
It was part of his final-year project	☐
It was part of his second-year project	☐

23.9 RÉPONDEZ AUX QUESTIONS EN UTILISANT DES EXPRESSIONS DILATOIRES, PUIS LISEZ LES PHRASES À VOIX HAUTE.

What is your proudest career moment?

Good question. *I think it'd be when I was promoted to senior manager.*

1 When have you worked as part of a team?

Well, _____

2 What do you know about our company?

Actually, _____

3 Where do you see yourself in five years?

Let's see. _____

4 Why do you think we should hire you?

Good question. _____

Les schémas complexes de verbes

Les verbes peuvent suivre différents schémas, et être suivis par un infinitif ou un gérondif.

⚙ **Grammaire** Verbe + infinitif / gérondif
Aa Vocabulaire Le monde du travail
🧩 **Compétence** Utiliser des schémas complexes de verbes

24.1 POINT CLÉ LES SCHÉMAS VERBE + INFINITIF

Certains verbes sont suivis d'un infinitif.

VERBE + INFINITIF

He **managed** to finish the report just in time.

D'autres verbes doivent avoir un objet devant l'infinitif.

VERBE + OBJET + INFINITIF

My computer **enables** me to work on two screens at once.

🔊

 24.2 BARREZ LES MOTS INCORRECTS DANS CHAQUE PHRASE.

I was delighted when the HR department offered me / offered to improve my salary.

① The new product launch caused the profits to rise / to rise the profits, which was excellent news.

② I recently lost my job, but I managed me / managed to find a new one quite quickly.

③ The employees were furious, so they threatened the boss / threatened to not work yesterday.

④ I always get scared when my boss invites me to / invites to me her office. It's never good news.

⑤ Sometimes it can be good to volunteer you / volunteer to do extra work. It'll impress your boss.

⑥ On Fridays, my manager sometimes allows me / allows to leave early to enjoy the weekend.

🔊

24.3 **POINT CLÉ** LES SCHÉMAS VERBE + GÉRONDIF

Certains verbes sont suivis d'un gérondif plutôt que d'un infinitif.

VERBE + GÉRONDIF

I really **enjoy** working **at the zoo. It's a lot of fun.**

D'autres verbes peuvent être suivis d'un objet et d'un gérondif.

VERBE + OBJET + GÉRONDIF

Hayley **heard the boss** interviewing **the new secretary.**

24.4 COMPLÉTEZ LES PHRASES AVEC LES MOTS DE LA LISTE.

I remember ___*mentioning*___ some changes to you briefly, so here's a little more information.

❶ Over the years we have enjoyed _____ the market when it comes to the environment.

❷ An auditor has advised us _____ some of our policies in order to improve further.

❸ One change we would like _____ is to no longer supply disposable cups.

❹ We're sure that you will approve of us _____ to become more environmentally friendly.

❺ The change will prevent our company _____ up to 25,000 cups each year.

❻ Bringing your own mug will enable us _____ to this new initiative.

❼ We hope that you approve of the company _____ a change like this. It's for a great cause.

❽ I'll send another quick memo on Friday to remind you _____ your own mug to work.

to stick	leading	throwing away	~~mentioning~~	to make
trying	to bring	making	to change	

24.5 POINT CLÉ LES VERBES QUI NÉCESSITENT UNE PRÉPOSITION

Certains verbes doivent être suivis d'une préposition spécifique avant un objet. Différentes prépositions suivent différents verbes.

VERBE + PRÉPOSITION

The head chef used to shout at the staff to encourage them to work harder.

24.6 AUTRES EXEMPLES LES VERBES QUI NÉCESSITENT UNE PRÉPOSITION

The café was counting on the new menu to impress its customers.

The head chef appealed to the manager to hire more kitchen staff.

The café advertised for another chef to join the team.

24.7 BARREZ LES MOTS INCORRECTS DANS CHAQUE PHRASE.

They planned for / at / on / to a babysitter to look after their son while they went to a dinner party.

❶ He appealed for / at / on / to the audience, asking them to stop booing the actors in the play.

❷ She always shouts for / at / on / to him when he doesn't take the dog for a walk.

❸ You should wait for / at / on / to Jane to arrive before talking to Max about this important issue.

❹ I'm sure that I can count for / at / on / to you to support your boss at this difficult time.

❺ I've arranged for / at / on / to the doctor to see you tomorrow morning at 10am.

❻ My children never listen for / at / on / to me when I tell them what to do.

24.8 LISEZ L'ARTICLE, PUIS RÉPONDEZ AUX QUESTIONS.

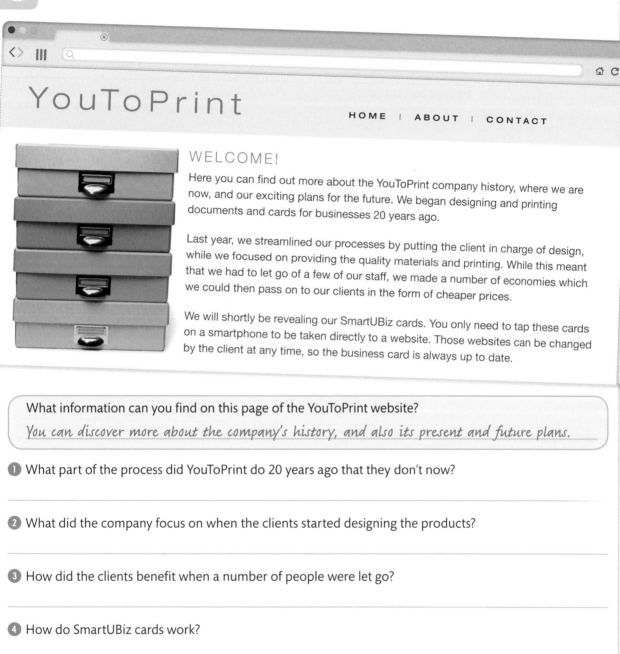

YouToPrint

HOME | ABOUT | CONTACT

WELCOME!

Here you can find out more about the YouToPrint company history, where we are now, and our exciting plans for the future. We began designing and printing documents and cards for businesses 20 years ago.

Last year, we streamlined our processes by putting the client in charge of design, while we focused on providing the quality materials and printing. While this meant that we had to let go of a few of our staff, we made a number of economies which we could then pass on to our clients in the form of cheaper prices.

We will shortly be revealing our SmartUBiz cards. You only need to tap these cards on a smartphone to be taken directly to a website. Those websites can be changed by the client at any time, so the business card is always up to date.

> What information can you find on this page of the YouToPrint website?
>
> *You can discover more about the company's history, and also its present and future plans.*

❶ What part of the process did YouToPrint do 20 years ago that they don't now?

_____

❷ What did the company focus on when the clients started designing the products?

_____

❸ How did the clients benefit when a number of people were let go?

_____

❹ How do SmartUBiz cards work?

_____

---

24 ✓ CHECK-LIST

⚙ Verbe + infinitif / gérondif ☐   **Aa** Le monde du travail ☐   🧩 Utiliser des schémas complexes de verbes ☐

25 Les verbes à double objet

Certains verbes peuvent être suivis soit par un complément d'objet direct, soit par un complément d'objet indirect. Les phrases qui utilisent ces verbes peuvent être ordonnées de plusieurs façons.

⚙ **Grammaire** Les verbes à double objet
Aa Vocabulaire Les nouvelles activités
🧩 **Compétence** Parler de créer une entreprise

25.1 POINT CLÉ LES VERBES À DOUBLE OBJET AVEC DES NOMS

Le complément d'objet direct est la personne ou la chose à qui l'action arrive. Le complément d'objet indirect bénéficie de cette même action. Si le focus est sur le complément d'objet indirect, celui-ci se place alors après le complément d'objet direct avec « to » ou « for ».

Le complément d'objet indirect peut aussi se placer avant le complément d'objet direct. Dans ce cas, aucune préposition n'est requise.

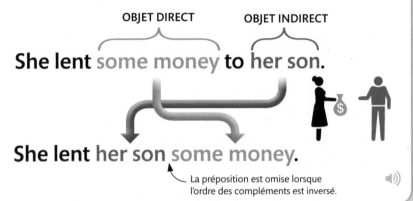

OBJET DIRECT   OBJET INDIRECT

She lent some money to her son.

She lent her son some money.

La préposition est omise lorsque l'ordre des compléments est inversé.

25.2 POINT CLÉ LES VERBES À DOUBLE OBJET AVEC DES PRONOMS

Si le complément d'objet direct est un pronom, il doit se placer devant le complément d'objet indirect.

She lent it to her son. ✔
She lent her son it. ✖

Si le complément d'objet indirect est un pronom, il peut se placer avant ou après le complément d'objet direct.

She lent him some money. ✔
She lent some money to him. ✔

25.3 RÉCRIVEZ LES PHRASES EN CORRIGEANT LES ERREURS.

He bought a house his daughter.
He bought a house for his daughter.

❶ Barbara gave it me.

_____

❷ We gave to them some candy.

_____

❸ James passed to me the documents.

_____

25.4 POINT CLÉ LES VERBES AVEC « TO » OU « FOR »

Certains verbes se construisent soit avec « to » soit avec « for », en fonction
du contexte. On utilise généralement « to » lorsque quelque chose est transféré,
et « for » lorsque quelqu'un bénéficie de quelque chose.

He sold the house to the family.
[The family bought the house.]

He sold the house for the family.
[He sold the house on behalf of the family.]

25.5 BARREZ LE MOT INCORRECT DANS CHAQUE PHRASE, PUIS RELIEZ LES PHRASES CORRESPONDANTES.

| The brothers bought the business. | = | She sold the business to / ~~for~~ the brothers. |

❶ The students received the homework.   =   The teacher gave homework **to** / **for** the students.

❷ The speech was promoting the business.   =   He made a speech **to** / **for** the business.

❸ He passed on his knowledge.   =   He gave advice **to** / **for** them.

❹ A charity worker is collecting money.   =   He's collecting money **to** / **for** the charity.

25.6 LISEZ L'ARTICLE, PUIS COCHEZ LES BONNES RÉPONSES.

> The museum has recently been built.
> **True** ☐   **False** ☐   **Not given** ☑

❶ Hugh Walker won an award at the ceremony.
True ☐   **False** ☐   **Not given** ☐

❷ People have donated money to help save the museum.
True ☐   **False** ☐   **Not given** ☐

❸ Walker is still in charge of the building.
True ☐   **False** ☐   **Not given** ☐

---

16   ART AND CULTURE

SAVE THE MUSEUM

Historian Hugh Walker last night gave an emotional speech to the audience at the Heritage Awards held in the newly renovated museum. He thanked all the people who had donated money to the "Save the Museum" campaign. He thanked them for preserving the historic museum for the benefit of thousands of future history enthusiasts. Walker, who bought the building five years ago, gave it to the charity to run last year.

25.7 ÉCOUTEZ L'ENREGISTREMENT, PUIS CORRIGEZ LES PHRASES.

 Colin raconte à son ami qu'il a décidé
de créer une nouvelle entreprise.

> Colin still has quite a lot of paperwork to do.
> *Colin has finished all of the paperwork.*

1 The business will start trading next year.

_____

2 Starting a business is expensive, but Colin has lots of money.

_____

3 Lots of companies have made walking map apps.

_____

4 If it fails, he will really regret opening the business.

_____

 **25.8 ÉCOUTEZ À NOUVEAU L'ENREGISTREMENT, PUIS COMPLÉTEZ
LES PHRASES AVEC LES EXPRESSIONS IDIOMATIQUES DE LA LISTE.**

I've been planning to start my own map shop for years, and finally I've done all the paperwork and all the

_____*red tape*_____ is out of the way. We don't formally open until next month, but I'm getting

everything ready now so we can really _____ . It hasn't been cheap though. Starting a

business is very expensive and I don't have a _____ to buy thousands of maps. The

walking map app is the _____ though. Not many people do those yet and I hope to

have _____ by the end of next year. Of course, it might all go horribly wrong, but

_____ , eh?

cornered the market	~~red tape~~	ace up my sleeve	blank check
	nothing ventured, nothing gained		hit the ground running

25.9 RÉCRIVEZ LES PASSAGES SURLIGNÉS EN CORRIGEANT LES ERREURS.

opening Saturday

1. _____
2. _____
3. _____
4. _____
5. _____
6. _____
7. _____

Colin's Maps will be openning Saturday!

For all you're map needs.

We are 20 years' experience in the map industry and have always moved with the times. Now, however, we are a head of the times. Colin's Maps will be lunching the new walking and leisure map app for your digital devices soon. This app will be avialable for all smartphones and tablets and you will be able to make digital notes on it as you walk or later, once you youve returned home.

We also have a enormous stock of traditional paper and waterproof maps.

Stop in to see us!

---

25 ✓ CHECK-LIST

⚙ Les verbes à double objet ☐   **Aa** Les nouvelles activités ☐   🧩 Parler de créer une entreprise ☐

⟳ BILAN L'ANGLAIS QUE VOUS AVEZ APPRIS DANS LES CHAPITRES 22-25

NOUVEAU POINT LINGUISTIQUE	EXEMPLE TYPE	☑	CHAPITRE
LES PRÉPOSITIONS ET LE GÉRONDIF	After graduating, I worked in a hospital.	☐	22.1
LES QUESTIONS INDIRECTES	Could you tell me what your career goals are? I'd like to know if you've worked in a café before?	☐	23.1 23.3
LES EXPRESSIONS DILATOIRES	Good question, I think I'd have to check first.	☐	23.7
LES SCHÉMAS COMPLEXES DE VERBES	He managed to finish writing the report just in time. She likes her boss telling her what's happening.	☐	24.1 24.3
LES VERBES QUI NÉCESSITENT UNE PRÉPOSITION	The café advertised for another chef to join the team.	☐	24.5
LES VERBES À DOUBLE OBJET	She lent some money to her son. She lent him some money.	☐	25.1
LES VERBES AVEC « TO » OU « FOR »	He sold the store to the family. He sold the store for the family.	☐	25.4

26.1 LES RÉUNIONS ET LES PRÉSENTATIONS

You will need to attend the finance meeting **tomorrow.**

attend a meeting
[go to a meeting]

I'd like you to give a presentation **on your research.**

give a presentation
[present a formal talk for a group of people]

The CEO has put forward an agenda **for tomorrow's meeting.**

put forward an agenda
[suggest what will be discussed in a meeting]

Our falling profits will be on the agenda **today.**

on the agenda
[included in a list of things to discuss]

OK, now you've all been introduced, let's get down to business.

get down to business
[start working or doing something that you have to do]

John is ill and so he will be absent **from the meeting.**

absent
[not present]

We've arranged a conference call **with our French and German managers.**

conference call
[a telephone call with a number of people at the same time]

Sanjay has been on the board of directors **for three years.**

board of directors
[a group of people who manage a business or organization]

Let's look at **last year's sales figures for this product.**

look at
[begin to consider or discuss]

On the one hand **it is affordable, but** on the other hand **it is not durable.**

on the one hand / on the other hand
[something to consider / a contrasting thing to consider]

Can we have a show of hands for those who agree with the idea?

show of hands
[a vote performed by raising hands to show agreement with a proposal]

It took hours to reach a consensus.

reach a consensus
[arrive at a position of agreement]

We reached a unanimous agreement on the plan.

unanimous
[when everyone is in agreement]

So, to sum up, we need to increase sales in this area.

sum up
[conclude]

Shall we set a date for the next meeting?

set a date
[agree on a date in the future]

I think we're finished unless there is any other business?

any other business (AOB)
[any matter discussed in a meeting that is not on the agenda]

I will take questions at the end of the presentation.

take questions
[listen to and answer questions]

We can't discuss replacing the printers because we've run out of time.

run out of time
[have no time left for something]

Maria will take the minutes of the meeting today.

take the minutes
[write the record of what was said during a meeting]

Let's start by reviewing the minutes of last month's meeting.

review the minutes
[look again at the written record of a past meeting]

27 Les pronoms réfléchis

Les pronoms réfléchis indiquent que le sujet d'un verbe est le même que son objet. Ils peuvent aussi être utilisés dans d'autres situations pour plus d'emphase.

⚙ **Grammaire** Les pronoms réfléchis
Aa Vocabulaire Le langage du milieu du travail
🧩 **Compétence** Parler de problèmes au travail

27.1 POINT CLÉ LES PRONOMS RÉFLÉCHIS

On ajoute les suffixes « -self » ou « -selves » aux pronoms simples pour former les pronoms réfléchis en anglais.

 I left **myself** a reminder about the meeting.

 Sarah sees **herself** as a natural team leader.

 We pride **ourselves** on our customer service.

 Not a single person let **themselves** down today.

🔊

27.2 CONSTRUCTION

I ➡	myself
you ➡	yourself
he ➡	himself
she ➡	herself
it ➡	itself
we ➡	ourselves
you ➡	yourselves
they ➡	themselves

🔊

 ## 27.3 BARREZ LE PRONOM RÉFLÉCHI INCORRECT DANS CHAQUE PHRASE.

You made ~~itself~~ / yourself sound good in your application.

① We had to run the meeting ourselves / yourselves.

② Do you ever send meeting reminders to myself / yourself?

③ I taught herself / myself how to play the guitar.

④ Do you and Priya see yourself / yourselves as team players?

⑤ He put himself / herself forward for a big promotion.

⑥ The company promotes itself / ourselves online.

🔊

27.4 POINT CLÉ UTILISER LES PRONOMS RÉFLÉCHIS POUR L'EMPHASE

On peut parfois utiliser les pronoms réfléchis pour ajouter de l'emphase, même s'ils ne sont pas essentiels à la grammaire de la phrase.

The company director gave the talk.

Cette phrase est correcte sans pronom réfléchi.

On souligne ici que l'action n'a pas été déléguée en ajoutant un pronom réfléchi à la fin de la phrase.

The company director gave the talk himself.

[The company director gave the talk, rather than getting someone else to do it.]

On accentue ici l'importance du sujet en plaçant le pronom réfléchi juste après.

The company director himself gave the talk.

[The company director, who is an important person, gave the talk.]

27.5 COMPLÉTEZ LES PHRASES AVEC LE PRONOM RÉFLÉCHI QUI CONVIENT.

The CEO _____himself_____ came in to discuss his views about the merger.

1 I'm very impressed that they planned this conference _____ !

2 I spent all evening doing research for this presentation _____ .

3 The area is traditional, but the city _____ is full of modern offices.

4 Nobody helped us. We won this contract _____ .

5 I couldn't believe it! The Queen _____ presented the award.

6 Marta writes summaries for her boss. He can't write them _____ .

7 It's very important that you fix these problems _____ , Jacob.

8 The company founders _____ will be making the final decision.

27.6 POINT CLÉ LES COLLOCATIONS AVEC PRONOM RÉFLÉCHI

De nombreuses collocations comprennent des pronoms réfléchis. Elles suivent souvent le schéma verbe + pronom réfléchi + préposition.

Try to tear yourself away from **the computer as often as possible.**

27.7 AUTRES EXEMPLES LES COLLOCATIONS AVEC PRONOM RÉFLÉCHI

The managers don't concern themselves with **minor issues.**

Remember to behave yourselves **when you are in public.**

She still has to familiarize herself with **company policy.**

Are you leaving early today? Enjoy yourself**!**

« You » est le sujet implicite dans cette phrase à l'impératif.

CONSEIL
Le sujet n'est pas toujours inclus mais sous-entendu par le pronom réfléchi.

 ## 27.8 COMPLÉTEZ LES PHRASES AVEC LES EXPRESSIONS RÉFLÉCHIES DE LA LISTE.

73 BUSINESS TODAY

STRANGE CIRCUMSTANCES
CEO leaves coworkers mystified following surprise resignation

Steven Strange, CEO of AngloEuroCorp, left the company in unusual circumstances last week. Acting CEO Don Black was called into the CEO's office by Strange, who said, "You should _familiarize yourself_ with this office and _____ at home." Another employee commented on Strange's odd behavior: "He usually _____ from our meetings because he didn't _____ with day-to-day matters. Last Friday was different. Mr. Strange _____ away from his office and attended the weekly meeting. He even thanked us for our hard work!" As he left, Strange supposedly announced: "Go home early and _____ !"

~~familiarize yourself~~

concern himself

make yourself

tore himself

absented himself

enjoy yourselves

27.9 ÉCOUTEZ L'ENREGISTREMENT, PUIS RELIEZ CHAQUE DÉFINITION AU VERBE À PARTICULE QUI LUI CORRESPOND.

have too much work to do	stay behind
❶ do things you haven't had time to do	knock off
❷ decide or agree to do something	be snowed under
❸ deal with a problem or situation	take on
❹ finish work	catch up
❺ remain somewhere after others have left	sort out

27.10 RÉCRIVEZ LES PHRASES EN CORRIGEANT LES ERREURS.

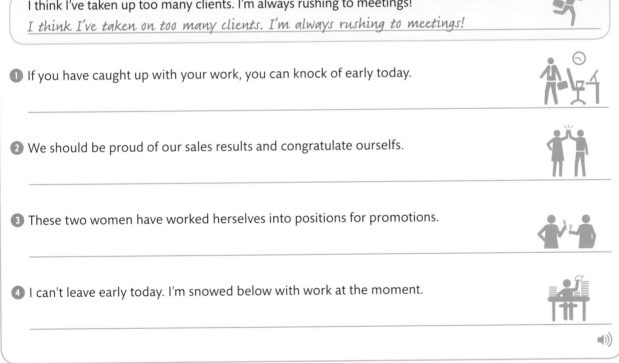

I think I've taken up too many clients. I'm always rushing to meetings!
I think I've taken on too many clients. I'm always rushing to meetings!

❶ If you have caught up with your work, you can knock of early today.

_____

❷ We should be proud of our sales results and congratulate ourselfs.

_____

❸ These two women have worked herselves into positions for promotions.

_____

❹ I can't leave early today. I'm snowed below with work at the moment.

_____

28 Les réunions et la planification

De nombreux verbes peuvent être suivis d'un autre verbe. Celui-ci peut être un infinitif en « to » (« want to eat ») ou un gérondif (« enjoy cooking »).

⚙ **Grammaire** Combiner les verbes

Aa Vocabulaire Les tâches de bureau

🧩 **Compétence** Participer à des réunions

28.1 POINT CLÉ LES VERBES SUIVIS DE « TO » OU « -ING » (AVEC AUCUN CHANGEMENT DE SENS)

Certains verbes peuvent être suivis d'un gérondif (une forme en « -ing ») ou d'un infinitif avec « to », avec peu ou pas de changement de sens. Vous pouvez souvent utiliser l'une ou l'autre de ces formes.

Emails are really awkward. I prefer { meeting / to meet } in person.

I like { working / to work } in an open-plan office with a team.

28.2 RELIEZ LE DÉBUT DE CHAQUE PHRASE À LA FIN QUI LUI CORRESPOND.

CONSEIL
Tous ces verbes peuvent être suivis de « to » ou « -ing » sans aucun changement de sens.

Oh no. It's James! Once he **starts** → talking, he never stops.

to run for the bus.

① He was fired because he **continued**

being cold and wet.

② How would you **propose**

writing to people by hand.

③ I was so late that I **began**

talking, he never stops.

④ Let's go inside. I really **can't stand**

to ignore his duties.

⑤ I have to say that I **prefer**

to raise the money?

28.3 POINT CLÉ LES VERBES SUIVIS DE « TO » OU « -ING » (AVEC CHANGEMENT DE SENS)

Certains verbes changent de sens en fonction de la forme du verbe qui les suit.

He stopped to talk to her in the office before lunch.

[He was walking around the office, and he stopped so that he could talk to her.]

She stopped talking to him and rushed to a meeting.

[She was talking to him, and she stopped in order to do something else.]

28.4 AUTRES EXEMPLES LES VERBES SUIVIS DE « TO » OU « -ING » (AVEC CHANGEMENT DE SENS)

En général, l'infinitif est utilisé pour décrire une action qui a lieu après celle du verbe principal. Le gérondif est souvent employé pour une action qui a lieu avant ou au même moment que celle du verbe principal.

VERBE + INFINITIF	VERBE + GÉRONDIF
She forgot to send the email, so her team never received the update. [She did not send the email.]	**She forgot sending the email, so she sent it a second time.** [She forgot that she had already sent the email.]
He went on to write the report once the meeting had finished. [He finished a meeting and then wrote the report.]	**He went on writing the report all evening. It took hours.** [He was writing the report, and continued to do so.]
I regret to tell you the unhappy news. Your flight has been delayed. [I have to tell you unhappy news, and I am sorry about this.]	**I regret telling you the unhappy news. I can see it has upset you.** [I wish I hadn't told you the unhappy news because you are very upset now.]
Did you remember to meet David? Your meeting was scheduled for today. [You were supposed to meet David. Did you remember to do that?]	**Did you remember meeting David? I'd forgotten that we had already met him.** [You had met David before. Did you remember that?]

28.5 BARREZ LE MOT INCORRECT DANS CHAQUE PHRASE.

> We regret to inform / ~~informing~~ you that the hotel will be closed for refurbishment.

1. I hope you remembered to put / putting the advertisement for the grand reopening in the newspaper?

2. Unfortunately, when the hotel reopened, they had forgotten advertising / to advertise, so it was empty.

3. I'll never forget to see / seeing the manager's face when there were no guests at the party.

4. Do you remember to plan / planning the grand opening party with Ceri last year?

5. Do you regret to ask / asking Tim to promote the reopening?

6. After the initial failure, the refurbished hotel went on to be / being a huge success.

7. Now it's famous and successful, the hotel will probably go on being / to be popular for many years.

🔊

28.6 COMPLÉTEZ LES PHRASES EN CONJUGUANT LES VERBES DE LA LISTE À LA BONNE FORME.

> I hope you ___remembered___ to finish your assignment from last week.

1. I need to _____ spending so much money on food at work.

2. My dad says he could never _____ meeting Elvis, even though it was a long time ago.

3. If I'm not busy tonight, I'd absolutely _____ to go to dinner with you.

4. My boss _____ talking on the phone to video calls.

5. Thanks for the offer. If you don't mind, I'd like to _____ to do my work instead.

6. After the book was published, he _____ to write an award-winning screenplay.

7. I _____ to inform you that the meeting has been postponed.

8. It looks like it will be expensive to get catering. I _____ making the food ourselves.

> propose   continue   ~~remember~~   go on   love   prefer   regret   forget   stop

🔊

LISEZ L'ARTICLE, PUIS COCHEZ LES BONNES RÉPONSES.

Should you have meetings to hand out information?
Yes ☐   No ☑

❶ Should you only have a meeting when it is needed?
Yes ☐   No ☐

❷ Should you ask participants to set meeting objectives?
Yes ☐   No ☐

❸ Should you use written objectives to help manage the meeting?
Yes ☐   No ☐

❹ Should you share the agenda on the day of the meeting?
Yes ☐   No ☐

❺ Should you stop meetings to ask people why they are late?
Yes ☐   No ☐

❻ Should you start late if some attendees are not yet present?
Yes ☐   No ☐

❼ Should you talk to latecomers after the meeting has finished?
Yes ☐   No ☐

98   BUSINESS WORLD

HOW TO RUN EFFECTIVE MEETINGS
Top tips from our experts

1 Make sure the meeting you propose having is necessary. Could a notice or email be used to hand out information more effectively? Remember many people can't stand attending unnecessary meetings. If you only have meetings when necessary, then participants will prepare properly and take them more seriously.

2 Remember to set objectives for meetings. This serves a number of purposes. First, everyone knows why the meeting is being held and so will see it as potentially useful. Second, if a participant starts bringing up unrelated topics, you can refer back to the objective.

3 Make sure everyone knows the meeting's objectives by sharing an agenda at least a few days before the meeting. Some people prefer to assign a pre-meeting task to ensure that the agenda is read.

4 Begin talking on time to show respect to those attendees who arrived on time. Don't stop to talk to latecomers. Deal with them later.

---

28 ✓ **CHECK-LIST**

⚙ Combiner les verbes ☐   **Aa** Les tâches de bureau ☐   🧩 Participer à des réunions ☐

29 Les descriptions qualificatives

Il existe plusieurs façons de qualifier ou d'ajouter des détails aux adjectifs. Certains types d'adjectifs ne peuvent être modifiés que de certaines manières.

⚙ **Grammaire** Les adjectifs non gradables
Aa Vocabulaire Les mots qualificatifs
🧩 **Compétence** Ajouter des détails aux descriptions

29.1 POINT CLÉ LES ADJECTIFS NON GRADABLES

La plupart des adjectifs peuvent être modifiés par des adverbes de gradation, tels que « slightly », « very » et « extremely ». Les adjectifs non gradables ne peuvent être modifiés de cette manière. Ces adjectifs ont tendance à se répartir en trois catégories : extrêmes, absolus et de classification.

Les adjectifs gradables comme « good » peuvent être modifiés par des adverbes de gradation tels que « extremely » et « very ».

Her arguments were extremely good.

Her arguments were fantastic!

Les adjectifs non gradables comme « fantastic » ne peuvent pas être modifiés par des adverbes de gradation.

LES ADJECTIFS EXTRÊMES

Les adjectifs extrêmes sont des versions plus fortes des adjectifs gradables, comme « awful », « hilarious », « fantastic » ou « terrifiant ».

Her presentation was awful.

Le sens de « extremely » est déjà incorporé ici.

LES ADJECTIFS ABSOLUS

Les adjectifs absolus ne peuvent pas être gradués dans la mesure où ils décrivent des qualités ou états fixes, tels que « unique », « perfect » ou « impossible ».

She has a unique presenting style.

Il est impossible d'être plus ou moins unique.

LES ADJECTIFS DE CLASSIFICATION

On utilise les adjectifs de classification pour dire que quelque chose est d'un type particulier ou d'une classe particulière, tels que « American », « nuclear » ou « medical ».

The audience was American.

🔊

29.2 ÉCRIVEZ LES ADJECTIFS DE LA LISTE DANS LES CATÉGORIES CORRESPONDANTES.

EXTREME	ABSOLUTE	CLASSIFYING
awful	*unique*	*organic*
___ ___	___ ___	___ ___
___ ___	___ ___	___ ___

unknown   ~~awful~~   digital   dead   enormous   right   ~~organic~~   wrong

chemical   industrial   superb   tiny   ~~unique~~   disgusting   electronic

◀))

29.3 COCHEZ LES PHRASES CORRECTES.

This new product is great. It's extremely perfect for kids. ☐
This new product is great. It's perfect for kids. ☑

1️⃣ Have you seen this very amazing designer watch? ☐
Have you seen this amazing designer watch? ☐

2️⃣ This new software is so slow. It's slightly awful. ☐
This new software is so slow. It's awful. ☐

3️⃣ Because it runs on solar power, it's extremely cheap. ☐
Because it runs on solar power, it's extremely cheaply. ☐

4️⃣ The instructions for this product are very impossible. ☐
The instructions for this product are impossible. ☐

5️⃣ The numbers on the watch are tiny! ☐
The numbers on the watch are slightly tiny! ☐

6️⃣ I need to replace my computer. It's extremely broken. ☐
I need to replace my computer. It's broken. ☐

◀))

113

29.4 POINT CLÉ LES ADVERBES NON GRADABLES

Certains adverbes peuvent être utilisés pour qualifier des adjectifs non gradables. On appelle ces adverbes des « adverbes non gradables ». Ils signifient souvent « entièrement » ou « presque entièrement ». On ne peut généralement pas les employer avec des adjectifs gradables.

Her presentation was absolutely awful**!**

She has a totally unique **presenting style.**

She had a completely American **audience.**

29.5 AUTRES EXEMPLES LES ADVERBES NON GRADABLES

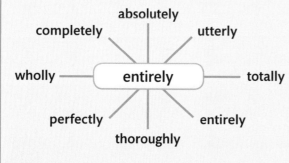

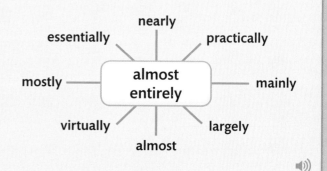

 29.6 BARREZ LE MOT INCORRECT DANS CHAQUE PHRASE.

If this new design is really popular, it will be an absolutely huge / ~~big~~ bonus for the company.

1. It is incredibly / perfectly important to know a lot about the product you are trying to sell.

2. Did you see that slightly / completely digital presentation by the marketing team?

3. Don't you think that this kind of product is extremely useful / excellent for teenagers?

4. To copy and then sell someone else's invention as your own is slightly / utterly wrong.

5. From the initial product design to marketing is a rather / completely long process.

6. The new designer in my department is absolutely / really fantastic.

7. I think the food at the conference was bad. I felt extremely sick / boiling this morning.

8. I have to say that I think it was an absolutely superb / okay presentation.

29.7 POINT CLÉ « REALLY », « FAIRLY » ET « PRETTY »

Quelques adverbes peuvent être utilisés avec à la fois
des adjectifs gradables et non gradables. Ces adverbes sont :
« really » (dans le sens de « very much »), « pretty » et « fairly »
(tous deux dans le sens de « quite a lot but not very »).

Gradable

What you need is a really { **good** / **brilliant** } **idea.**

Non gradable

You need to be fairly { **confident** / **certain** } **it works.**

Inventing a new product is pretty { **difficult** / **impossible** } **.**

CONSEIL

Notez que « fairly » peut
avoir une connotation
négative et n'est par
conséquent pas normalement
utilisé pour suggérer que
quelque chose est très
bon ou nécessaire.

29.8 ÉCOUTEZ L'ENREGISTREMENT, PUIS COCHEZ LES BONNES RÉPONSES.

Deux partenaires commerciaux, James et Maria, viennent d'assister
à des présentations réalisées par des concepteurs de produit.
Ils discutent des produits dans lesquels ils veulent investir.

What did James think of the presentations?
- **Liked them a lot** ✓
- **Hated them** ☐
- **Liked them a little** ☐

1 What did Maria think about how the
smartwatch looked?
- **Liked it a lot** ☐
- **Hated it** ☐
- **Liked it a little** ☐

2 What did they both think about the
smartwatch functionality?
- **Really good** ☐
- **Really bad** ☐
- **Not very good** ☐

3 What did they think about the cardboard
coffee capsules idea?
- **Liked it a lot** ☐
- **Hated it** ☐
- **Liked it a little** ☐

4 What did Maria think about how the
coffee machine looked?
- **Liked it a lot** ☐
- **Hated it** ☐
- **Didn't like it very much** ☐

5 What did James think of the air freshener?
- **Liked it a lot** ☐
- **Hated it** ☐
- **Didn't like it very much** ☐

29.9 POINT CLÉ « QUITE »

Vous pouvez utiliser « quite » avec les adjectifs gradables et non gradables. En anglais américain, « quite » signifie « very ». En anglais britannique, il affaiblit les adjectifs gradables et signifie « not very », mais renforce les adjectifs non gradables et signifie « very » ou « completely ».

Her invention is quite incredible.

[Her invention is absolutely fantastic.]

Her idea was quite good.

[Her idea was really good.] (US)

[Her idea was good, but not great.] (UK)

29.10 LISEZ LA CRITIQUE, PUIS COCHEZ LES BONNES RÉPONSES.

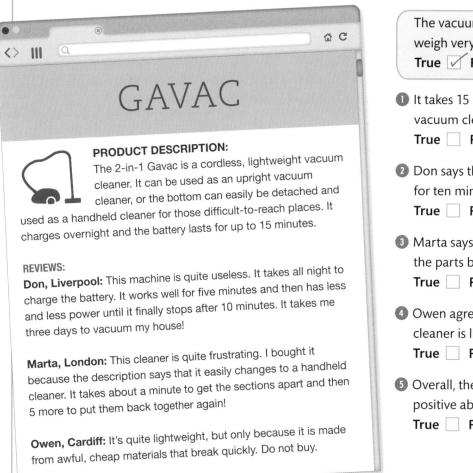

GAVAC

PRODUCT DESCRIPTION:
The 2-in-1 Gavac is a cordless, lightweight vacuum cleaner. It can be used as an upright vacuum cleaner, or the bottom can easily be detached and used as a handheld cleaner for those difficult-to-reach places. It charges overnight and the battery lasts for up to 15 minutes.

REVIEWS:
Don, Liverpool: This machine is quite useless. It takes all night to charge the battery. It works well for five minutes and then has less and less power until it finally stops after 10 minutes. It takes me three days to vacuum my house!

Marta, London: This cleaner is quite frustrating. I bought it because the description says that it easily changes to a handheld cleaner. It takes about a minute to get the sections apart and then 5 more to put them back together again!

Owen, Cardiff: It's quite lightweight, but only because it is made from awful, cheap materials that break quickly. Do not buy.

The vacuum cleaner does not weigh very much.
True ✓ **False** ☐

① It takes 15 minutes to charge the vacuum cleaner.
True ☐ **False** ☐

② Don says the vacuum works well for ten minutes.
True ☐ **False** ☐

③ Marta says it is difficult to put the parts back together.
True ☐ **False** ☐

④ Owen agrees that the Gavac cleaner is lightweight.
True ☐ **False** ☐

⑤ Overall, the reviews are quite positive about the Gavac.
True ☐ **False** ☐

HOME SHOPPING TODAY

New gadgets for your home

Inventions and innovations to make your home life easier and more comfortable. Order now for next-day delivery!

Envirocaff

The Envirocaff is a coffee machine like no other. Not only does it look absolutely amazing, but it also makes fantastic-tasting coffee every time. Unlike any other machine, the coffee capsules are made entirely from cardboard and can be recycled. Great coffee that doesn't cost the earth.
$85 for the machine
$5.99 / 12 coffee capsules

Blingtech3000

This sleek, fashionable watch face can be combined with a number of different designer straps from traditional leather through to modern rubber. The software is cutting edge and ensures all the functionality you would hope for from a smartwatch: email alerts, a fitness suite, and, of course, a watch. $259

AirFresh 4ever

This everlasting air freshener will bring all the smells of the countryside into your home forever! Unlike our rivals' products, there are no costly refills. There is just a great fragrance to make your house smell fresh forever. Enjoy AirFresh in three incredible fragrances: Country, Sea, and Highland fragrances. $24.99

Coz-E-Slip

The amazing new self-warming slippers. You can choose when to heat them up by using the timer or you can use the completely self-regulating thermostat option and have cozy, toasty, ready-to-go slippers at any time of day. Stay warm this winter with Coz-E-Slip.
$45.99 / batteries not included

The Envirocaff makes coffee that is _remarkably tasty_ .

1. The coffee capsules are _____ .

2. The Blingtech3000 is an _____ timepiece.

3. The Blingtech3000's software is _____ .

4. Most air freshener refills are _____ .

5. Coz-E-Slip slippers have a _____ thermostat.

6. The slippers are supposed to be _____ .

wholly recyclable

utterly stylish

~~remarkably tasty~~

extremely expensive

totally automatic

incredibly comfortable

absolutely state-of-the-art

---

29 ✓ CHECK-LIST

⚙ Les adjectifs non gradables ☐   **Aa** Les mots qualificatifs ☐   🧩 Ajouter des détails aux descriptions ☐

30 Exprimer le but

Il y a plusieurs façons d'exprimer le but, ou la raison, d'une action. Diverses expressions permettent de décrire la fonction d'un objet.

⚙ **Grammaire** « In order to » et « so that »
Aa Vocabulaire Les mots pour s'excuser
🧩 **Compétence** Exprimer le but

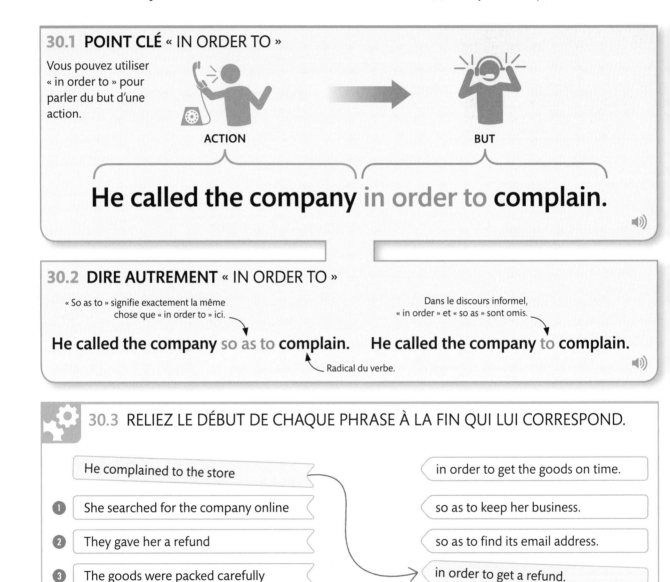

30.1 POINT CLÉ « IN ORDER TO »

Vous pouvez utiliser « in order to » pour parler du but d'une action.

ACTION

BUT

He called the company in order to **complain.**

30.2 DIRE AUTREMENT « IN ORDER TO »

« So as to » signifie exactement la même chose que « in order to » ici.

Dans le discours informel, « in order » et « so as » sont omis.

He called the company so as to **complain.**   **He called the company** to **complain.**

Radical du verbe.

30.3 RELIEZ LE DÉBUT DE CHAQUE PHRASE À LA FIN QUI LUI CORRESPOND.

He complained to the store	in order to get the goods on time.
① She searched for the company online	so as to keep her business.
② They gave her a refund	so as to find its email address.
③ The goods were packed carefully	in order to get a refund.
④ They paid for express delivery	so as to be able to relax on my trip.
⑤ I booked an expensive hotel	to protect them.

30.4 POINT CLÉ « SO THAT »

« So that » a une signification similaire à « in order to » et « so as to » mais est moins formel.

He complained so that he would get a refund.

« So that » est suivi du sujet + verbe.

« So that » est souvent suivi de verbes modaux tels que « can », « could » et « would ».

30.5 AUTRES EXEMPLES « SO THAT »

He reported the problem so that it could be fixed in other machines.

Si le verbe principal est au passé, le verbe après « so that » fait normalement référence au passé.

They check goods for damage so that customers don't receive broken items.

Si le verbe principal est au présent, le verbe après « so that » fait normalement référence au présent ou au futur.

30.6 ÉCOUTEZ L'ENREGISTREMENT, PUIS COCHEZ LES BONNES RÉPONSES.

Peter travaille au service client d'une société d'appareils électroménagers. Il parle d'une commande avec un client.

The customer bought the product in a store.
True ☐ **False** ☐ **Not given** ☑

① The customer is happy with what she received.
True ☐ **False** ☐ **Not given** ☐

② The product arrived broken.
True ☐ **False** ☐ **Not given** ☐

③ The company tries to pack the product well.
True ☐ **False** ☐ **Not given** ☐

④ The customer number is MN80.
True ☐ **False** ☐ **Not given** ☐

⑤ The replacement will arrive the same day.
True ☐ **False** ☐ **Not given** ☐

⑥ The replacement will arrive at 3pm.
True ☐ **False** ☐ **Not given** ☐

⑦ Peter offers 25 percent off the next purchase.
True ☐ **False** ☐ **Not given** ☐

30.7 RÉCRIVEZ LES PHRASES EN UTILISANT L'EXPRESSION DE BUT ENTRE PARENTHÈSES.

> I always go to Austria on vacation. I like to go skiing. [so that]
> *I always go to Austria on vacation so that I can go skiing.*

❶ Last year we had to complain. We wanted to get a bigger room. [in order to]

_____

❷ I usually go to the same resort. I like staying in the same hotel. [so that]

_____

❸ He bought the latest model. He wanted to impress his friends. [to]

_____

❹ I pack very carefully. I don't want to forget anything. [so as not to]

_____

❺ I went to the top of the highest mountain. I wanted to race down. [so that]

_____

❻ I went to a hospital. I needed to get an X-ray of my leg. [in order to]

_____

🔊

30.8 **POINT CLÉ** LE BUT GÉNÉRAL

Il se peut que vous vouliez parler de la raison qu'a une chose d'exister ou de sa fonction. Vous pouvez décrire un but général en utilisant « to » et « for ».

| « TO » + INFINITIF | **You can use this watch to track your heart rate.** |

Vous pouvez utiliser l'infinitif avec « to » lorsque le sujet d'une phrase est une personne.

| « FOR » + GÉRONDIF | **The device is perfect for improving your health.** |

Cette construction répond couramment à la question : « À quoi ça sert ? »

| « FOR » + NOM | **It is designed for people who love technology.** |

🔊

30.9 COMPLÉTEZ LES PHRASES AVEC « FOR » OU « TO ».

This form is ____*for*____ complaining about product quality and customer service.

1 Special "outlet" stores are known _____ selling excess goods at reduced prices.

2 This process is for customers who want _____ complain about the products they have received.

3 People are employed _____ check the quality of the goods before they are sent to stores.

4 These notes are here _____ help you complete the form and submit your complaint.

5 There is a telephone number _____ unhappy customers who wish to make further complaints.

6 I think a large number of people only complain _____ get refunds.

7 This new product is _____ busy people who want to make their lives simpler.

---

30 ✓ CHECK-LIST

⚙ « In order to » et « so that » ☐   **Aa** Les mots pour s'excuser ☐   🧩 Exprimer le but ☐

🔄 BILAN L'ANGLAIS QUE VOUS AVEZ APPRIS DANS LES CHAPITRES 27-30

NOUVEAU POINT LINGUISTIQUE	EXEMPLE TYPE	✓	CHAPITRE
LES PRONOMS RÉFLÉCHIS	I left myself a reminder about the meeting. The company director gave the talk himself.	☐	27.1, 27.4
LES VERBES SUIVIS DE « TO » OU « -ING » (AUCUN CHANGEMENT DE SENS)	I prefer to meet in person. I prefer meeting in person.	☐	28.1
LES VERBES SUIVIS DE « TO » OU « -ING » (AVEC CHANGEMENT DE SENS)	He stopped to talk to her in the office. She stopped talking to him and rushed off.	☐	28.3
LES ADJECTIFS GRADABLES ET NON GRADABLES	Her arguments were extremely good. Her arguments were fantastic!	☐	29.1
LES ADVERBES NON GRADABLES	Her presentation was absolutely awful!	☐	29.4
« REALLY », « FAIRLY », « PRETTY » ET « QUITE »	What you need is a really good idea. Her invention is quite brilliant.	☐	29.7, 29.9
« IN ORDER TO » ET « SO THAT »	He called the company in order to complain. He complained so that he could get a refund.	☐	30.1, 30.4

31.1 L'ENVIRONNEMENT

Factory emissions contribute to global warming.

global warming
[the increase in the Earth's temperature]

The protesters wanted to raise awareness of climate change.

climate change
[changes in the Earth's weather patterns]

Carbon dioxide is a well-known greenhouse gas.

greenhouse gases
[gases that cause the greenhouse effect, heating up the Earth]

Coal and oil are fossil fuels, **which produce carbon dioxide.**

fossil fuels
[fuels based on oil, coal, and gas]

This process consumes **a lot of fuel.**

consume
[use a supply of something, such as fuel or energy]

Flying less will help reduce your carbon footprint.

reduce your carbon footprint
[lower the level of carbon dioxide produced by your actions]

We need new laws if we are going to tackle pollution.

tackle pollution
[deal with the problem of pollution]

It is essential that we start using more types of alternative energy.

alternative energy
[energy that does not use fossil fuels]

Wind and solar are fairly green energy sources.

green energy sources
[types of energy that do not damage the environment]

It is more economical to use renewable energy.

renewable energy
[energy from sources that do not run out]

These big cars can be very harmful to the environment.

harmful to the environment
[causing damage to the environment]

Polluted rivers have dire consequences for local wildlife.

dire consequences
[very bad results]

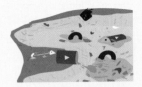

Some people use solar power to heat their water.

solar power
[energy created using sunlight]

A lot of the houses here have solar panels on their roofs.

solar panel
[equipment needed to turn sunlight into electricity]

Here we use turbines to turn wind power into electricity.

wind power
[energy created using the wind]

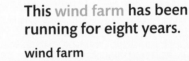

This wind farm has been running for eight years.

wind farm
[a place with many turbines for generating wind power]

After years of poaching, the white rhino is endangered.

endangered
[at risk of extinction]

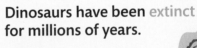

Dinosaurs have been extinct for millions of years.

extinct
[no longer existing]

It's terrible to see the destruction of the rainforests.

destruction
[the act of damaging something so badly that it cannot survive or be repaired]

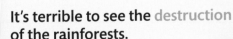

As the planet heats up, it will undergo irreversible change.

irreversible change
[permanent change that cannot be undone]

32 Les conditionnels

Vous pouvez utiliser le troisième conditionnel pour décrire un passé irréel ou des événements qui n'ont pas eu lieu. Ce temps est utile pour parler de regrets que vous avez concernant le passé.

Grammaire Le troisième conditionnel
Aa Vocabulaire Les menaces environnementales
Compétence Parler d'un passé irréel

32.1 POINT CLÉ LE TROISIÈME CONDITIONNEL

DEUXIÈME CONDITIONNEL

On utilise le deuxième conditionnel pour décrire des situations irréelles dans le présent.

If I lived in New York, I would go running in Central Park.

TROISIÈME CONDITIONNEL

On utilise le troisième conditionnel pour décrire une situation irréelle dans le passé.

If we had left earlier, we would have caught the train.

32.2 CONSTRUCTION LE TROISIÈME CONDITIONNEL

« IF »	« HAD » + PARTICIPE PASSÉ	« WOULD/COULD/ MIGHT »	« HAVE » + PARTICIPE PASSÉ
If	we had left earlier,	we would	have caught the train.

La proposition avec « if » est la condition passée irréelle.

Vous pouvez modifier le degré de certitude du résultat imaginé en utilisant différents modaux.

La proposition au conditionnel est le résultat irréel.

32.3 DIRE AUTREMENT LE TROISIÈME CONDITIONNEL

Le past perfect continu peut aussi suivre « if » au troisième conditionnel.

If you'd been wearing a coat, you would have stayed warm.

We would've caught the train if we'd left on time.

« Have » est souvent contracté à l'oral.

Les phrases au troisième conditionnel peuvent être réordonnées sans virgule avec la proposition en « if » en seconde position.

32.4 COMPLÉTEZ LES PHRASES EN CONJUGUANT LES VERBES AU TEMPS QUI CONVIENT POUR FAIRE DES PHRASES AU TROISIÈME CONDITIONNEL.

If he ___had asked___ (ask) me to marry him, I ___would have said___ (would / say) yes.

1 If I _____ (choose) the trip, we _____ (would / go) to Spain.

2 If we _____ (arrive) earlier, we _____ (would/ not miss) the show.

3 I _____ (could / help) them if they _____ (call) me earlier.

4 If we _____ (stop) eating earlier, we _____ (might / not feel) so sick.

5 She _____ (would / pass) her exam if she _____ (work) a bit harder.

6 If you _____ (shut) the door, we _____ (might / not be) so cold.

🔊

32.5 POINT CLÉ L'INVERSION FORMELLE

Vous pouvez rendre le troisième conditionnel plus formel en inversant le sujet et « had » et en ôtant « if ».

If you had attended **the meeting, you would have met the manager.**

Had you attended **the meeting, you would have met the manager.**

L'inversion est davantage utilisée en anglais écrit académique et en anglais formel.

🔊

32.6 ÉCOUTEZ L'ENREGISTREMENT, PUIS ENTOUREZ LES ÉVÉNEMENTS QUI ONT VRAIMENT EU LIEU.

32.7 PRONONCIATION LES FORMES CONTRACTÉES

En anglais parlé, vous entendrez souvent les formes contractées de « would have », « could have » et « might have ». Le son voyelle avant le « v » final est un son paresseux « uve ».

would've

could've

might've

🔊

32.8 LISEZ LES PHRASES À VOIX HAUTE EN UTILISANT LES FORMES CONTRACTÉES.

They would have taken my car if I had not paid the bill.

They would've taken my car if I hadn't paid the bill.

1 I might have worked harder if I had been paid more.

2 If more people had voted for him, he would have won.

3 If you had left earlier, we would have arrived on time.

4 She might have finished on time if she had started sooner.

🔊

 ## 32.9 RÉCRIVEZ LES PHRASES EN CORRIGEANT LES ERREURS.

If Jack had visited sooner, he will have seen us.
If Jack had visited sooner, he would have seen us.

1 If you'll have kept the fire alight, we wouldn't have been so cold.

_____

2 You might slept better if you had brought a sleeping bag!

_____

3 If she'd wore her boots, she wouldn't have had such wet feet.

_____

4 If they'd keep the river clean, the fish not might have died.

_____

🔊

32.10 LISEZ L'ARTICLE, PUIS COCHEZ LES BONNES RÉPONSES.

There are only a few rhinos left in Java.
True ☑ **False** ☐

① The last Javan rhino in Vietnam died of old age.
True ☐ **False** ☐

② It is important to protect the rhinos' habitat.
True ☐ **False** ☐

③ Rhinos naturally live in tropical forests.
True ☐ **False** ☐

④ It is quite cheap to buy rhino horn.
True ☐ **False** ☐

⑤ Rhino horn is mostly used in cooking.
True ☐ **False** ☐

⑥ The leaflet says there is nothing that readers can do.
True ☐ **False** ☐

CONSERVATION WEEKLY

Save the Javan rhino

In 2010, the last surviving Javan rhino in Vietnam was killed for its horn. How can we make sure that the same does not happen to the few remaining rhinos on Java? What can we do differently?

Firstly, if the rhinos' habitat had been better protected, the rhinos would have had a much greater chance of survival.

Not only does their natural tropical rainforest habitat provide a place for the rhinos to live and find food but it also acts as a place to hide from hunters and poachers.

We also need to stop the market in rhino horns. Prices are so high that poachers take huge risks to get them. Had we persuaded more people not to use rhino horn in traditional medicines, we might have saved that last Javan rhino in Vietnam. We must do all we can to stop the illegal trade in rhino horn.

Go to our website for more information.

 32.11 ÉCOUTEZ L'ENREGISTREMENT, PUIS COCHEZ LE BON RÉSUMÉ.

① In the 1930s more than three-quarters of Java was covered in forest. The Javan tiger was classified as endangered in 1976 and now it is nearly extinct. The population of its main food source, the Rusa deer, has also declined. ☐

② In the 1930s nearly a quarter of Java was covered in forest. The Javan tiger was last seen in the wild in 1976 and is now classified as extinct. The population of its main food source, the Rusa deer, has also declined. ☐

③ In the 1930s more than half of Java was covered in forest. The Javan tiger was last seen in the wild in 1952 and is now classified as extinct. The population of its main food source, the Rusa deer, has increased significantly. ☐

32.12 POINT CLÉ « I WISH »

REGRETS PRÉSENTS

Vous pouvez utiliser « I wish » pour exprimer des regrets concernant le présent d'une façon similaire au deuxième conditionnel

The snow is amazing!
I wish I knew **how to ski.**

↖ « Wish » + passé = sens présent.

REGRETS PASSÉS

Vous pouvez utiliser « I wish » pour exprimer des regrets concernant le passé d'une façon similaire au troisième conditionnel.

My camera has no power.
I wish I'd charged **the battery.**

↖ « Wish » + « had » + participe passé = sens passé.

🔊

32.13 DIRE AUTREMENT « I WISH »

REGRETS PRÉSENTS

Vous pouvez exprimer des regrets plus forts concernant le présent en utilisant « if only » suivi du passé.

These mountains are incredible!
If only I knew **how to ski.**

REGRETS PASSÉS

Vous pouvez exprimer des regrets plus forts concernant le passé en utilisant « if only » avec « had » et le participe passé.

I really wanted to take pictures.
If only I'd charged **the battery.**

🔊

 ## 32.14 BARREZ LE MOT INCORRECT DANS CHAQUE PHRASE.

> There wasn't much wildlife. I wish I had seen / s̶a̶w̶ more animals!

1 I wish we weren't / hadn't been outdoors right now.

2 I think about the trip a lot. I wish I took / had taken more photos.

3 I feel sick. If only I had eaten / ate fewer of those berries.

4 The bus has broken down! If only the driver had known / knew how to fix it.

5 I'm so exhausted! If only I sleep / 'd slept a little more.

🔊

32.15 COMPLÉTEZ LES PHRASES AVEC « I WISH » ET « IF ONLY ».

I was so hot in the sun today. I wish <u>*I had remembered my hat!*</u> (remember / hat).

❶ I missed the bus again. I wish _____ (set / alarm).

❷ I caught a huge fish yesterday. If only _____ (take / photo).

❸ I can't afford those boots. If only _____ (not spend / money).

❹ I was so cold this winter. I wish _____ (buy / coat).

32.16 LISEZ L'ARTICLE, PUIS COMPLÉTEZ LES PHRASES.

I wish I'd _____*gone*_____ sailing with him.

❶ He wished he'd _____ the fishermen from killing the seal.

❷ He thought, if only he'd _____ something to protect the seals.

❸ If I hadn't helped, I know I would've _____ guilty forever.

❹ If he'd seen me become a campaigner, he'd have _____ very proud.

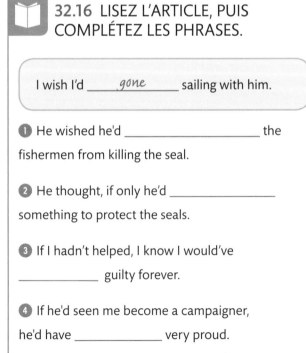

76 ENVIRONMENT UPDATE

WHY ARE YOU A CAMPAIGNER?

My grandfather was a sailor and explored the world by sea. He'd tell me stories of his adventures. He never asked me to go sailing with him, though I would have loved to. Once, in the 1930s, he saw fishermen killing a Caribbean monk seal. He wanted to stop the fishermen, and always felt bad that he did not do anything. After about 20 years, he read that the very last Caribbean monk seal had been killed. He always regretted not doing anything to protect these seals. Many years later when I was in Greece, I saw a leaflet about the endangered Mediterranean monk seal. I knew I had to help or else I'd feel guilty forever. Unfortunately my grandfather never knew I became a campaigner. He'd be very proud.

---

32 ✓ **CHECK-LIST**

⚙ Le troisième conditionnel ☐   **Aa** Les menaces environnementales ☐   🧩 Parler d'un passé irréel ☐

33 Les regrets

Vous pouvez utiliser « should have » et « ought to have » pour parler d'erreurs passées. Ces deux tournures indiquent que vous souhaiteriez avoir fait quelque chose différemment dans le passé.

🔧 **Grammaire** « Should have » et « ought to have »

Aa Vocabulaire Les marqueurs temporels

🧩 **Compétence** Exprimer des regrets

33.1 POINT CLÉ « SHOULD HAVE » ET « OUGHT TO HAVE »

On utilise « should have » et « ought to have » pour exprimer des regrets au sujet de quelque chose qui n'a pas eu lieu dans le passé. « Ought to » est moins courant que « should » et est généralement plus formel.

This bill is so big. I { **should have** / **ought to have** } **used less electricity.**

33.2 AUTRES EXEMPLES « SHOULD HAVE » ET « OUGHT TO HAVE »

Perhaps I ought to have used energy-saving light bulbs.

La forme négative « ought not to have » est grammaticalement correcte mais rarement utilisée.

I shouldn't have fallen asleep with the TV on.

33.3 COMPLÉTEZ LES PHRASES AVEC « SHOULD HAVE » ET « SHOULDN'T HAVE ».

We ___*shouldn't have*___ damaged the environment. It's becoming a long-term problem.

① People _____ thrown things in the river. The fish population has declined dramatically.

② Factories _____ reduced pollution in accordance with environmental agreements.

③ Companies _____ used fewer vehicles in order to lower their carbon footprint.

④ Factories _____ released pollution into the water. It has poisoned the ecosystem.

33.4 RÉCRIVEZ LES PHRASES EN CORRIGEANT LES ERREURS.

You really should have not watched a horror film on your own.
You really shouldn't have watched a horror film on your own.

1 I ought have gone to bed earlier last night. I'm feeling really exhausted now.

_____

2 We really shouldn't to have eaten so much at lunchtime. I'm feeling sleepy now.

_____

3 You should drove more carefully on the wet road. You could have had an accident.

_____

4 Should have I bought this desktop computer, or would the laptop have been better?

_____

◀))

33.5 LISEZ L'ARTICLE, PUIS COCHEZ LES BONNES RÉPONSES.

Humans intentionally introduce non-native species.
True ☑ **False** ☐

1 New species are introduced to help other animals.
True ☐ **False** ☐

2 Sometimes no animals hunt the introduced species.
True ☐ **False** ☐

3 The Small Indian Mongoose is not native to Mauritius.
True ☐ **False** ☐

4 The mongooses killed the rats on Mauritius.
True ☐ **False** ☐

5 The mongooses also killed all the local animals.
True ☐ **False** ☐

MONGOOSE MADNESS
Mongooses wreak havoc on Mauritius.

One surprising environmental problem caused by humans is the introduction of non-native species of animals to solve local problems.

The new species is supposed to eat the animal that is causing a problem for humans. The difficulties arise when there are no predators for this newly introduced species or when it decides to feed on plants and animals that we do want. For example, the Small Indian Mongoose was introduced to Mauritius and should have dealt with an ever-growing rat population. The mongooses killed the rats, but then they also killed many local animals which then became extinct on the island.

33.6 VOCABULAIRE LES MARQUEURS TEMPORELS

1980s	1990s

Initially, the factories were quite small.

[At first, the factories were quite small.]

During the 1980s, people invested money in the factories.

[At some point in the 1980s, people invested in the factories.]

Throughout the 1990s, the factories grew in size.

[From the beginning to the end of the 1990s, the factories grew in size.]

 ## 33.7 ÉCOUTEZ L'ENREGISTREMENT, PUIS NUMÉROTEZ LES IMAGES DANS LE BON ORDRE.

Ⓐ ☐   Ⓑ ① 1   Ⓒ ☐   Ⓓ ☐   Ⓔ ☐

Aa ## 33.8 ÉCOUTEZ À NOUVEAU L'ENREGISTREMENT, PUIS COMPLÉTEZ LES PHRASES EN UTILISANT LES MOTS DU VOCABULAIRE 33.6.

___*Initially*___ , Easter Island was expansively forested.

❶ _____ the rise of a new civilization, the islanders built statues to honor their ancestors.

❷ _____ this time, the islanders were cutting down lots of trees.

❸ _____ his visit, the first European explorer noticed that there weren't many trees.

❹ The ship HMS Blossom visited in 1825, and _____ , the statues had been toppled over.

❺ An airport was built in 1987 and _____ , lots of tourists have visited Easter Island.

2004   2005

Pollution peaked in 2004. that time **many trees had died.**

[At the start of 2004, many trees had already died.]

Following **new laws in 2005, pollution levels dropped.**

[After new laws were passed in 2005, pollution levels dropped.]

Since then, **there have been some signs of a recovery.**

[From that point onward, there has been a slight recovery.]

◀))

33.9 LISEZ L'ARTICLE, PUIS COCHEZ LES BONNES RÉPONSES.

Humans are producing less waste now than they used to.
True ☐   False ☐   Not given ☑

① Radioactive waste is the most widespread problem.
True ☐   False ☐   Not given ☐

② All the waste is poured into rivers.
True ☐   False ☐   Not given ☐

③ The kind of waste humans produce has changed over time.
True ☐   False ☐   Not given ☐

④ Modern plastics can be difficult to dispose of effectively.
True ☐   False ☐   Not given ☐

THE PROBLEM WITH POLLUTION
Pollution levels rising across the globe.

The growing human population is producing more and more waste, ranging from sewage and smog to radioactive fuel. Dealing with all this waste is a huge problem. Much of it is just dumped, pumped into the atmosphere, or even poured into rivers and oceans. The resulting pollution is damaging nature.

One of the main issues is the kind of waste humans are now producing. Until the mid-20th century, most of the waste was buried and it just slowly decayed. Nowadays, however, modern plastics make up a large portion of what we throw away. These plastics are almost indestructible by any natural process, so they just pile up, creating huge heaps of waste.

---

33 ✓ CHECK-LIST

⚙ « Should have » et « ought to have » ☐   **Aa** Les marqueurs temporels ☐   🧩 Exprimer des regrets ☐

Contrairement à de nombreuses parties du discours, les prépositions ont souvent peu de sens en elles-mêmes, mais elles permettent de modifier le sens des mots qui les entourent.

⚙ **Grammaire** Les prépositions dépendantes
Aa Vocabulaire Les actions et les conséquences
🧩 **Compétence** Changer l'accentuation de la phrase

34.1 POINT CLÉ LES PRÉPOSITIONS DÉPENDANTES

Certains mots doivent s'accompagner de prépositions dépendantes spécifiques.

I am late for **my meeting!**

« Late » ne pourrait pas être associé à une autre préposition dans ce contexte.

We agreed about **the idea.**

He's really afraid of **flying.**

There was an increase in **sales.**

🔊

Aa **34.2 COMPLÉTEZ LES PHRASES AVEC AVEC LES LOCUTIONS DE LA LISTE.**

Recently, there has been a ⟨ *lack of* ⟩ energy in the team.

1 Please make sure you [   ] help if you need it.

2 Who is giving the lecture? I have never [   ] him.

3 My brother and I are always [   ] current affairs.

4 The global [   ] natural resources is worrying.

5 Thank you so much! I am so [   ] all you have done.

6 When you're stressed, it is good to [   ] problems.

7 The [   ] the economic crisis is enormous.

8 Most of the population [   ] climate change.

9 All of the scientific evidence [   ] one direction.

decline in
talk about
arguing about
grateful for
~~lack of~~
knows about
heard of
points in
ask for
effect of

🔊

134

34.3 COMPLÉTEZ CHAQUE PHRASE AVEC LA PRÉPOSITION QUI CONVIENT.

> Have you ever heard __*of*__ Esperanto?

① Why do they always argue _____ everything?

② There was a decline _____ the number of birds.

③ There's a lot to be grateful _____ .

④ This demonstrates a real lack _____ talent.

⑤ How do I ask _____ directions in Greek?

⑥ I don't think we'll ever agree _____ this.

⑦ I really don't want to be late _____ work.

⑧ My mother is very afraid _____ heights.

⑨ What is the long-term effect _____ this?

34.4 POINT CLÉ LES MOTS AVEC PLUS D'UNE PRÉPOSITION DÉPENDANTE

Certains mots peuvent être accompagnés de plus d'une préposition spécifique. Le choix de la préposition change souvent le sens de la phrase.

He talked to the teacher.
[He had a conversation with the teacher.]

He talked about the teacher.
[He had a conversation with someone else about the teacher.]

34.5 ÉCOUTEZ L'ENREGISTREMENT, PUIS BARREZ LES PRÉPOSITIONS INCORRECTES.

> Technology is a great way to increase interest in / ~~interest with~~ the environment.

① I'm so bored with / bored about their constant fighting about policies.

② They've made a new app for / of children to learn about the Earth.

③ Do you have any objection to / objection for this environmental policy?

④ I often worry to / worry about the future of our planet.

⑤ You need to apologize to / apologize for them to / for the things you said.

⑥ Do you think a policy like this is suitable with / suitable for a country like ours?

34.6 PRONONCIATION L'ACCENTUATION AU SEIN DE LA PHRASE

Vous pouvez changer le sens d'une phrase en accentuant différents mots lorsque vous les prononcez.

The journalist called the mayor today.

[Her assistant didn't make the call.]

The journalist called the mayor today.

[She didn't email.]

The journalist called the mayor today.

[She didn't call the mayor's secretary.]

The journalist called the mayor today.

[She didn't call yesterday.]

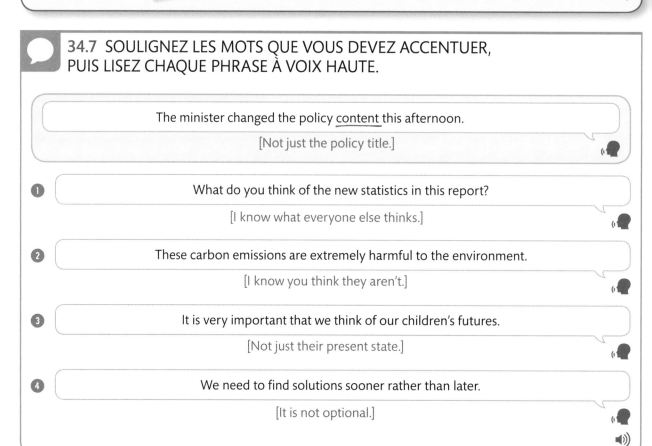

34.7 SOULIGNEZ LES MOTS QUE VOUS DEVEZ ACCENTUER, PUIS LISEZ CHAQUE PHRASE À VOIX HAUTE.

The minister changed the policy content this afternoon.

[Not just the policy title.]

1. What do you think of the new statistics in this report?

[I know what everyone else thinks.]

2. These carbon emissions are extremely harmful to the environment.

[I know you think they aren't.]

3. It is very important that we think of our children's futures.

[Not just their present state.]

4. We need to find solutions sooner rather than later.

[It is not optional.]

Aa 34.8 LISEZ L'ARTICLE, PUIS COMPLÉTEZ LES PHRASES AVEC LES MOTS DE LA LISTE.

93 ENVIRONMENT NEWS WEEKLY

GROWTH AND DECAY

The complex effects of urbanization in a rapidly changing world

Urbanization (the population shift from rural areas to towns and cities) has been happening for centuries. However, the rate and extent of population shift has reached astonishing levels. Some Asian cities, such as Osaka, Jakarta, Mumbai, Seoul, and Beijing, already have populations of more than 20 million people.

What are the environmental ____consequences____ of urbanization on such a massive scale? One major

effect of urbanization is the creation of "urban heat islands." Rural areas can remain cooler

_____ the sun evaporating the moisture from the vegetation and the soil. However, in

the cities there is much less soil and vegetation. _____ , the sun beating on the buildings

and roads _____ to an increase in temperatures. Additional heat from vehicles, factories,

and cooling units also increases temperatures. This heat then _____ changes in local

weather patterns.

Not only is there increased air pollution, but also higher levels of rainfall, _____ in

flooding within the cities themselves and also downstream. Another _____ of

urbanization is the increased consumption of food, energy, and durable goods. This has a

far-reaching _____ on levels of natural resources.

---

causes   impact   ~~consequences~~   due to   Consequently   consequence   leads   resulting

---

34 ✅ CHECK-LIST

⚙️ Les prépositions dépendantes ☐   **Aa** Les actions et les conséquences ☐   🧩 Changer l'accentuation de la phrase ☐

137

35 « Few » ou « little » ?

Le choix des mots utilisés pour décrire des quantités dépend de nombreux facteurs, notamment s'il s'agit de quelque chose de dénombrable ou d'indénombrable.

⚙ **Grammaire** « Few », « little », « fewer », « less »
Aa Vocabulaire La nature et l'environnement
🧩 **Compétence** Décrire des quantités

35.1 POINT CLÉ « FEW » POUR PARLER DE PETITS NOMBRES

Utilisez « few » avec un nom pluriel dénombrable pour dire qu'il n'y a pas beaucoup de quelque chose. « Few » indique à quel point ce nombre est faible. On emploie « a few » pour dire « some ». « A few » souligne que le nombre, bien que faible, est suffisant.

few = not many

**There are few rare birds here.
We probably won't see any.**

a few = some

**There are a few rare birds here.
We might see one.**

🔊

35.2 POINT CLÉ « LITTLE » POUR PARLER DE FAIBLES QUANTITÉS

Utilisez « little » avec un nom pluriel indénombrable pour dire qu'il n'y a pas beaucoup de quelque chose. « Little » indique à quel point cette quantité est faible. On emploie « a little » pour dire « some ». « A little » souligne que la quantité, bien que faible, est suffisante.

CONSEIL
Vous pouvez ajouter « very » à « few » et « little » pour dire « presque pas ».

little = not much

I have little money left. I can't afford to visit the wildlife park.

a little = some

I have a little money left. Should we visit the wildlife park?

🔊

35.3 DIRE AUTREMENT UTILISER « LITTLE » ET « FEW » POUR PARLER DE PETITES QUANTITÉS

Vous pouvez utiliser « a (little) bit of » au lieu de « a little » de manière informelle.

There's a little bit of the park that we haven't seen yet.

Vous pouvez également utiliser « little » et « few » comme pronoms pour dire « not much/many ».

Little can be done when few are willing to contribute.

🔊

35.4 BARREZ LES MOTS INCORRECTS DANS CHAQUE PHRASE.

 I'm so excited. I've got ~~few~~ / a few hours to explore the city tonight.

1 I'm afraid we have little / a little time to catch the train. We must hurry.

2 That cake is delicious. I'll have little / a little bit more.

3 Sadly, there are few / a few examples of this quality craftmanship left.

4 Great! We have little / a little spare money. Should we go out for dinner?

5 Wow! Look at all these monkeys! I think there are few / a few different species here.

6 Unfortunately, I have few / a few friends. It's quite lonely here.

35.5 OBSERVEZ LES IMAGES, PUIS COMPLÉTEZ LES PHRASES AVEC « (A) FEW » OU « (A) LITTLE ».

There is ___little___ water left in the bottle. I'm so thirsty!

1 Great! There are _____ magazines to choose from.

2 Sadly, there are _____ fish in my aquarium.

3 There is very _____ cake left, I'm afraid.

4 It should be OK. We have _____ time left.

5 The café is closing soon. There are so _____ customers.

35.6 POINT CLÉ « QUITE A FEW » ET « QUITE A BIT(OF) » POUR DE GRANDES QUANTITÉS

Les locutions « quite a bit » et « quite a few » sont des euphémismes
qui signifient en fait « a lot » ou « many ».

| quite a few = many |

The park has been open for quite a few **years.**

| quite a bit of = a lot of |

They collected quite a bit of **money for charity.**

🔊

35.7 COMPLÉTEZ LES PHRASES EN UTILISANT « (A) FEW » ET « (A) LITTLE ».

Ninety-year-old Ken Wilson has finally decided to have ___*a little*___

time off after volunteering at his local wildlife park for 30 years. Ken

started volunteering _____ years after he retired from

teaching. He says, "I started making coffee for people in the little

visitor center, but I've had quite _____ different roles

since then."

Ken has been a guide, he's surveyed butterflies, and he even managed

to get his hands dirty quite _____ times clearing up litter. What

does he like so much about the park? "Well, there are _____

green places left like this in big cities. For _____ or no money, a

family can explore all day and learn _____ about local wildlife.

It's _____ bit of calm in a busy world."

What will he do now? "I'd like quite _____ days sitting in the

park doing nothing." After three decades looking after the wildlife, it's

time for Ken to take _____ break.

35.8 POINT CLÉ « FEWER » ET « LESS »

La confusion entre « less » et « fewer » est très commune. N'oubliez pas d'utiliser « less » avec des noms indénombrables, et « fewer » avec des noms pluriels dénombrables.

« Issues » est un nom pluriel dénombrable.

There are fewer issues with electric cars these days.

It would be great to use less fuel.

« Fuel » est un nom indénombrable.

35.9 AUTRES EXEMPLES « FEWER » ET « LESS »

There are fewer whales in the oceans nowadays.

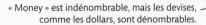

We need to spend less money.

« Money » est indénombrable, mais les devises, comme les dollars, sont dénombrables.

Fewer people enjoy gardening these days.

There is much less traffic today.

35.10 RELIEZ CHAQUE DÉBUT DE PHRASE À LA FIN QUI LUI CORRESPOND.

People are spending much less	volunteers than last year.
❶ Protesters have demanded fewer	wildlife near big factory sites.
❷ The charity has fewer	money on organic food than expected.
❸ The new light bulbs use far less	electricity than the old ones.
❹ Unsurprisingly, there is much less	pollution in the capital city.
❺ Since the new traffic laws, there is a lot less	harmful emissions by 2025.

35.11 POINT CLÉ « FEWER THAN » ET « LESS THAN »

Utilisez « less than » lorsque vous parlez de quantités, de distances, de temps et d'argent.
Utilisez « fewer than » pour parler de groupes de personnes ou de choses.

There are fewer than 3,500 tigers in the wild.

Baby elephants weigh less than 300 pounds.

35.12 AUTRES EXEMPLES « FEWER THAN » ET « LESS THAN »

The charity survives with fewer than 20 volunteers.

Charity workers are paid less than $10 an hour.

There are fewer than 50 tickets left for the charity concert.

You can donate less than the recommended amount.

35.13 ÉCOUTEZ L'ENREGISTREMENT, PUIS COCHEZ LES BONNES RÉPONSES.

Une station de radio locale présente un reportage
sur le récent succès d'un militant environnemental.

	True	False
Environmental campaigner Rachel Roberts is 70 years old.	☐	☑
❶ The proposal was to build houses on the site of the lake.	True ☐	False ☐
❷ Rachel's family used to have family picnics near Lake Lucid.	True ☐	False ☐
❸ There were only modern pictures at the photography exhibition.	True ☐	False ☐
❹ After 25 days, the exhibition had raised just under $3,000.	True ☐	False ☐
❺ People have come to visit the lake from other countries.	True ☐	False ☐
❻ The plans for the bypass are delayed, but are still going ahead.	True ☐	False ☐

35.14 COMPLÉTEZ LES PHRASES DU RÉSUMÉ DE L'ENREGISTREMENT DE L'EXERCICE 35.13 AVEC LES MOTS DE LA LISTE.

___Few___ people would have believed the government would change their minds.

1. Rachel also had the help of _____ friends during her campaign.

2. Rachel knew that _____ people held the same opinion as her.

3. The area is home to _____ 500 plant and animal species.

4. The photography exhibition raised $25,000 in _____ a week.

5. _____ people sent messages of support via social media sites.

6. Making Lake Lucid a popular tourist site will only take _____ years.

| ~~Few~~ | a few | more than | quite a few | less than | Quite a few | a few |

---

35 ✓ CHECK-LIST

⚙ « Few », « little », « fewer » et « less » ☐   **Aa** La nature et l'environnement ☐   🧩 Décrire des quantités ☐

♻ BILAN L'ANGLAIS QUE VOUS AVEZ APPRIS DANS LES CHAPITRES 32-35

NOUVEAU POINT LINGUISTIQUE	EXEMPLE TYPE	☑	CHAPITRE
LE TROISIÈME CONDITIONNEL	If we had left earlier, we would have caught the train.	☐	32.1
« I WISH » ET « IF ONLY »	I wish I knew how to ski. If only I'd charged the battery.	☐	32.12, 32.13
« SHOULD HAVE » ET « OUGHT TO HAVE »	This bill is so big, I should have used less electricity.	☐	33.1
LES PRÉPOSITIONS DÉPENDANTES	I am late for my meeting!	☐	34.1, 34.4
« FEW » ET « LITTLE »	There are few rare birds here. I have little money left.	☐	35.1, 35.2
« FEWER » ET « LESS »	There are fewer issues with electric cars. It would be great to use less fuel.	☐	35.8

36.1 LES TRADITIONS ET LES SUPERSTITIONS

I told a white lie and said the dress looked good on her.

tell a white lie
[say something that is not true to avoid upsetting someone]

She always drops hints about the presents she wants.

drop a hint
[say something indirectly]

Varinder started a rumor that Sonia stole some money.

start / spread a rumor
[to start / continue saying things that may or may not be true]

Paulo loves to gossip. He's always talking behind people's backs.

gossip
[talk about other people, often in a negative way]

I have a sneaking suspicion that he won't come to the party tonight.

have a sneaking suspicion
[have a persistent idea about something with little evidence]

I don't believe in ghosts.

believe in something
[think that something exists or is true]

I haven't ever broken a bone. Knock on wood!

knock on wood (US)
touch wood (UK)
[wish for good luck, or avert bad luck]

Close your eyes and make a wish.

make a wish
[hope for something to happen]

I have serious misgivings about this new policy.

have serious misgivings / doubts
[have a strong feeling that something is not right]

She was such a tattletale at school.

tattletale (US) / telltale (UK)
[somebody who tells an authority figure when another person has done something wrong]

The best type of publicity is word of mouth.

word of mouth
[information or news transmitted by people telling other people]

I want you to tell me the truth, not another fairy tale.

fairy tale
[a traditional story with magic, or a story designed to mislead others]

That story about the haunted hotel is just an urban myth.

urban myth
[a modern story which is untrue but believed by many]

A black cat is seen as both a good and bad omen.

good / bad omen
[a positive / negative sign about something that will happen]

Winning that car was a real stroke of luck.

a stroke of luck
[a single piece of good fortune]

Winning that game was just beginner's luck.

beginner's luck
[have good fortune the first time you do something]

This is a game of pure luck.

pure luck
[good fortune with no skill involved]

I've just read a book about Chinese folklore.

folklore
[stories, sayings, and traditions from a certain area or culture]

That generation has a different set of beliefs to ours.

set of beliefs
[a group of values]

She has an unshakable belief in the goodness of people.

unshakeable belief
[a firm and unchangeable conviction]

37 Les possibilités passées

Vous pouvez utiliser divers modaux pour parler d'événements possibles dans le passé et pour indiquer si vous êtes d'accord ou pas avec des hypothèses émises.

⚙ **Grammaire** « Might/may/could » dans le passé
Aa Vocabulaire Les légendes urbaines
🧩 **Compétence** Parler de possibilités passées

37.1 POINT CLÉ LES POSSIBILITÉS PASSÉES

Vous pouvez utiliser cette construction pour parler de quelque chose qui, selon vous, a probablement eu lieu dans le passé.

The copier isn't working. It { **might may could** } **have run out of paper.**

[He thinks it is possible that the copier has run out of paper.]

Vous pouvez utiliser cette construction pour parler de quelque chose qui n'a probablement pas eu lieu dans le passé.

You { **might not may not** } **have plugged it in properly.**

[He thinks it is possible that the printer wasn't plugged in properly.]

« Could not » ne peut être utilisé que lorsque le locuteur est certain que quelque chose a eu lieu.

You couldn't have changed the ink properly earlier.

[He is certain that the ink wasn't changed properly.]

37.2 BARREZ LES MOTS INCORRECTS DANS CHAQUE PHRASE.

 I feel a bit sick. I might / ~~may not~~ / ~~could not~~ have eaten something bad.

 ① It was raining, so I could / might not / could not have gone sunbathing even if I had wanted to.

 ② Look at him! Do you think he might / may not / could not have won the lottery?

 ③ If I had left the house a little earlier, I may / might not / could not have missed the bus.

 ④ I don't know where she is. She could / may not / could not have gone for a run. She loves exercise.

37.3 ÉCOUTEZ L'ENREGISTREMENT, PUIS RÉPONDEZ AUX QUESTIONS.

  Sophie raconte à son amie une légende urbaine dont elle a entendu parler.

What is an urban myth?
An urban myth is a modern story that isn't true, but lots of people think it is.

① How did Sophie's opinion change about about her brother's story?

_____

② Why were the golfers celebrating?

_____

③ What did they do after they knocked over the kangaroo?

_____

④ What did the kangaroo do when it woke up?

_____

⑤ Why couldn't the golfers continue driving home?

_____

37.4 POINT CLÉ LE DISCOURS INDIRECT

Au discours indirect, le verbe principal passe souvent au passé. Les références de temps et de lieu de la phrase doivent parfois aussi changer.

I don't **believe** these **ghost stories.**

Le présent simple « don't » devient le prétérit « didn't ».

He said that he didn't **believe** those **ghost stories.**

« These » est remplacé par « those », plus éloigné.

Dans les questions ouvertes rapportées, le sujet se place avant le verbe et on n'utilise pas la forme interrogative.

What are you reading?

I asked her what she was reading.

Dans les questions fermées rapportées (avec une réponse en « yes/no »), on utilise « if » ou « whether ».

Are you enjoying it?

I asked her { if / whether } **she was enjoying it.**

37.5 RÉCRIVEZ LES PHRASES AU DISCOURS INDIRECT.

> Amal has bought a book about ghosts.
> Amal said _____ *that she had bought a book about ghosts.*

❶ Amal's reading a scary story.

Amal mentioned _____

❷ Amal's finished the book.

Amal told me _____

❸ Are you going to the movies?

I asked her _____

❹ What kind of movie are you going to see?

I asked her _____

❺ Did you enjoy it?

I asked her _____

37.6 LISEZ LE COURRIEL, PUIS COCHEZ LES BONNES RÉPONSES.

Carl went to New Zealand before Australia.
True ☐ **False** ☐ **Not given** ☑

1 Last week Sophie visited their father.
True ☐ **False** ☐ **Not given** ☐

2 Their father had received an email from the bank.
True ☐ **False** ☐ **Not given** ☐

3 The email looked genuine.
True ☐ **False** ☐ **Not given** ☐

4 The police have found the email scammers.
True ☐ **False** ☐ **Not given** ☐

5 Their father cannot get the money back.
True ☐ **False** ☐ **Not given** ☐

To: Carl Underwood

Subject: Update from home

Hi Carl,

Your Australian vacation photos look great. I'm just writing to keep you up to date with events while you're away.

I've been looking after Dad and I went to see him last week. I'm afraid he looked quite a sorry sight. He said that he'd received an email asking for his bank details. He sent them and then someone stole money out of his account!

At first sight, the email really looked like one from his bank, but it turned out to be fake.

Well, I saw red and called the police and the bank immediately, and luckily they agreed to refund his money. I've told him to call me if another email like that arrives!

Other than that, everything is fine here.

Keep having fun!

Sophie

37.7 COMPLÉTEZ LES PHRASES AVEC LES EXPRESSIONS IDIOMATIQUES DE LA LISTE.

The detectives said they were [*looking into*] the case.

1 I was so angry that I just [   ] and shouted.

2 The poor dog had been left in the cold and was a very [   ].

3 The watch looked genuine [   ], but it wasn't.

4 I'll just have to [   ] about my English test results.

| at first sight | saw red | ~~looking into~~ | sorry sight | wait and see |

38 Les hypothèses et les déductions

Vous pouvez utiliser des verbes modaux pour décrire des événements passés avec différents degrés de certitude. Ces constructions sont utiles pour évoquer des événements dont vous n'avez pas été témoin.

⚙ **Grammaire** Les autres emplois des verbes modaux
Aa Vocabulary Les verbes à particule avec « out »
✤ **Compétence** Émettre des hypothèses et déduire

38.1 POINT CLÉ LES VERBES MODAUX POUR ÉMETTRE DES HYPOTHÈSES ET DÉDUIRE

Lorsque vous évoquez le passé et que vous êtes sûr que quelque chose a eu lieu, utilisez « must have » avec le participe passé.

He just disappeared. Aliens must have abducted him.

Le locuteur est sûr.

Lorsque vous n'êtes pas sûr que quelque chose s'est produit, remplacez « must » par « may », « might » ou « could ».

They { **might / may / could** } **have taken him to another planet.**

Le locuteur n'est pas sûr.

Si vous êtes certain que quelque chose n'a pas eu lieu, utilisez « can't » ou « couldn't ».

Hold on! It { **can't / couldn't** } **have been aliens, they don't exist.**

Le locuteur est sûr que cela n'est pas possible.

🔊

38.2 RELIEZ LES PHRASES CORRESPONDANTES.

| He drove his car into the water! | He must have hurt his legs. |

① He's walking with crutches.

② Those teenagers look very tired today.

③ The plants are all dry and dead.

④ Someone's left the gate open again.

⑤ The girl next door looks really happy.

It could have been the delivery man.

They may have had a party last night.

He couldn't have seen the "flood" sign.

She might have passed her exam.

It can't have rained all week.

🔊

38.3 RÉCRIVEZ LES PHRASES EN CORRIGEANT LES ERREURS.

She broke her arm falling off a horse. It might have hurt.
She broke her arm falling off a horse. It must have hurt.

❶ The ground is dry so it can't rained last night.

_____

❷ She ate two more slices of cake, so it could have tasted nice.

_____

❸ A police car just drove past. There might have was a robbery.

_____

❹ He doesn't have any money. He can't not have bought that car himself.

_____

❺ They were in the same store as us. They have might buy the same coat.

_____

 38.4 BARREZ LES MOTS INCORRECTS DANS CHAQUE PHRASE.

 He had a brand new waterproof coat on. He must / ~~might~~ / ~~can't~~ have stayed dry.

❶ I missed a call. It must / may / couldn't have been Diego, he said he might call.

❷ I haven't checked my emails yet, so she must / might / can't have replied already, I'm not sure.

❸ After the run, he drank a whole bottle of water. He must / might / can't have been really thirsty.

❹ She loved both dresses, but she must / might / can't have bought both, as they were too expensive.

❺ She hadn't slept for two days. She must / might / can't have been exhausted.

38.5 DÉCRIVEZ CE QUE CHAQUE PERSONNE A DÛ FAIRE AVEC LES MOTS DE LA LISTE, PUIS LISEZ LES PHRASES À VOIX HAUTE.

He must have scored a goal.

passed her driving test   eaten too much candy   ~~scored a goal~~

won the lottery   slept through his alarm   failed their exams

---

38.6 ÉCOUTEZ L'ENREGISTREMENT, PUIS COCHEZ LE RÉSUMÉ CORRECT.

Un présentateur radio parle du mystère non résolu du SS *Ourang Medan.*

① The ship sent out a call saying that most of the crew had passed out. The *Silver Star* went to check out the ship and found that everyone on board was dead except the dog, which had passed out. ☐

② The ship sent out a call saying that a few of the crew were dead. The *Silver Star* went to check out the ship and the sailors freaked out when they saw the dead crew. However, the dog was still alive. ☐

③ The ship sent out a call saying that most of the crew were dead. The *Silver Star*'s crew went to check out the ship and found that everyone on board, including the dog, had died with their eyes still open. ☐

38.7 COMPLÉTEZ LES PHRASES AVEC LES VERBES DE LA LISTE.

I was so scared on the roller coaster ride that I nearly _____*passed out*_____ .

1 Every month my company _____ a newsletter to all its customers.

2 Every time my sister sees a spider, she _____ and starts screaming.

3 Should we go to the movie theater and _____ what's showing?

4 He isn't like anyone else. He really _____ from the crowd.

5 I can't _____ what this guy's written. His handwriting is awful.

| ~~passed out~~ | sends out | stands out | check out | work out | freaks out |

38.8 LISEZ L'ARTICLE, PUIS COCHEZ LES BONNES RÉPONSES.

Lateral thinking puzzles give you a lot of information.
True ☐   False ☑

1 Pete lives on the 10th floor of the apartment building.
True ☐   False ☐

2 Pete always gets out of the elevator at the right floor for his apartment.
True ☐   False ☐

3 Pete doesn't like walking, but he sometimes climbs two flights of stairs.
True ☐   False ☐

4 The article tells you the solution to the puzzle about Pete.
True ☐   False ☐

GAMES AND PUZZLES

Lateral Thinking Puzzles

With a lateral thinking puzzle, you are given an unusual situation and a little information. Your task is to discover the explanation. Can you work this one out?

A young boy, Pete, lives on the 12th floor of an apartment building. Every morning he takes the elevator down to the lobby. In the evening, he gets into the elevator, and, if there's someone else there, he goes up to his floor directly. Otherwise, he goes to the 10th floor and walks up two flights of stairs to his apartment. He does this even though he hates walking. Why?

The solution to this puzzle is that the young boy is too short to reach the buttons for those floors numbered above 10.

38 ✓ CHECK-LIST

⚙ Les autres emplois des verbes modaux ☐   **Aa** Les verbes à particule avec « out » ☐   🧩 Émettre des hypothèses et déduire ☐

153

39 Les conditionnels mixtes

Vous pouvez utiliser différents types de déclarations au conditionnel pour parler de situations hypothétiques. Les conditionnels mixtes comprennent plus d'une de ces déclarations dans une même phrase.

⚙ **Grammaire** Les conditionnels mixtes
Aa Vocabulaire Les traits de caractère
🧩 **Compétence** Parler de situations hypothétiques

39.1 POINT CLÉ LES CONDITIONNELS MIXTES

LE DEUXIÈME CONDITIONNEL

Utilisez le deuxième conditionnel pour parler de situations hypothétiques dans le présent.

PRÉTÉRIT

If I didn't believe in astrology, I wouldn't read my horoscope.

« WOULD » + INFINITIF

LE TROISIÈME CONDITIONNEL

Utilisez le troisième conditionnel pour parler de situations hypothétiques dans le passé.

PAST PERFECT

If I had known he was an Aquarius, I would not have gone out with him.

« WOULD » + « HAVE » + PARTICIPE PASSÉ

CONDITIONNEL MIXTE

Les conditionnels mixtes combinent le deuxième et le troisième conditionnel.

If you had been born a month earlier, you would be a Virgo like me.

🔊

39.2 AUTRES EXEMPLES LES CONDITIONNELS MIXTES

Les conditionnels mixtes servent souvent à exprimer le regret.

If I had finished my assignment sooner, I could be out with my friends today.

You would be starting a new school tomorrow **if you hadn't failed your exams.**

Vous pouvez utiliser des conditionnels mixtes pour parler de situations futures.

 🔊

39.3 RELIEZ LE DÉBUT DE CHAQUE PHRASE À LA FIN QUI LUI CORRESPOND.

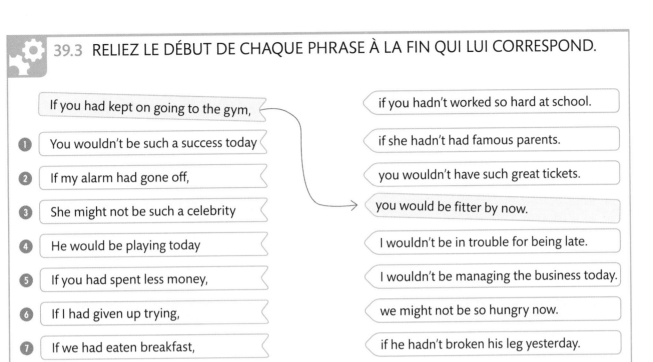

If you had kept on going to the gym,

if you hadn't worked so hard at school.

1. You wouldn't be such a success today

if she hadn't had famous parents.

2. If my alarm had gone off,

you wouldn't have such great tickets.

3. She might not be such a celebrity

you would be fitter by now.

4. He would be playing today

I wouldn't be in trouble for being late.

5. If you had spent less money,

I wouldn't be managing the business today.

6. If I had given up trying,

we might not be so hungry now.

7. If we had eaten breakfast,

if he hadn't broken his leg yesterday.

39.4 COMPLÉTEZ LES PHRASES EN CONJUGUANT LES VERBES AU TEMPS QUI CONVIENT.

If he ___*had not fixed*___ (not fix) my car, I would still be walking to work every day.

1. If Clara _____ (not stay) up so late, she might not be so tired now.

2. She might not be a famous actress today if she _____ (not go) to that first audition.

3. If he _____ (keep) playing the guitar, he would be in a famous band by now.

4. If Juan _____ (listen) to all his critics, he would not be a world-famous chef today.

5. He would not be playing for a premier team if he _____ (not train) every day.

6. If she _____ (say) "yes" to your proposal, you could be married by now.

7. They would not be so confident if they _____ (see) their team training yesterday.

155

39.5 ÉCOUTEZ L'HOROSCOPE, PUIS COCHEZ LES BONNES RÉPONSES.

You have had good ideas, but you haven't used them sensibly.
True ☑ **False** ☐

1 You need to get others to invest in your business.
True ☐ **False** ☐

2 You should be braver in promoting your ideas at work.
True ☐ **False** ☐

3 You should have said sorry for something yesterday.
True ☐ **False** ☐

4 You will definitely have an exciting weekend, especially Sunday.
True ☐ **False** ☐

5 If it's your birthday, today is a good day to care for your friends.
True ☐ **False** ☐

Aa 39.6 COMPLÉTEZ LES PHRASES AVEC LES ADJECTIFS DE LA LISTE.

He reads lots of books and loves going to museums. He's very___*intellectual*___.

1 You need _____ staff who turn up on time and do their work.

2 He's so _____. He just jumped into the fire to save the kitten.

3 My husband is really _____. He even cries during romantic films.

4 If he hadn't been so violent and _____, he would not be in jail today.

5 If she hadn't been so _____, she might not be such a successful singer.

6 Jane is very _____. She can fix the car and put up shelves.

intellectual   sensitive   determined   courageous   reliable   quick-tempered   practical

IN YOUR STARS?

HOME | ENTRIES | ABOUT | CONTACT

Diane Carter (24), Scorpio (Oct 24–Nov 22)

I'm a Scorpio and I check my stars every day. I've got an app on my smartphone and it's one of the first things I read in the mornings. If the horoscope says I shouldn't do something, I won't. For example, if it says "Don't travel," then there's no chance of me getting on a plane that day. I know that, logically, it's very unlikely that anything will happen, but I don't want to take the risk. I'm a typical Scorpion because I'm quite passionate about things, but I'm also a little obsessive. I guess that's why I have to check my stars every day!

Richard Davis (22), Sagittarius (Nov 24–Dec 22)

I'm Sagittarius, I think, but I never think about horoscopes. I think that it's all nonsense. I mean, when you read the things that they say will happen to you on a certain day, there's a fair chance that they will happen to most people on most days. Things like "You'll get some news" or "You'll talk to a stranger." I also think that, if you believe in these things, then it is inevitable that the predictions will suit what happens because you will make them fit. I mean, if you wear red because your stars tell you to, and everything is OK, then you can say that the horoscope was right. Apparently, I'm supposed to be intellectual and superficial. I'm not sure how I can be both!

> Diane reads her stars in the newspaper first thing every day.
> *Diane reads her stars on a phone app first thing every day.*

❶ Diane would not change her plans because of her horoscope's advice.

_____

❷ Diane thinks she's a typical Scorpio because she's not very passionate about things.

_____

❸ Richard thinks that things a horoscope says will happen are unlikely.

_____

❹ He says it's surprising how many times horoscopes make correct predictions.

_____

39 ✓ CHECK-LIST

⚙ Les conditionnels mixtes ☐   **Aa** Les traits de caractère ☐   🧩 Parler de situations hypothétiques ☐

40 Ajouter « -ever » aux mots interrogatifs

Ajouter « -ever » aux mots interrogatifs change leur sens.
Ce suffixe signifie « no matter » ou « it doesn't matter ».

🔧 **Grammaire** Les mots avec « -ever »

Aa Vocabulaire Les expressions liées à la météo
et à la chance

🧩 **Compétence** Lier une proposition à une phrase

40.1 POINT CLÉ LES MOTS INTERROGATIFS AVEC « -EVER »

Vous pouvez utiliser les mots en « -ever » comme sujets, objets ou adverbes dans leur proposition.
Ces mots peuvent également être utilisés pour lier une proposition au reste d'une phrase.

I'm still going to the game, whatever the weather's like.

[It doesn't matter what the weather is like. I'm still going.]

Ici, « whichever » est objet.

We can take a taxi or walk, whichever you prefer.

[It doesn't matter to me which you choose, taxi or walking.]

Ici, « whoever » est sujet.

Whoever invented the umbrella was a very clever person indeed.

[I don't know who invented the umbrella, but they were very clever.]

It always seems to rain whenever I go away.

[Any time I go away, it rains.]

I always check the forecast for wherever I'm going to be.

[I check the forecast for the place I am going to be, no matter where it is.]

Ici, « however » est adverbe.

If there's a chance of rain, however small, I'll take an umbrella.

[I'll take an umbrella, no matter how small the risk of rain.]

🔊

40.2 BARREZ LE MOT INCORRECT DANS CHAQUE PHRASE.

~~Whoever~~ / Whatever choice you make, you know we'll support you.

1 Buy red or green peppers, however / whichever is the cheapest.

2 She moves every few years to wherever / whatever her company asks her to go.

3 I love going to concerts and watching live music, whenever / whoever is playing.

4 My mother never likes my brother's girlfriends, however / whoever nice they are.

5 The company director visits our office whenever / wherever she's in town.

6 The competition winner deserves praise, however / whoever they are.

7 The company is in a difficult situation, whichever / however way you look at it.

🔊

40.3 COMPLÉTEZ LES PHRASES AVEC LES MOTS DE LA LISTE.

I'm happy to go _____ *wherever* _____ you like for a vacation, as long as there's a beach.

1 She's an excellent cook. I'm sure _____ cake I choose will be delicious.

2 Sometimes I just can't start my car _____ I do. It's really frustrating.

3 I don't think I'll ever be a good long-distance runner, _____ hard I try.

4 During the winter months, we can visit the castle for free _____ we want.

5 I will give my full support to the next head chef, _____ it is.

| whatever | whichever | whoever | whenever | ~~wherever~~ | however |

🔊

159

40.4 LISEZ LE COURRIEL, PUIS RÉPONDEZ AUX QUESTIONS.

✉

To: Eleri Roberts

Subject: Update from home

Hi Eleri, I hope you're having a great time in Chile! I've had an unusual week here. I got an email saying that I'd won a competition for two free bungee jumps. It was a bit of a bolt from the blue because I'd completely forgotten that I'd even entered the competition!

I was on cloud nine, so I told my sister. I thought she would be overjoyed like me, but she was so moody! You know what she's like, always wanting to get all the attention and trying to steal my thunder. Well, I asked her if she'd do it with me. I thought it would be really funny because she hates heights.

The jump was all planned for Thursday, but as I was driving to her house, she sent me a text message saying that she had the flu and so would have to take a rain check. I thought this was a bit odd because she was as right as rain the night before.

Anyway, I had already decided that I was doing this jump come rain or shine, so I went without her. I jumped off the canal bridge. It was absolutely awesome! So now I'm just going to throw caution to the wind and do a sky dive next year. I already can't wait!

Matt

> Where is Eleri at the moment?
>
> *At the moment, Eleri is in Chile.*

① Why was the email from the adventure activity company a surprise?

_____

② Why wasn't Matt's sister happy about his prize?

_____

③ Why did Matt's sister say that she couldn't do the bungee jump?

_____

④ Where did Matt do the bungee jump?

_____

⑤ What is Matt planning to do next year?

_____

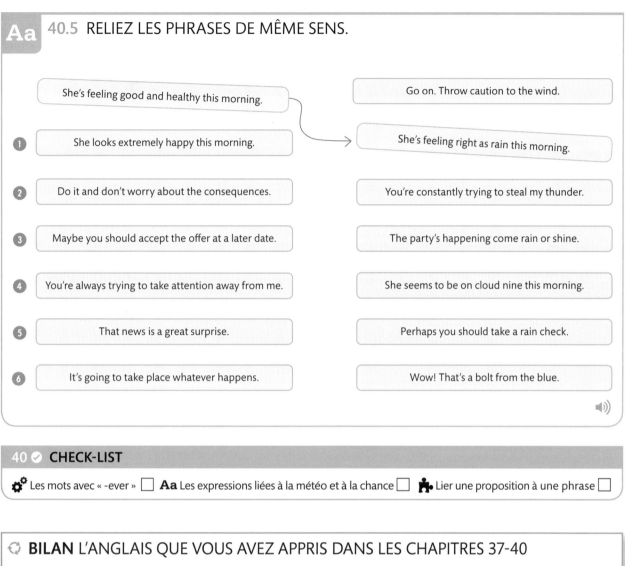

She's feeling good and healthy this morning.

Go on. Throw caution to the wind.

1 She looks extremely happy this morning.

She's feeling right as rain this morning.

2 Do it and don't worry about the consequences.

You're constantly trying to steal my thunder.

3 Maybe you should accept the offer at a later date.

The party's happening come rain or shine.

4 You're always trying to take attention away from me.

She seems to be on cloud nine this morning.

5 That news is a great surprise.

Perhaps you should take a rain check.

6 It's going to take place whatever happens.

Wow! That's a bolt from the blue.

---

40 ✓ CHECK-LIST

⚙ Les mots avec « -ever » ☐   **Aa** Les expressions liées à la météo et à la chance ☐   🧩 Lier une proposition à une phrase ☐

♺ BILAN L'ANGLAIS QUE VOUS AVEZ APPRIS DANS LES CHAPITRES 37-40

NOUVEAU POINT LINGUISTIQUE	EXEMPLE TYPE	☑	CHAPITRE
LES POSSIBILITÉS PASSÉES	The printer isn't working. It might have run out of paper.	☐	37.1
LE DISCOURS INDIRECT	He said that he didn't believe those ghost stories.	☐	37.4
LES SPÉCULATIONS ET LES DÉDUCTIONS	Aliens might have taken him to another planet.	☐	38.1
LES CONDITIONNELS MIXTES	If you had been born a month earlier, you would be a Virgo like me.	☐	39.1
LES MOTS INTERROGATIFS AVEC « -EVER »	I'm still going to the game, whatever the weather's like.	☐	40.1

41.1 LES MÉDIAS ET LES CÉLÉBRITÉS

The newspapers always sensationalize things.

sensationalize
[make something more dramatic or exciting than it is]

The journalist exposed the politician's lies.

expose
[reveal something hidden]

I honestly think that the newspaper exploited that politician.

exploit
[use something or someone for your own gain]

Nowadays you can become a celebrity without being talented.

become a celebrity
[become a famous person]

He's a household name in lots of countries.

be a household name
[be known by most people]

My son has always wanted to have his name in lights.

have your name in lights
[be very famous]

All of the publicity has gone to her head.

go to somebody's head
[make somebody feel more important than they are]

She's always been in the public eye. Perhaps she's used to it!

be in the public eye
[be seen and well known by the public]

Have you seen this morning's newspaper headline?

newspaper headline
[the large text at the top of a newspaper page]

It seems like her love life is always headline news.

headline news
[news that is widely reported]

The internet has supported the rise of celebrity culture.

celebrity culture
[the popular culture which surrounds famous people]

His real claim to fame was that he could eat five burgers in a row.

claim to fame
[the thing that somebody or something is known for, often said jokingly]

I always vote for my favorites on talent shows.

talent show
[a competition with performances by entertainers showcasing their skills]

There are so many reality shows on TV nowadays.

reality show
[a show based on or around real-life events]

I would hate to be followed everywhere by the paparazzi.

paparazzi
[photographers who take pictures of famous people]

All the stars went to the opening night in Hollywood.

opening night
[the first night of a show or film]

The stars were all on the red carpet this evening.

red carpet
[a carpet for important guests to walk or stand on at an event]

She's had a truly meteoric rise in the film industry.

meteoric rise
[a very rapid rise, often in a career]

Join us for an exclusive interview with the stars of the movie.

exclusive interview
[an interview that no other source has obtained]

She always wears such attention-grabbing outfits.

attention-grabbing
[something designed to get your attention quickly]

42 Rapporter avec le passif

Une façon de se distancier des faits est d'utiliser la voix passive et des verbes rapporteurs. Cette technique est couramment utilisée par les journalistes.

⚙ **Grammaire** Rapporter avec la voix passive
Aa Vocabulaire Les mots pour rapporter des faits
🧩 **Compétence** Se distancier des faits

42.1 POINT CLÉ RAPPORTER AVEC LE PASSIF

Un certain nombre de constructions et de verbes rapporteurs peuvent être utilisés à la voix passive pour distancier l'auteur ou le locuteur des faits énoncés.

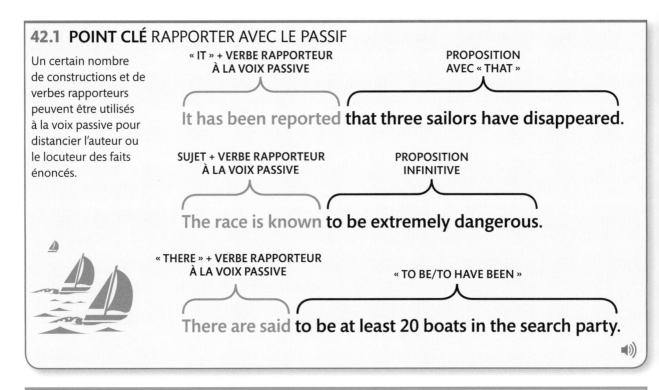

« IT » + VERBE RAPPORTEUR À LA VOIX PASSIVE — PROPOSITION AVEC « THAT »

It has been reported **that three sailors have disappeared.**

SUJET + VERBE RAPPORTEUR À LA VOIX PASSIVE — PROPOSITION INFINITIVE

The race is known **to be extremely dangerous.**

« THERE » + VERBE RAPPORTEUR À LA VOIX PASSIVE — « TO BE/TO HAVE BEEN »

There are said **to be at least 20 boats in the search party.**

🔊

⚙ 42.2 RELIEZ LE DÉBUT DE CHAQUE PHRASE À LA FIN QUI LUI CORRESPOND.

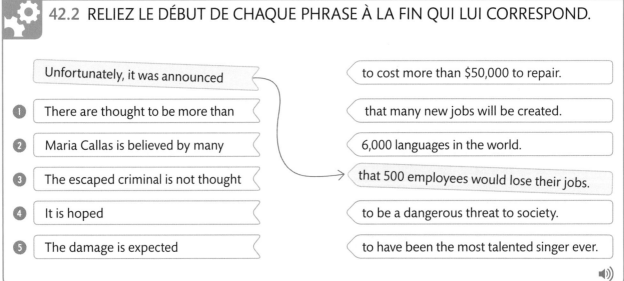

Unfortunately, it was announced	to cost more than $50,000 to repair.
1 There are thought to be more than	that many new jobs will be created.
2 Maria Callas is believed by many	6,000 languages in the world.
3 The escaped criminal is not thought	that 500 employees would lose their jobs.
4 It is hoped	to be a dangerous threat to society.
5 The damage is expected	to have been the most talented singer ever.

🔊

42.3 POINT CLÉ LES MODAUX À LA VOIX PASSIVE

Les modaux au présent peuvent devenir passifs en remplaçant le radical du verbe principal par « be » suivi du participe passé.

You should tell Barbara the exciting news.
[The important thing is that you tell her the news.]

Barbara should be told the exciting news.
[The important thing is that Barbara is told the news, not who tells her.]

Les modaux au passé peuvent devenir passifs en remplaçant « have » par « have been ».

The managers should have given Daniel more time.
[The main issue is what the managers failed to do.]

Daniel should have been given more time.
[The main issue is what Daniel did not get, not the people responsible.]

42.4 AUTRES EXEMPLES LES MODAUX À LA VOIX PASSIVE

Modal exprimant l'interdiction.

Phones must not be used in school.

Modal exprimant la désirabilité.

Homeless youngsters should be housed here.

Extra tickets may be sold on the day.

Modal exprimant la possibilité.

It must have been mentioned on the news.

Modal exprimant une forte probabilité.

 42.5 BARREZ LES MOTS INCORRECTS DANS CHAQUE PHRASE.

With no exceptions, seat belts must ~~worn~~ / be worn at all times in the vehicle.

1. I'm so sorry! You should have been / be introduced to each other earlier this evening.

2. Thirty people are expected to have been / be awarded top prizes at the ceremony later.

3. It would help if the school children could be given / give different instruments to try.

4. It's been a strange tournament, and there have been / are thought to be more surprises to come.

42.6 RÉCRIVEZ LES PHRASES À LA VOIX PASSIVE.

CONSEIL
N'oubliez pas que vous pouvez parfois omettre l'agent (la personne ou la chose qui exécute l'action) si le sens reste clair.

Industry experts must have written the report.

The report _must have been written by industry experts._

① Somebody should have thanked the hosts of the party before we left.

The hosts _____

② The journalist reported that 20 people were injured in the stampede.

It has _____

③ Many people think that Pelé was the best soccer player ever.

Pelé is _____

42.7 EN VOUS AIDANT DES IMAGES, COMPLÉTEZ LES PHRASES EN UTILISANT LA VOIX PASSIVE, PUIS LISEZ-LES À VOIX HAUTE.

FIVE RESTAURANTS CLOSED

Since the flood, it has been reported
that five restaurants have closed.

②
TORNADO DESTROYS HOMES

Many homes are said _____
_____

YOUTH TEAM WINS CUP

① It has been announced that the Cup
_____

COUPLE MARRIES IN PARIS

③ This celebrity couple are reported
_____

42.8 COMPLÉTEZ LES PHRASES AVEC LES VERBES DE LA LISTE EN UTILISANT LA FORME CORRECTE.

16   THE DAILY HERALD

CRIMINAL NEGLIGENCE

The police in Longerton had a suprisingly easy arrest when a robber was foolish enough to incriminate himself.

Bank robber Mark Thomas is _____*spending*_____ the night in jail before going to court to be

_____ tomorrow.

Last June, Mr. Thomas, dressed in a mask and hat and armed with a knife, demanded $10,000 from the

cashier of a local bank. He was _____ the money, but at this point

Mr. Thomas' planning skills must be _____ . Instead of escaping the area, Mr. Thomas

took off his hat and mask and walked into the bank next door. He tried to deposit the money and gave the

cashiers his full name, address, and bank details. Fortunately, the police had been _____

by the original bank and Mr. Thomas was quickly _____ .

He is understood to have been _____ the robbery for many months. He stated that

he had been _____ for a vacation, but it was taking too long to raise enough money.

It is _____ that he will be given a lengthy sentence, so he will have to wait even longer

for his trip abroad.

question	sentence	~~spend~~	save	call	predict	arrest	plan	give

43 Formuler des énoncés indirects

Vous voudrez parfois éviter de formuler des faits établis ou des opinions personnelles. On appelle cette technique « hedging » (éluder) en anglais. Certains mots et énoncés indirects peuvent vous y aider.

⚙ **Grammaire** Les énoncés indirects
Aa Vocabulaire Les mots élusifs
🧩 **Compétence** Exprimer l'incertitude

43.1 POINT CLÉ ÉLUDER

Les mots et expressions élusifs peuvent être ajoutés à une phrase pour la rendre moins définie ou directe.

| VERBES ÉLUSIFS | **Polls suggest that locals dislike the new statue.** |

| ADVERBES ÉLUSIFS | **It is arguably the strangest statue around.** |

| LOCUTIONS ÉLUSIVES | **To some extent, locals feel their views are being ignored.** |

43.2 COMPLÉTEZ LES PHRASES EN UTILISANT LES MOTS ÉLUSIFS DE LA LISTE.

_____*Often*_____ people use hedging language if they do not have exact figures.

1 There are _____ five hundred employees in this factory.

2 These new figures _____ a downward trend in sales.

3 The director _____ took all of the money from the company.

4 This kind of market behavior _____ an underlying problem.

5 _____ by some that her opinions are controversial.

6 _____ they are not enjoying the film very much.

7 Academics _____ to use hedging language if something is not proven.

| allegedly | indicate | It looks like | tend | approximately | ~~Often~~ | It has been said | suggests |

🔊

43.3 POINT CLÉ « SEEM » ET « APPEAR »

Vous pouvez utiliser « seem » et « appear »
pour vous distancier d'une affirmation.
Cela est utile si vous n'êtes pas sûr de sa véracité.

The prisoners $\left\{ \begin{array}{l} \textbf{seem} \\ \textbf{appear} \end{array} \right\}$ to have **vanished.**

« Seem » et « appear » sont souvent suivis
d'un autre verbe à l'infinitif.

It $\left\{ \begin{array}{l} \textbf{seems} \\ \textbf{appears} \end{array} \right\}$ that **the prison cell was left unguarded.**

Vous pouvez aussi utiliser « it seems » ou « it
appears » suivis d'une proposition avec « that ».

It would $\left\{ \begin{array}{l} \textbf{seem} \\ \textbf{appear} \end{array} \right\}$ that **a file was used to saw the bars.**

« Would » introduit
encore plus de distance
ou d'incertitude.

 43.4 BARREZ LES MOTS INCORRECTS DANS CHAQUE PHRASE.

> The detectives seem / ~~suggest~~ to have found an important piece of information.

❶ It appears / believes that two prisoners have escaped from the police station.

❷ I don't trust her. I think it tends / looks like she is guilty of both crimes.

❸ They seem / suggest to have found more important evidence to support their case.

❹ I believe / indicate that the police have made a mistake and arrested the wrong man.

❺ I don't know, but it would appear / tend that he stole the car when the owner was inside.

❻ With a huge number of hit records, the Beatles are arguably / allegedly the best band ever.

❼ After a difficult year, all our figures appear / indicate that sales are finally improving.

❽ It's too soon to judge. He probably / approximately committed the crime, but we're not sure.

❾ We used to go to Spain a lot. Sometimes we drove there, but we often / probably flew.

43.5 LISEZ L'ARTICLE, PUIS REPORTEZ LES MOTS ÉLUSIFS DANS LES ENCADRÉS CORRESPONDANTS.

THE DAILY POST

NEWS | BUSINESS | LIFE

LATEST NEWS

Town in chaos as burglar strikes again

POSTED TUESDAY, 7:00AM

In the lastest incident in what is arguably the most unusual series of crimes in the area, the Daylight Burglar has apparently struck again. It looks like this time he has targeted cheese from victims' refrigerators. It has only been a few days since the last series of burglaries, but it seems that the Daylight Burglar's spree is not over yet. If anything, these new crimes suggest that he has no plans to stop soon.

The Daylight Burglar tends to take fairly unusual items of little value. Last week, single socks were taken from approximately 20 homes. Before that, it was teapots.

It could be said that this burglar is harmless, but that is not how the victims feel. Often, they are left traumatized by the fact that someone has broken into their homes. "It's very scary. To some extent we no longer feel safe at home. We all assume it's a local person, probably a someone we all know," said burglary victim Sasha Johnson.

It would appear that each week the burglar targets one unusual item to steal from people's homes. We believe that the police have no clue who the burglar is, but the evidence indicates that it is someone who likes tea and cheese.

WEATHER   SPORT   TRAVEL   ARTS

ADVERBS	VERBS	PHRASES
arguably	suggest	it looks like

170

43.6 ÉCOUTEZ L'ENREGISTREMENT, PUIS COCHEZ LES BONNES RÉPONSES.

Une station de radio locale présente un reportage
sur une vidéo populaire publiée en ligne.

	True	False
The report is about a video that was famous last year.	☐	☑
1 The video was recorded on Sara's mother's smartphone.	☐	☐
2 The video has been watched just under a million times.	☐	☐
3 The cat screeched and waved her paws at the hissing snake.	☐	☐
4 The snake, or a similar one, had been seen on other properties.	☐	☐
5 The animal charity said that these snakes often attack young people.	☐	☐

43.7 COMPLÉTEZ LES PHRASES DU RÉSUMÉ AVEC LES MOTS ÉLUSIFS DE LA LISTE.

It _____looks_____ like three-year-old Sara Wilson is fine after her brush with a snake last week.

1 An online video _____ shows her pet cat, Mini, protecting her.

2 _____ that the snake was frightened away by Mini.

3 Interviews with neighbors _____ that the snake had been seen on other properties.

4 A local animal charity _____ that it would be unusual for such a snake to attack.

5 The charity said that these snakes _____ to be extremely shy.

6 They also stated that _____ these kinds of snakes are pets that have escaped.

~~looks~~	tend	often	suggested	indicate	apparently	It would appear

🔊

44 Ajouter de l'emphase

Vous pouvez ajouter de l'emphase, ou même un sens du drame, à une déclaration au travers de la grammaire et de la prononciation. L'inversion est une manière efficace d'y parvenir.

⚙ **Grammaire** L'inversion après les locutions adverbiales
Aa Vocabulaire Les médias et les célébrités
🧩 **Compétence** Ajouter de l'emphase aux déclarations

44.1 POINT CLÉ L'INVERSION APRÈS LES LOCUTIONS ADVERBIALES NÉGATIVES

Dans les textes plus formels ou littéraires, l'inversion (lorsque l'ordre normal des mots est inversé) est utilisée pour ajouter de l'emphase après des locutions adverbiales négatives comme « not only », « not since » ou « only when ».

Dans cette phrase simple, le sujet vient avant le verbe.

She is a famous singer. **She is** also a very good actor.

Not only is she a famous singer, but **she's** also a very good actor.

Après la locution adverbiale, le sujet et le verbe sont inversés.

🔊

44.2 AUTRES EXEMPLES L'INVERSION APRÈS LES LOCUTIONS ADVERBIALES NÉGATIVES

Les locutions adverbiales négatives sont généralement suivies d'un auxiliaire + sujet.

Not since I was a teenager have I enjoyed a performance so much.
Not until the performance was over did he look up at the audience.

Lorsqu'il n'y a pas d'auxiliaire, on utilise « do ».

Only if it stops raining will the race go ahead this afternoon.
Only when he emerged from the car did the fans start cheering.
Only after the race did he realize what he had achieved.

Little do they know how lucky they are to be successful.
Little did they realize how difficult fame would be.

🔊

172

44.3 BARREZ LES MOTS INCORRECTS DANS CHAQUE PHRASE.

 Not since 2003 ~~we had~~ / had we seen such a dramatic match.

❶ Little he did / **did he** know that someone else had already invented the same thing.

❷ Only after living there for two weeks **did they** / they did notice the smell.

❸ Not when / **until** we spoke to the manager did the company admit their mistake.

❹ Not since the children were little **had we** / we had been on such a fun day out.

❺ Only **when** / until she won the award did people start taking her writing seriously.

44.4 COMPLÉTEZ LES PHRASES AVEC LES MOTS DE LA LISTE.

Not ___*since*___ the 1990 World Cup has the team reached the quarter finals.

❶ _____ if the company invests more money can the project be completed.

❷ _____ until the wedding day did the groom see the bride's dress.

❸ Little did they _____ that the weather would be absolutely terrible for the festival.

❹ Not _____ the final encore did the audience begin to leave their seats at the concert.

❺ Only _____ she was paying for the album did she realize she already owned it.

❻ Not _____ will you be famous, but you will also be rich beyond your wildest dreams.

❼ Only _____ she got home from the party did she notice how late it was.

~~since~~	Not	when	realize	after	until	Only	only

44.5 POINT CLÉ L'INVERSION APRÈS LES LOCUTIONS ADVERBIALES TEMPORELLES

Vous pouvez aussi ajouter de l'emphase à un événement passé en utilisant des locutions adverbiales temporelles comme « no sooner » et « never before ».

Dans cette phrase simple, le sujet vient avant le verbe.

Tina had just released an album when she starred in her first movie.

No sooner had Tina released an album than she starred in her first movie.

Le sujet (« Tina ») et l'auxiliaire (« had ») échangent leur place.

44.6 AUTRES EXEMPLES L'INVERSION APRÈS LES LOCUTIONS ADVERBIALES TEMPORELLES

Hardly had she stepped out of the car when fans surrounded her.

Never before had a song reached the top of the charts so quickly.

Rarely do you meet a celebrity with such talent and style.

 ## 44.7 RÉCRIVEZ LES PHRASES POUR TRANSFÉRER L'EMPHASE À PARTIR DES AMORCES.

They don't go to the movies together often. [rarely]
Rarely do they go to the movies together.

❶ He only felt safe at home. [only when]

_____

❷ Fans chanted his name as soon as he walked on stage. [hardly]

_____

❸ They became the number one band and then split up immediately. [no sooner]

_____

❹ It was the first time anyone had seen so many fans in one place. [never before]

_____

44.8 ÉCOUTEZ L'ENREGISTREMENT, PUIS COCHEZ LES BONNES RÉPONSES.

Deux amis, Marta et Jeremy, discutent de célébrités et de leurs enfants.

Marta has just seen Don and Sara Moran on a television show. **True** ☐ **False** ☑

1 Don has always encouraged people to photograph his children. **True** ☐ **False** ☐

2 Jeremy thinks the parents may have made a deal with the photographers. **True** ☐ **False** ☐

3 Marta dislikes photos of celebrities' children in the papers. **True** ☐ **False** ☐

4 Marta suspects that Don and Sara want their children to be famous. **True** ☐ **False** ☐

44.9 ÉCRIVEZ LES MOTS SUIVANTS DANS LE BON ORDRE AFIN DE RECONSTITUER LES PHRASES.

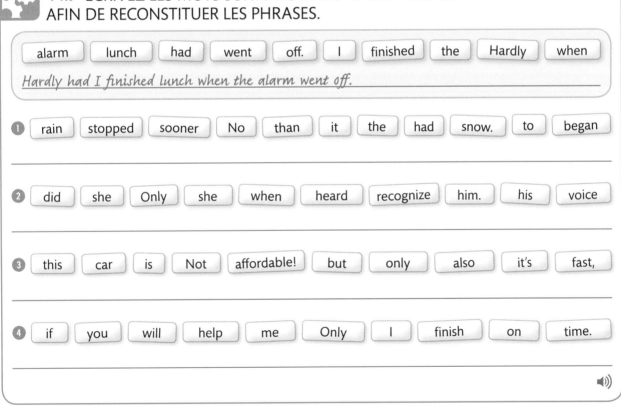

| alarm | lunch | had | went | off. | I | finished | the | Hardly | when |

Hardly had I finished lunch when the alarm went off.

1 | rain | stopped | sooner | No | than | it | the | had | snow. | to | began |

_____

2 | did | she | Only | she | when | heard | recognize | him. | his | voice |

_____

3 | this | car | is | Not | affordable! | but | only | also | it's | fast, |

_____

4 | if | you | will | help | me | Only | I | finish | on | time. |

_____

44 ✓ CHECK-LIST

⚙ L'inversion après les locutions adverbiales ☐ **Aa** Les médias et les célébrités ☐ 🧩 Ajouter de l'emphase aux déclarations ☐

45 Déplacer la focalisation

En anglais, vous pouvez ajouter de l'emphase sur une partie de la phrase en séparant celle-ci en deux propositions. Cela permet d'attirer l'attention sur l'information nouvelle ou importante.

⚙ **Grammaire** Mettre en relief avec des propositions
Aa Vocabulaire Les expressions de l'emphase
🧩 **Compétence** Déplacer la focalisation

45.1 POINT CLÉ METTRE EN RELIEF AVEC DES PROPOSITIONS AVEC « WHAT »

Vous pouvez ajouter le verbe « be » à un énoncé simple pour le rendre plus emphatique. Cette construction est souvent utilisée avec des verbes exprimant les émotions, tels que « love, « hate », « like » et « want ».

Would you like to go to a movie?

No, thanks. What I really want is to go to bed early.

Cette tournure est plus emphatique que « I really want to go to bed early ».

Ajoutez « what » au début de la phrase.

L'information que vous voulez mettre en relief est en dehors de la proposition avec « what ».

45.2 AUTRES EXEMPLES METTRE EN RELIEF AVEC DES PROPOSITIONS AVEC « WHAT »

What we hated was the bad service.   **What I like here** is the weather.

What they loved the most were the museums.

45.3 RELIEZ LE DÉBUT DE CHAQUE PHRASE À LA FIN QUI LUI CORRESPOND.

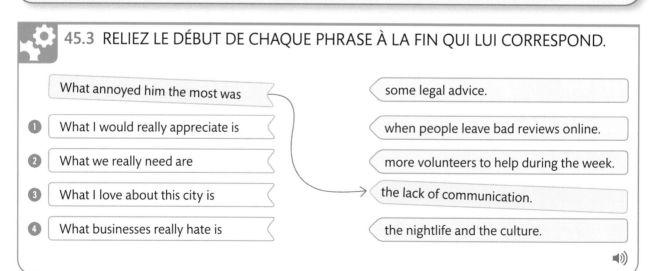

What annoyed him the most was —— the lack of communication.

1 What I would really appreciate is   some legal advice.

2 What we really need are   when people leave bad reviews online.

3 What I love about this city is   more volunteers to help during the week.

4 What businesses really hate is   the nightlife and the culture.

45.4 POINT CLÉ METTRE EN RELIEF AVEC UN NOM

Si le sujet de la phrase ne peut pas être remplacé par « what » (par exemple avec les personnes, les lieux ou les marqueurs temporels), vous pouvez utiliser un nom général au sens similaire.

I've been to many countries.
The place **I most enjoyed visiting** was Nepal.

I've read about some great people.
The woman **I respect the most** is Marie Curie.

I don't know why the show was canceled.
The reason **they gave** was not good enough.

I have lots of fun memories.
The evening **I most remember** is my first concert.

🔊

45.5 COMPLÉTEZ LES PHRASES AVEC LES NOMS DE LA LISTE.

The ___*city*___ I'd most like to visit is Kyoto in Japan for its amazing gardens.

❶ The _____ she gave for being late for work was not good enough.

❷ The _____ in history that fascinates me most is the Jurassic period.

❸ A _____ that we'd really love to visit is Ha Long Bay in Vietnam.

❹ One _____ I'll never forget is when my first grandchild was born.

❺ The _____ I don't understand is why the instructions are so complicated.

| natural wonder | justification | period | moment | thing | ~~city~~ |

🔊

45.6 POINT CLÉ METTRE EN RELIEF AVEC DES PROPOSITIONS AVEC « IT »

Vous pouvez aussi mettre en relief une partie de la phrase en ajoutant « it is » ou « it was » et « that ».

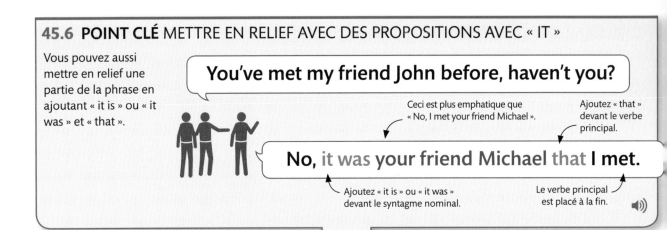

You've met my friend John before, haven't you?

Ceci est plus emphatique que « No, I met your friend Michael ».

Ajoutez « that » devant le verbe principal.

No, it was your friend Michael that I met.

Ajoutez « it is » ou « it was » devant le syntagme nominal.

Le verbe principal est placé à la fin.

45.7 AUTRES EXEMPLES METTRE EN RELIEF AVEC DES PROPOSITIONS AVEC « IT »

La seconde proposition est plus communément introduite par « that », « but », « which » ou « who ». « When » et « where » peuvent aussi être utilisés, quoique moins fréquemment.

It is the engine that I need to replace.

It was the doctor who I needed to call.

It was 1998 when I last saw my cousins.

45.8 RÉPONDEZ AUX QUESTIONS EN METTANT EN RELIEF VOTRE RÉPONSE, PUIS LISEZ-LES PHRASES À VOIX HAUTE.

Did your father teach you how to play the electric guitar?

No, ___it was___ my brother ___who___ taught me.

① Did you say that you want to visit Hong Kong?

Actually, _____ I most want to visit _____ Istanbul.

② Did you start learning English quite recently?

Actually, _____ a while ago_____ I started.

③ Would you say that you admire Bill Gates the most?

No, _____ I most admire _____ Albert Einstein.

45.9 ÉCOUTEZ L'ENREGISTREMENT, PUIS COCHEZ LES BONNES RÉPONSES.

Un expert en éducation des enfants donne une interview au sujet des réseaux sociaux et des compétences parentales numériques.

The expert says it's easy to keep up-to-date with digital trends.	**True** ☐	**False** ☑

1. She says that there is a lot of online help for parents. **True** ☐ **False** ☐

2. She encourages parents to set up their own social networking accounts. **True** ☐ **False** ☐

3. She says young people should only think carefully about what they post publicly. **True** ☐ **False** ☐

4. It is quite easy to change or delete your digital footprint. **True** ☐ **False** ☐

5. The CEO said people might have to change their names in the future. **True** ☐ **False** ☐

---

45 ✓ CHECK-LIST

⚙ Mettre en relief avec des propositions ☐　　**Aa** Les expressions de l'emphase ☐　　🧩 Déplacer la focalisation ☐

🔄 BILAN L'ANGLAIS QUE VOUS AVEZ APPRIS DANS LES CHAPITRES 42-45

NOUVEAU POINT LINGUISTIQUE	EXEMPLE TYPE	☑	CHAPITRE
RAPPORTER AVEC LE PASSIF	It has been reported that **three sailors have disappeared.**	☐	42.1
LES MODAUX À LA VOIX PASSIVE	**Barbara** should be told **the exciting news.**	☐	42.3
ÉLUDER	**It is** arguably **the strangest statue around.** The prisoners seem to have **vanished.**	☐	43.1, 43.3
L'INVERSION APRÈS LES LOCUTIONS ADVERBIALES NÉGATIVES	Not only is she **a famous singer, but she's also a very good actor.**	☐	44.1
L'INVERSION APRÈS LES LOCUTIONS ADVERBIALES TEMPORELLES	No sooner had Tina **released an album than she starred in her first movie.**	☐	44.5
METTRE EN RELIEF DES PROPOSITIONS AVEC « WHAT » ET AVEC UN NOM	What **I really want** is to go to bed early. The place **I most enjoyed visiting** was Nepal.	☐	45.1, 45.4
METTRE EN RELIEF AVEC DES PROPOSITIONS AVEC « IT »	**No,** it was your friend Michael that **I met.**	☐	45.6

46.1 LA CRIMINALITÉ ET LE DROIT

He refused to admit he had committed a crime.

commit a crime
[break the law]

I got away with cheating in my last exam.

get away with something
[do a bad thing without being caught]

She denied all knowledge of the gang and their activities.

deny all knowledge
[say that you know nothing about something or somebody]

The jury was chosen from a random group of people.

jury
[the people who decide whether a person is guilty of a crime]

It took the jury several hours to reach a verdict.

reach a verdict
[come to a decision about somebody's guilt or innocence]

In the end the jury found him guilty of the robbery.

find somebody (not) guilty
[officially decide that someone has (not) broken the law]

They were sure beyond reasonable doubt that she did it.

(beyond) reasonable doubt
[(without) uncertainty about somebody's guilt]

The jury convicted the criminal and the judge sent him to prison.

convict a criminal
[find somebody guilty of a crime]

She was sentenced to 80 hours of community service.

sentence somebody to something
[decide on a punishment in accordance with the law]

This morning the judge passed sentence on the attacker.

pass sentence
[say what punishment a criminal will have]

He was released from prison after serving a sentence of five years.

serve a sentence
[spend time in prison]

The police help enforce the law.

enforce
[make people obey a rule or a law]

After he left prison, he never offended again.

offend
[break a law or a rule]

They arrested the woman for damaging cars.

arrest
[use the power of the law to take and question somebody]

In most countries it is the law that all cars must be insured.

be insured
[be covered by insurance]

After the burglary I made a claim on my insurance.

make a claim
[request that an insurance company pays you money]

It can be difficult to get a job with a criminal record.

criminal record
[a list of crimes that a person has committed]

Fewer police officers on the street may lead to a crime wave.

crime wave
[a lot of crimes happening suddenly in the same area]

The rate of street crime, such as mugging, has risen.

street crime
[crime committed in a public place]

Police are training more experts to deal with white-collar crime.

white-collar crime
[financial, nonviolent crime]

Les propositions relatives

Les propositions relatives sont des parties de phrase qui apportent un complément d'information sur un nom dans l'énoncé principal. Elles peuvent être définissantes ou non définissantes.

⚙ **Grammaire** Les propositions relatives
Aa Vocabulaire La criminalité et les criminels
🧩 **Compétence** Préciser et détailler

47.1 POINT CLÉ LES PROPOSITIONS RELATIVES DÉFINISSANTES

Une proposition relative est constituée d'un sujet, d'un verbe et généralement d'un objet. Elle débute habituellement par un pronom relatif, qui peut être soit le sujet, soit l'objet de cette proposition relative. Les propositions relatives définissantes apportent des précisions sur la personne ou la chose dont vous parlez dans la proposition principale.

Ici, le pronom relatif « who » est le sujet de la proposition relative.

PROPOSITION PRINCIPALE
SUJET + VERBE + OBJET

PROPOSITION RELATIVE
SUJET + VERBE + OBJET

I'm writing about people who are in prison.

« Who » est le sujet de « are ».

Ici, le pronom relatif « which » est l'objet de la proposition relative.

PROPOSITION PRINCIPALE
SUJET + VERBE + OBJET

PROPOSITION RELATIVE
OBJET + SUJET + VERBE

This is the car which the criminal stole.

« Which » est l'objet de « stole ».

« The criminal » est le sujet de « stole ».

47.2 INDIQUEZ SI LE PRONOM RELATIF EST LE SUJET OU L'OBJET DE LA PROPOSITION RELATIVE.

This is the criminal that I saw.
Subject ☐ **Object** ✓

❶ The man who went to prison was innocent.
Subject ☐ **Object** ☐

❷ This is the man who called the police.
Subject ☐ **Object** ☐

❸ That's the bank that she robbed last week.
Subject ☐ **Object** ☐

❹ Did you believe the story that he told you?
Subject ☐ **Object** ☐

❺ Some police wear jackets that protect them.
Subject ☐ **Object** ☐

❻ Did you see the man who was driving the car?
Subject ☐ **Object** ☐

❼ That's the security alarm that I told you about.
Subject ☐ **Object** ☐

47.3 POINT CLÉ LES PRONOMS RELATIFS

L'anglais utilise différents pronoms relatifs pour parler de personnes ou de choses.

PERSONNES

CHOSES

who   **that**   **which**

47.4 CONSTRUCTION LES PROPOSITIONS RELATIVES DÉFINISSANTES

Si le pronom relatif est le sujet de la proposition relative, il doit apparaître dans la phrase.

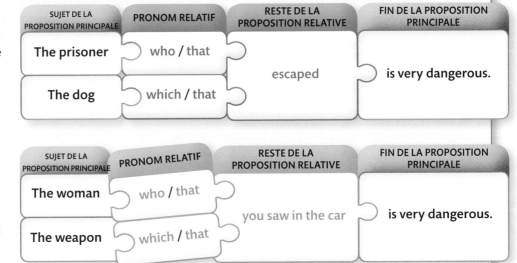

SUJET DE LA PROPOSITION PRINCIPALE	PRONOM RELATIF	RESTE DE LA PROPOSITION RELATIVE	FIN DE LA PROPOSITION PRINCIPALE
The prisoner	who / that	escaped	is very dangerous.
The dog	which / that		

Si le pronom relatif est l'objet de la proposition relative, il peut être omis. Vous pouvez utiliser « whom » lorsqu'une personne est l'objet, mais ce pronom est très formel.

SUJET DE LA PROPOSITION PRINCIPALE	PRONOM RELATIF	RESTE DE LA PROPOSITION RELATIVE	FIN DE LA PROPOSITION PRINCIPALE
The woman	who / that	you saw in the car	is very dangerous.
The weapon	which / that		

◀))

47.5 RELIEZ LES TROIS PARTIES DE LA MÊME PHRASE.

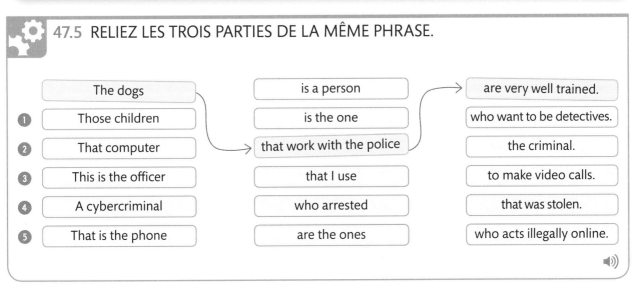

	The dogs	is a person	are very well trained.
❶	Those children	is the one	who want to be detectives.
❷	That computer	that work with the police	the criminal.
❸	This is the officer	that I use	to make video calls.
❹	A cybercriminal	who arrested	that was stolen.
❺	That is the phone	are the ones	who acts illegally online.

◀))

47.6 POINT CLÉ LES PROPOSITIONS RELATIVES NON DÉFINISSANTES

Les propositions relatives non définissantes apportent plus d'informations sur le nom de la proposition principale. La proposition principale aurait toujours un sens sans la relative.

PROPOSITION PRINCIPALE

PROPOSITION RELATIVE NON DÉFINISSANTE

We spoke to Linda, who had recently been mugged.

Une virgule sépare les propositions.

Lorsqu'elles sont placées au milieu d'une phrase, elles sont séparées de la proposition principale par deux virgules.

PROPOSITION PRINCIPALE

PROPOSITION RELATIVE NON DÉFINISSANTE

FIN DE LA PROPOSITION PRINCIPALE

Her necklace, which she'd just bought, **was stolen.**

Il y a une virgule avant et après la proposition relative.

47.7 AUTRES EXEMPLES LES PROPOSITIONS RELATIVES NON DÉFINISSANTES

The suspect, whom we had been following, **was arrested.**

« Whom » n'est utilisé que dans les situations très formelles.

All the burglars were arrested, which was a great relief.

Le pronom relatif peut faire référence à la totalité de la proposition précédente.

47.8 RÉCRIVEZ LES PHRASES EN AJOUTANT DES VIRGULES SI NÉCESSAIRE.

The burglars who were arrested last night will be in court today.

The burglars, who were arrested last night, will be in court today.

① The violent criminals were not sent to jail which surprised the victim.

② Detective Smith who arrested the fraudster works in a special department.

③ Vivian Jones who had worked for the bank for 10 years was arrested yesterday.

47.9 ÉCOUTEZ L'ENREGISTREMENT, PUIS COCHEZ LES BONNES RÉPONSES.

On demande à 5 personnes comment elles réduiraient la criminalité dans la ville.

When does Joan think young people should be banned from the city center?

On Saturdays ☐
Before 10pm ☐
After 10pm ☑

1 Where does Derrick think there should be more surveillance cameras?

On every street corner ☐
On a few street corners ☐
In bars and restaurants ☐

2 What should bars and restaurants do, according to Maxine?

Help to clear up the trash ☐
Stop serving takeout food ☐
Charge more money for takeout food ☐

3 What does Javier think should happen to troublemakers?

They ought to spend a night in a police cell. ☐
They ought to be banned from the city. ☐
They ought to be fined. ☐

4 What does Tamal think should happen to the young people?

Other places should be built for them. ☐
They should be banned from city centers. ☐
They should annoy other people instead. ☐

47.10 LISEZ L'ARTICLE, PUIS COCHEZ LES BONNES RÉPONSES.

32 LOCAL NEWS

PIZZA POLICE!

Police deliver two years for a pizza craving.

Burglar Dan Weatley let his need for a pizza get him into big trouble last month. One afternoon, he broke into a house and stole jewelry, a laptop, and a credit card. As soon as the owner returned home, she called the police and then her bank to report the stolen credit card. Meanwhile Dan, who felt hungry after his busy day, ordered a pizza using the victim's card. The bank alerted the police about the use of the credit card. The police officers, who went with the pizza delivery man to Weatley's home address, found all the day's stolen goods and more from previous burglaries. Mr. Weatley, who admitted committing the burglaries, was yesterday sent to prison for two years.

Weatley carried out the crime in the daytime.
True ☑ False ☐ Not given ☐

1 The victim called the police and her bank.
True ☐ False ☐ Not given ☐

2 The pizza company told the police that the stolen credit card had been used.
True ☐ False ☐ Not given ☐

3 Weatley ordered a pizza to the house he had broken into.
True ☐ False ☐ Not given ☐

4 Weatley had previously been to jail for burglary.
True ☐ False ☐ Not given ☐

---

47 ✓ **CHECK-LIST**

⚙ Les propositions relatives ☐   **Aa** La criminalité et les criminels ☐   🧩 Préciser et détailler ☐

48 Plus de propositions relatives

Les mots relatifs définissent ou décrivent un nom d'une partie principale de la phrase. On utilise des mots relatifs différents en fonction des noms auxquels ils se rapportent.

⚙️ **Grammaire** « Where », « when », « whereby »,et « whose
Aa » **Vocabulaire** Les expressions du tribunal
🧩 **Compétence** Utiliser des mots relatifs

48.1 POINT CLÉ « WHERE », « WHEN » ET « WHEREBY »

« Where » est le pronom relatif utilisé pour faire référence à un lieu.

That is the place where the judge sits.

[The judge sits there.]

« When » est le mot relatif utilisé pour faire référence à un moment.

He is looking forward to the day when he'll be released from prison.

[He's looking forward to the day of his release.]

« Whereby » est le mot relatif utilisé pour faire référence à un processus.

A trial is the process whereby a person is found guilty or innocent of a crime.

[To be found guilty, you must go through a trial process.]

🔊

48.2 BARREZ LES MOTS INCORRECTS DANS CHAQUE PHRASE.

That is the restaurant where / ~~when~~ / ~~whereby~~ we first met.

❶ Courtrooms are places where / when / whereby lawyers argue their cases in front of a judge.

❷ Thursday is the night where / when / whereby we usually go to the movies.

❸ Sentencing is the legal process where / when / whereby a judge decides the punishment.

❹ Morning coffee break is the time where / when / whereby we gossip most.

❺ A police station is the place where / when / whereby most criminals are taken at first.

🔊

48.3 COMPLÉTEZ LES PHRASES AVEC LES SYNTAGMES DE LA LISTE ET « WHERE », « WHEN » OU « WHEREBY ».

Prison is the place _____*where most criminals*_____ serve their sentences.

1 The camera's timer let the police know the exact time _____ .

2 They have developed a system _____ for life outside jail.

3 Do you know the date _____ goes to court?

4 This is the café _____ great food for the public.

5 Conveyancing is a process _____ to another.

6 I remember the day _____ to become a lawyer.

7 This cell is the place _____ are held until a verdict is reached.

one person sells property	~~most criminals~~	prisoners can prepare	the suspect
the robbery took place	the suspects	the prisoners cook	my sister decided

48.4 ÉCOUTEZ L'ENREGISTREMENT, PUIS COCHEZ LES BONNES RÉPONSES.

Deux membres d'un jury discutent d'un procès pour cambriolage.

The man is unsure if the defendant is guilty.
True ☐ **False** ☐ **Not given** ☑

1 The woman suggests that they take a vote.
True ☐ **False** ☐ **Not given** ☐

2 Most of the people think that he's guilty.
True ☐ **False** ☐ **Not given** ☐

3 The defendant had been to jail before.
True ☐ **False** ☐ **Not given** ☐

4 The woman says the defendant was well dressed.
True ☐ **False** ☐ **Not given** ☐

5 The defendant appeared on security video footage.
True ☐ **False** ☐ **Not given** ☐

6 Several computers were stolen in the burglary.
True ☐ **False** ☐ **Not given** ☐

7 The defendant said that he was unable to drive.
True ☐ **False** ☐ **Not given** ☐

48.5 POINT CLÉ « WHOSE »

« Whose » est le mot relatif utilisé pour indiquer la possession ou l'appartenance.

This is the lawyer whose client lied in court.

[This lawyer's client lied in court.]

48.6 AUTRES EXEMPLES « WHOSE »

« Whose » peut être utilisé pour parler de choses qui appartiennent à des pays, des organisations, des villes etc.

The UK is an example of a country whose traffic laws are very strict.

[This UK has very strict traffic laws.]

Smith & Smith, whose success rate is very high, is a very well-respected law firm.

[Smith & Smith has a very high success rate.]

48.7 RÉCRIVEZ LES PHRASES AVEC « WHOSE ».

Judge Wright hand writes all her letters. Her computer skills are not very good.
Judge Wright, whose computer skills are not very good, hand writes all her letters.

1 Rodrigo deserves to be successful. His training regime is rigorous.

_____

2 My sister has become very famous. Her first book was a huge success.

_____

3 My neighbor Sara loves training dogs. Her dogs always win competitions.

_____

4 That company has excellent trading figures. Its employees work very hard.

_____

5 That school is very well respected. Their students always do well in exams.

_____

JURY FINDS HOCKLY GUILTY

Burglar sentenced to 18 months for theft

Burglar Gavin Hockly was jailed for 18 months yesterday. The jury, who had taken two days to reach a decision, finally found Hockly guilty last week. He was accused of stealing a computers from a small technology firm. Hockly, had pleaded not guilty, but the jury did not believe his evidence.

Police originally arrested Hockly when they checked security video footage of the street in front of the burgled premises. He was seen walking around the area each of the six days leading up to the burglary. Hockly said that he was visiting a friend in the area, but when the police asked for more details, he could not remember the full name of his friend or where he lived.

The stolen computers were taken by car to a garage where they were later discovered by police. Despite saying that he could not drive, the jury was shown videos found on social media of Hockly driving a car.

The most important evidence against Hockly was that his fingerprints were found on the stolen computers. Hockly said that someone had asked him to help carry the computers from the back of a van into the garage. The jury clearly did not believe his account of events.

How long did the jury take to find Gavin Hockly guilty?

The jury took two days to find him guilty.

① What made the police arrest Hockly in the first place?

_____

② Why couldn't the police interview the friend Hockly was visiting?

_____

③ Why did the jurors not believe that Hockly could not drive?

_____

④ Why did Hockly say his fingerprints were on the computers?

_____

---

48 ✓ **CHECK-LIST**

⚙️ « Where », « when », « whereby », « whose » ☐   **Aa** Les expressions du tribunal ☐   🧩 Utiliser des mots relatifs ☐

49 Les verbes modaux au futur

Certains verbes modaux changent de forme lorsqu'on les utilise pour parler du futur. D'autres ne peuvent pas être utilisés au futur et doivent être remplacés par d'autres modaux ou syntagmes.

⚙ **Grammaire** « Will be able to » et « will have to »
Aa Vocabulaire Les termes juridiques
🧩 **Compétence** Exprimer des capacités et des obligations futures

---

49.1 POINT CLÉ « CAN » AU FUTUR

On ne peut grammaticalement pas parler du futur en utilisant « can ». On utilise « will be able to » à la place.

At the moment, I can play the trombone quite well.

If I work harder, I will be able to play at concerts.

— « Will can » est incorrect.

La forme négative est construite avec « not able to » ou « unable to ».

Unfortunately, I can't read music very well.

If I don't learn, I won't be able to join the orchestra.

— Vous pouvez également utiliser « will be unable to », mais cette tournure est moins courante.

🔊

49.2 RÉCRIVEZ LES PHRASES AU FUTUR.

Can the police find a way to stop people from littering?
Will the police be able to find a way to stop people from littering?

❶ Unfortunately, he can't pay his parking fines.
_____

❷ Can you install a security camera in the store?
_____

❸ I can't understand all these legal regulations.
_____

❹ Hopefully, my sister can explain it all to me. She's a lawyer.
_____

🔊

49.3 POINT CLÉ « MUST » ET « HAVE TO » AU FUTUR

Il n'y a pas de forme future pour « must ». Le futur de « have to » est formé avec l'auxiliaire « will » et « have ».

In some countries, people $\left\{ \begin{matrix} \text{must} \\ \text{have to} \end{matrix} \right\}$ recycle. It's the law.

In the future, I think everyone will have to recycle.

« Will must » est incorrect.

La forme négative est construite en ajoutant « not » entre « will » et « have ».

One day, I hope I will not have to work so hard.

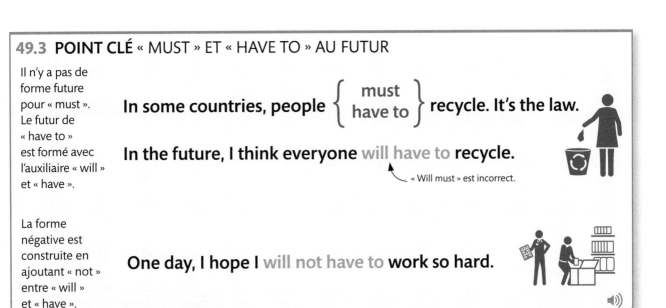

49.4 ÉCRIVEZ LES MOTS SUIVANTS DANS LE BON ORDRE AFIN DE RECONSTITUER LES PHRASES.

I | parking | fine? | have | Will | pay | to | a

Will I have to pay a parking fine?

1. have | You | will | to | longer | work | soon. | hours

2. able | you | be | won't | here. | to | park | Tomorrow

3. able | them? | Will | police | arrest | to | be | the

4. police. | will | I | have | the | to | call

5. law? | Will | enforce | they | to | new | be | able | the

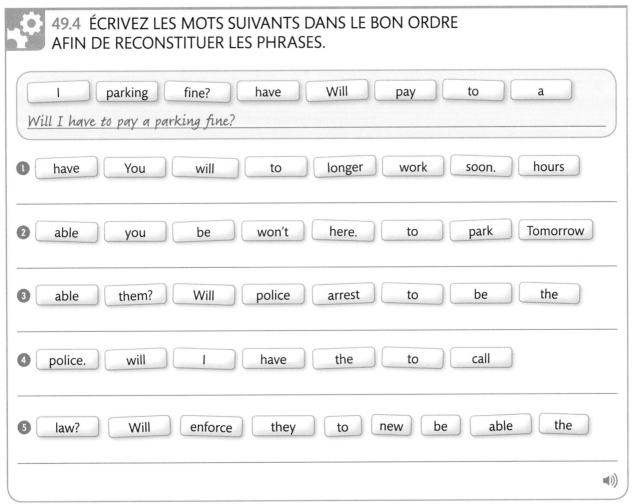

191

WORLD

GET OUT OF MY LANE!

Two-speed walking lanes are becoming increasingly common in shopping malls.

More and more shopping malls around the world are planning to introduce two-speed walking lanes for shoppers, consisting of a fast lane and a slow lane. The fast lanes are for shoppers who are in a hurry, but anyone who wants to browse slowly or use their phone as they walk has to use the slow lane.

Shopping malls in cities such as Chongqing, Antwerp, and Liverpool have already introduced this system. The idea is that faster people will be able to overtake slower shoppers. Researchers have found that younger shoppers in particular are really frustrated by people walking slowly. Mall owners worry that this frustration might encourage people to stay away and shop online instead.

However, the plans are not without their downsides. Some people argue that officials will not be able to enforce the new rules effectively. And in Chongqing, it has been reported that many shoppers were too busy looking at their phones to notice that they were straying into the wrong lane!

Who are the two different walking lanes for?

One is for fast walkers and one is for those who want to walk slowly.

① Where have these lanes already been introduced?

② Who are particularly frustrated by slower shoppers?

③ Why are shopping malls concerned about these frustrated shoppers?

④ What difficulty might officials face with the two-speed lanes system?

⑤ What was one of the problems with the scheme when it was introduced in Chongqing?

49.6 ÉCOUTEZ L'ENREGISTREMENT, PUIS COMPLÉTEZ LES PHRASES AVEC LES MOTS DE LA LISTE.

 Une émission de radio évoque une nouvelle loi pour les fermiers.

A new law has just been _____*passed*_____ by the government. This new law _____

members of the public to walk on farmers' land. Walkers will have to _____ reasonable rules

set by the landowners. If they _____ these rules, they could be _____ from

walking in the area or they could even be _____. Some farmers, however, think that the

police will not be able to _____ the law.

permits	banned	break	observe	enforce	~~passed~~	arrested

Aa 49.7 LISEZ LES INDICES, PUIS ÉCRIVEZ LES MOTS DE LA LISTE AU BON ENDROIT DANS LA GRILLE.

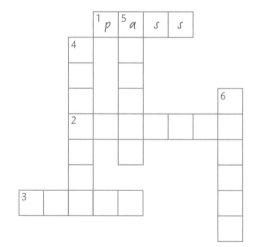

① To make a new law or rule official

② To follow a rule or law

③ To not follow a rule or law

④ To make sure a rule or law is obeyed

⑤ To stop someone and take them to a police station

⑥ To allow something to happen

enforce	~~pass~~	permit
break	arrest	observe

---

49 ✓ CHECK-LIST

✿ « Will be able to » et « will have to » ☐ **Aa** Les termes juridiques ☐ 🏃 Exprimer des capacités et des obligations futures ☐

Vue d'ensemble des verbes modaux

Les verbes modaux permettent de parler de probabilité, de capacité, de permission et d'obligation. Ils font souvent référence à des situations hypothétiques.

⚙ **Grammaire** Utiliser les verbes modaux
Aa **Vocabulaire** Les verbes modaux
🧩 **Compétence** Demander, offrir et prédire

50.1 POINT CLÉ LES VERBES MODAUX

Les verbes modaux ont des points communs : ils ne changent pas de forme en fonction du sujet ; ils sont toujours suivis d'un infinitif ; et leurs formes interrogatives et négatives sont construites sans « to ».

Logical deductions	It **can't** be Jane because she's on vacation. It **could** / **might** / **may** be Dave. I don't know. It **should** be my dad. He said he'd call me. It **must** be Tom, since nobody else ever calls.
Obligation	You **must** arrive on time for work. 
Permission	You **can** have more cake if you want. You **may** take as much as you like.
Ability	I **can** speak three languages. I **can't** read Latin because it's too difficult. I **couldn't** study it when I was at school.
Requests	**Can** / **Could** you give me a ride home later? **Would** you email James for me, please? **Will** you lock up the office tonight?
Advice and suggestions	You **should** / **ought to** go to the doctor. You **could** try the new medicine.
Offers	**Can** I help you with those? **Shall** I carry some of your bags? 

50.2 COMPLÉTEZ LES PHRASES AVEC LES VERBES MODAUX DE LA LISTE.

The rules say that you _____ *must* _____ finish before 5pm.

1 I appreciate that it's difficult, but I think you _____ talk to him about it.

2 Finally, after months of studying, I _____ read music.

3 I'm sorry, but I'm terribly busy at the moment, Mr. Jones. _____ tomorrow be okay?

4 I followed the recipe, so it _____ to taste great, but sometimes it doesn't.

5 I've tried really hard, but I just _____ make these figures add up.

6 I'm feeling very unwell. _____ I be excused?

| can't | can | ~~must~~ | should | May | would | ought |

50.3 BARREZ LES MOTS INCORRECTS DANS CHAQUE PHRASE.

Before you drive a car on your own, you ~~will~~ / ~~could~~ / must pass a test.

1 It's very hot in here. Would / Should / Shall you open a window, please?

2 This coffee has sugar in it! It will / must / ought to be yours.

3 I don't know when the movie will finish. It can / shall / might not be until after 10pm.

4 Shall / Would / Will I help you carry those dishes to the kitchen?

5 My lawnmower has broken. Could / Should / Would I borrow yours, please?

6 I can't / should / ought to swim very well at all, but my sister is an excellent swimmer.

50.4 RÉCRIVEZ LES PHRASES EN CORRIGEANT LES ERREURS.

You should have took your shoes off when you enter the building.
You should have taken your shoes off when you entered the building.

❶ She was was the lead singer in the band because she did could sing very well.

_____

❷ Do you would pick me up from work this evening, please?

_____

❸ The tree looks like it may to fall down soon.

_____

❹ If she doesn't study hard enough, she doesn't might get into medical school.

_____

◀))

50.5 LISEZ LE TEXTE, PUIS RÉPONDEZ AUX QUESTIONS.

Little cultural differences often shock students the most.
True ✓ **False** ☐

❶ Some students are surprised that British houses have shutters.
True ☐ **False** ☐

❷ Some students think British people eat a lot of potatoes.
True ☐ **False** ☐

❸ One student said that he ate mashed potatoes every night with his host family.
True ☐ **False** ☐

❹ In the UK, most animals must stay outside at night.
True ☐ **False** ☐

LIFESTYLE

Student surprises!

What surprises exchange students when they stay with British families?

More often than not, it's the small cultural differences that shock students the most when they stay with British families. Some students, for example, are surprised that houses have curtains, rather than shutters. Other students say they are shocked by the amount of potatoes that British people eat. One student once said to me, "Tonight, it could be mashed, it might be fried or it may even be boiled but, whatever it is, it will be potatoes!"

The British love of pets can also surprise students, and the fact that pets can sleep inside the house or even in bedrooms can be shocking for some. In many cultures, animals must stay outside.

50.6 ÉCOUTEZ L'ENREGISTREMENT, PUIS COCHEZ LES BONNES RÉPONSES.

Simon raconte à ses amis son dernier voyage aux États-Unis.

What does Simon say about the internal flights?

They cost too much ☐
They were easy to book ☐
They were fairly cheap ☑

❷ According to Simon, what should you **not** do with chopsticks?

Leave them standing in rice ☐
Eat rice with them ☐
Use the same pair more than once ☐

❶ What type of accommodation did Simon stay in?

Hotels ☐
B&Bs ☐
Family homes ☐

❸ What did Simon think about spending time with a Native-American family?

It was really interesting ☐
It was fairly interesting ☐
It was really boring ☐

---

50 ✔ CHECK-LIST

⚙ Utiliser les verbes modaux ☐ **Aa** Les verbes modaux ☐ 🧩 Demander, offrir et prédire ☐

♺ BILAN L'ANGLAIS QUE VOUS AVEZ APPRIS DANS LES CHAPITRES 47-50

NOUVEAU POINT LINGUISTIQUE	EXEMPLE TYPE	☑	CHAPITRE
LES PROPOSITIONS RELATIVES DÉFINISSANTES	I'm writing about people who are in prison. This is the car which the criminal stole.	☐	47.1
LES PROPOSITIONS RELATIVES NON DÉFINISSANTES	We spoke to a Linda, who had been mugged. Her necklace, which she'd just bought, was stolen.	☐	47.6
« WHERE », « WHEN » ET « WHEREBY »	That is the place where the judge sits.	☐	48.1
« WHOSE »	This is the lawyer whose client lied in court.	☐	48.5
« CAN » AU FUTUR	If I work harder, I will be able to play at concerts.	☐	49.1
« MUST » ET « HAVE TO » AU FUTUR	In the future, I think everyone will have to recycle.	☐	49.3
LES VERBES MODAUX	You must arrive on time for work. You should go to the doctor if you feel sick.	☐	50.1

Vocabulaire

51.1 LES COUTUMES ET LES CULTURES

My father believes that family values are very important.

values
[the principles and beliefs that somebody holds]

We taught our children to follow the same practices as us.

practices
[ways of doing things, often traditional]

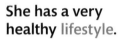

We lead a quiet way of life in the country.

way of life
[a typical routine or pattern of behavior]

She has a very healthy lifestyle.

lifestyle
[the way a person leads their life]

They loved being in the stadium soaking up the atmosphere.

soak up
[take time to absorb and enjoy experiences as much as possible]

I try to blend in on vacation and not look like a tourist.

blend in
[look or seem similar to the surrounding place or people]

I'm so sorry! I didn't mean to cause offense.

cause offense
[do something that upsets others]

It took me a while to acclimate to the weather.

acclimate (US) / acclimatize (UK)
[get used an environment, surroundings, or culture]

I like to try traditional dishes when I travel.

traditional
[part of old customs or beliefs]

There are some interesting local customs and dances.

local custom
[something that is done locally as part of tradition]

My friend speaks a southern dialect.

dialect
[the way that a language is spoken in a certain area]

Many religions have rituals that haven't changed for centuries.

ritual
[an action that is always performed in the same way]

Countries often have a great deal of cultural diversity within them.

diversity
[range or variety]

Many different nationalities were at the conference.

nationality
[people from a nation with a shared culture and language]

Some people believe globalization is bad for local customs.

globalization
[the increasing similarity between different cultures across the world]

A lot of stereotypes are false.

stereotype
[a fixed, often incorrect, idea about what a person or thing is like]

My parents like children who have good manners.

manners
[polite or accepted social behavior]

She picked up lots of bad habits from her brother.

bad habit
[something wrong that you do regularly]

The city is steeped in history.

steeped in something
[be completely involved in or surrounded by something]

I don't usually eat with chopsticks, but when in Rome.

when in Rome (do as the Romans do)
[when you travel, act as the local people do]

52 Parler de groupes

Vous voudrez peut-être parfois parler de groupes
de personnes ou de nationalités différentes de manière
générale. Il est important de connaître la façon correcte
de le faire.

⚙ **Grammaire** Utiliser des adjectifs comme noms
Aa Vocabulaire Les pays et les nationalités
🧩 **Compétence** Généraliser poliment

52.1 POINT CLÉ LES ADJECTIFS DE NATIONALITÉ COMME NOMS

Pour parler en général des personnes provenant d'un pays précis, il suffit de modifier l'adjectif de nationalité.
Si l'adjectif se termine en « -ch », « -sh », « -ese » ou « -ss », vous devez généralement ajouter « the ».
La plupart des autres nationalités prennent un « -s », mais pas le « the ».

-CH / -SH / -ESE / -SS

**Chinese design history is
really fascinating.**

**The Chinese have invented
many great things.**

LA PLUPART DES AUTRES NATIONALITÉS

**Australian rugby is
very competitive.**

**Australians love to
watch their team play.**

🔊

52.2 AUTRES EXEMPLES LES ADJECTIFS DE NATIONALITÉ COMME NOMS

 The Spanish   The Japanese   The British   Americans   Greeks   Russians

🔊

52.3 ÉCRIVEZ LE NOM CORRECT POUR CHAQUE GROUPE DE PERSONNES.

 German = *Germans*

❶ ➕ Swiss = _____

❷ ◉ Brazilian = _____

❸ Swedish = _____

❹ Indian = _____

❺ French = _____

❻ Korean = _____

❼ Kenyan = _____

🔊

52.4 POINT CLÉ « THE » AVEC ADJECTIFS POUR CERTAINS GROUPES

On fait aussi référence à certains groupes ou classes de personnes en utilisant des noms formés à partir d'adjectifs.

Rich people have bought most of the new houses in this town.

⬇

Almost all the houses here are owned by the rich.

52.5 AUTRES EXEMPLES « THE » AVEC ADJECTIFS POUR CERTAINS GROUPES

 Emergency treatment for the injured **is essential.**

 The media sometimes portrays the young **as lazy.**

 Many charities try to protect the poor.

 The elderly **often need the support of their families.**

52.6 COMPLÉTEZ LES PHRASES AVEC LES MOTS DE LA LISTE.

Not every country's government gives financial help to the ___unemployed___.

1 The _____ are often without a house as a result of some very bad luck.

2 Often, the _____ are described as being addicted to gadgets and phones.

3 The _____ often give lots of money to charity, but we don't know about it.

4 Many countries have laws to ensure that the _____ can access public transportation.

5 After the accident, the _____ were all taken to a nearby hospital.

6 The _____ have often cared for others all their lives and deserve care in return.

| unemployed | elderly | homeless | rich | young | injured | disabled |

THE SOCIAL CONTRACT

HOME | FORUM | NEWS | CONTACT

POSTED BY JEN AT 10:38AM

Who is responsible?

Sometimes I feel very sad for those people in my country who are unable to provide for themselves. Everything is about money, not about caring. How do you think your country treats vulnerable people in society?

Mi (Hanoi): The Vietnamese have many public and private hospitals to help the sick. We respect the elderly and do whatever we can to take care of them. Often, public transportation isn't easily accessible for the disabled, but usually people will offer help.

Pepe (Milan): Italians are very proud of how they care for the elderly. It would be very wrong for me to leave my mother or father in a difficult situation. They looked after me as I was growing up, and now it's my responsibility to look after them.

Simon (Oxford): As the young have to spend more and more time working to earn money for their own family's needs, it becomes harder to have time to spend with parents. But we still respect the elderly and often help pay for their care.

Jen thinks her country's citizens care more about money than people. **True** ✓ **False** ☐

① Jen only wants to know how different people treat the sick. **True** ☐ **False** ☐

② Pepe believes that Italians have no time to look after the elderly. **True** ☐ **False** ☐

③ Pepe thinks his parents should be able to look after themselves. **True** ☐ **False** ☐

④ Mi says that Vietnam has both public and private hospitals. **True** ☐ **False** ☐

⑤ Mi says that all public transportation in Vietnam has disabled access. **True** ☐ **False** ☐

⑥ Simon says that the English spend a lot of their time at work. **True** ☐ **False** ☐

⑦ According to Simon, the English do respect the elderly. **True** ☐ **False** ☐

52.8 ÉCOUTEZ L'ENREGISTREMENT, PUIS NUMÉROTEZ LES PHRASES DANS LE BON ORDRE.

Une enseignante dans une école multiculturelle urbaine, parle des recherches sur les stéréotypes qu'elle a menées avec ses élèves.

A "I might come from a cold country, but I still get cold over here. Nobody believes me!" ☐

B "It's annoying. People think I should cook all the time, but I don't like it." 1

C "People thought I wasn't allowed to get my hair cut whenever I wanted." ☐

D "I know that my country is rich, but it doesn't mean everyone from there is." ☐

E "Lots of times people are shocked or surprised that I'm not a vegetarian." ☐

F "Not everyone from my country can run long distances. I'm a terrible runner!" ☐

52.9 RÉPONDEZ AUX QUESTIONS DE L'ENREGISTREMENT, PUIS LISEZ LES RÉPONSES À VOIX HAUTE.

In professional sports, what happens when people hurt themselves?

The injured _leave the field and are treated by medical staff._

1 What happens if someone loses their job in your country?

The unemployed _____

2 How do young people in your country treat old people?

The elderly _____

3 Do you think young people are represented fairly by the media?

The young _____

52 ✓ CHECK-LIST

⚙ Utiliser des adjectifs comme noms ☐　　　**Aa** Les pays et les nationalités ☐　　　🧩 Généraliser poliment ☐

Les situations nouvelles peuvent parfois sembler étranges, mais elles deviennent familières avec le temps. Vous pouvez dans ce cas utiliser des phrases contenant « be used to » et « get used to ».

⚙ **Grammaire** « Be used to » et « get used to »

Aa **Vocabulaire** S'installer et vivre à l'étranger

🧩 **Compétence** Parler de situations passées et nouvelles

53.1 POINT CLÉ « BE USED TO » ET « GET USED TO »

« To get used to (doing) something » signifie que vous vous adaptez à des circonstances nouvelles ou différentes de sorte qu'elles deviennent familières.

« To be used to (doing) something » signifie que vous avez effectué cette action suffisamment longtemps pour qu'elle soit devenue normale et familière.

Waking up early for my new job was difficult at first, but eventually I got used to it.

I've lived in the city for years, so I am used to the bad pollution.

53.2 AUTRES EXEMPLES « BE USED TO » ET « GET USED TO »

When I travel, I get used to different customs very quickly.
[I find it easy to adapt to different customs when I travel.]

I got used to the cold weather within a couple of weeks.
[I adapted to the cold weather within two weeks.]

I am used to spicy food as I've always eaten it.
[I am accustomed to eating spicy food.]

We were used to the old teacher, so it was a shame when she left.
[We were accustomed to our previous teacher, but then she left.]

CONSEIL
Ne confondez pas ces phrases avec « used to » (sans « be » ou « get ») qu'on utilise lorsque quelqu'un parle d'une action passée régulière.

53.3 BARREZ LES MOTS INCORRECTS DANS CHAQUE PHRASE.

> When I visit the UK, it takes me a while to get / ~~be~~ used to driving on the left side of the road.

1 My parents are / get used to living in an old building, but the creaking floorboards scare me!

2 They were / get used to eating with chopsticks, but it was new to me. I found it hard!

3 My friend said I'd am / get used to eating my dinner later at night after a few weeks.

4 It took a while, but now I get / am used to recycling all my paper and plastic each week.

5 His friends found it strange, but he was / get used to doing things without using the computer.

6 It was difficult at first, but I was / got used to the new routine after a few months.

7 We were / get used to the old system at work, but then it changed completely.

8 Eventually I got / am used to answering the phone in English. It almost feels natural now!

53.4 RÉCRIVEZ LES PHRASES EN CORRIGEANT LES ERREURS.

> It has taken me a long time to get use to cycling in the city.
> *It has taken me a long time to get used to cycling in the city.*

1 I don't think I will ever got used to the noise in my street at night.

_____

2 I'm so used drinking coffee every morning that I can't function without it.

_____

3 They said that they could not be used to the icy weather.

_____

4 Don't worry. After a while you'll got used to the cold water.

_____

5 Do you think that you'll used to the long hours in your new job?

_____

53.5 RÉVISION « USED TO »

Vous pouvez utiliser « used to » (sans « be » ou « get ») avec l'infinitif pour parler d'habitudes passées. Vous pouvez aussi l'utiliser pour parler d'états figés dans le passé, mais uniquement dans le cadre d'une période indéterminée.

Fait référence à une habitude passée.

We used to play tennis every day, but now we prefer golf.

Fait référence à un état passé.

We used to live in London before we moved to Sydney.

53.6 COMPLÉTEZ LES PHRASES EN CONJUGUANT LES VERBES DE LA LISTE À LA FORME QUI CONVIENT.

When I was living abroad, I used to ____go out____ a lot so that I could meet people and make friends. Even though I was nervous, I used to _____ to any offer people made to try something new. Also, I didn't _____ things to fit around my old routines, but got used to _____ things in line with local customs instead. These were quite unusual at first, but I _____ used to them now. The staff in my local café are used to me _____ mistakes when I talk, but they always appreciate the effort and help me.

| be | agree | make | force | ~~go out~~ | do |

53.7 RELIEZ LE DÉBUT DE CHAQUE PHRASE À LA FIN QUI LUI CORRESPOND.

You may have to get used to days — when you are homesick. It's not unusual.

you're used to. That's the adventure!

① Be sure to experiment and try not

they got used to the different culture.

② Visit the country before you move

to start getting used to the culture.

③ Ask other people from abroad how

when you are homesick. It's not unusual.

④ Don't worry if things aren't what

is a great way to get to know new people.

⑤ Trying activities in your new country

to only do things you used to do at home.

53.8 ÉCOUTEZ L'ENREGISTREMENT, PUIS COCHEZ LES BONNES RÉPONSES.

On demande à Julie Holmes, journaliste internationale, de décrire ses plus grands chocs culturels.

How does Julie feel now when people ask her personal questions?

She feels surprised and offended ☐
She is surprised but not upset ☐
She is no longer surprised by it ☑

1 What examples of personal information has Julie been asked for?

Her age and whether she is married ☐
Her salary and when she will have children ☐
Her age and when she will have children ☐

2 What was a pleasant culture shock for Julie when she was in Spain?

Friends inviting her to family lunches ☐
Lunches lasting a long time ☐
Lunches being quick and efficient ☐

3 What happened after Julie missed her train?

She got a taxi to her home town ☐
She stayed overnight with a friend ☐
She got the last bus home that night ☐

4 What happened in a busy road in Hanoi?

Julie helped an old lady cross the road ☐
Julie crossed the road on her own ☐
An old lady helped Julie cross the road ☐

53.9 RÉPONDEZ AUX QUESTIONS DE L'ENREGISTREMENT, PUIS LISEZ LES PHRASES À VOIX HAUTE.

These festivals are so noisy. Do you think it'll bother you?

Yes, but we'll have to _get used to_ the noise.

0 You always stay up so late! Don't you feel tired the next day?

Not any more. I _____ _____ it now.

2 Why does everyone in the village paint that pattern on their doors?

It's tradition! We _____ _____ doing it.

3 Is it still strange for you to see people dressed in these costumes?

It was at first, but now I _____ them.

4 Were you able to cope with the hot weather when you first moved here?

No, it took me many years to _____ it.

---

53 ✓ **CHECK-LIST**

⚙️ « Be used to » et « get used to » ☐   **Aa** S'installer et vivre à l'étranger ☐   🧩 Parler de situations passées et nouvelles ☐

207

54 Les articles

L'article est l'un des mots les plus courts et communs de la langue anglaise. Des règles précisent quel article, si article il y a, doit être utilisé.

⚙ **Grammaire** Les articles
Aa Vocabulaire Les fautes d'orthographe les plus courantes
🧩 **Compétence** Prononcer les mots avec des lettres muettes

54.1 POINT CLÉ L'ARTICLE DÉFINI

Utilisez l'article défini « the » lorsque la personne ou la chose dont vous parlez est facilement identifiable.

We went on a tour and the guide was excellent.

Il est évident d'après le contexte que cela signifie « the tour guide ».

Cela inclut les situations où une personne ou une chose a déjà été mentionnée.

There's a bus trip or a lecture. I'd prefer the bus trip.

Le voyage en bus a déjà été mentionné.

Utilisez l'article défini devant les superlatifs.

The Colosseum is probably the most famous site in Rome.

L'article défini est utilisé devant les superlatifs comme « most famous ».

On utilise aussi l'article défini pour parler d'objets uniques.

I'm going to the Trevi Fountain before I check out.

La fontaine de Trevi est un monument unique.

On l'utilise également pour parler de personnes portant des titres uniques.

« Pope » est un titre.

The Pope is visiting another country this week.

54.2 POINT CLÉ L'ARTICLE INDÉFINI

Utilisez les articles indéfinis « a » et « an » lorsque vous ne connaissez pas précisément la personne ou la chose dont vous parlez.

We are trying to choose a vacation.

On introduit les vacances pour la première fois.

On utilise aussi l'article indéfini pour parler d'une catégorie entière de personnes ou de choses en général.

India is a fascinating country to visit.

54.3 BARREZ LES MOTS INCORRECTS DANS CHAQUE PHRASE.

Many of ~~a / an~~ / the largest cities in the world are in China.

❶ I want to visit a / an / **the** really modern city like Tokyo.

❷ I've always wanted to go up a / an / **the** Empire State Building.

❸ Should we go to a / an / **the** restaurant we ate at on Friday?

❹ Did you ride on a / an / **the** gondola in Venice?

54.4 **POINT CLÉ** L'ARTICLE ZÉRO

L'article n'est pas nécessaire avec les noms pluriels et indénombrables, lorsque vous voulez parler de quelque chose de manière générale plutôt que de manière précise. On appelle cela l'« article zéro ».

« Sand » est un nom indénombrable.

I don't like the beach. I get sand everywhere.

You can see famous sights all over New York City.

Le nombre de vues est indéfini.

54.5 RÉCRIVEZ LES PHRASES EN CORRIGEANT LES ERREURS.

The Maracanã stadium in Rio de Janeiro is in a north of the city.
The Maracanã stadium in Rio de Janeiro is in the north of the city.

❶ Have you ever been on guided tour of Rio de Janeiro?

_____

❷ The Christ the Redeemer statue in Rio de Janeiro is a largest statue of its type.

_____

❸ A soccer is a hugely popular sport in Rio and Brazil in general.

_____

❹ There is famous lagoon in central Rio called Lagoa Rodrigo de Freitas.

_____

54.6 COMPLÉTEZ LES PHRASES EN CHOISISSANT L'ARTICLE APPROPRIÉ. LAISSEZ UN BLANC POUR L'ARTICLE ZÉRO.

The Republic of Costa Rica in Central America has _____ estimated population of just under 5 million people and one of _____ highest life expectancy levels in the West. Its incredible beauty and the diverse nature of the flora and fauna in its rainforests make _____ Costa Rica a top destination for tourists. Indeed, tourism is _____ country's number one source of foreign exchange. As well as famous cash crops like bananas and coffee, Costa Rica boasts 1,000 species of orchids and _____ huge number of bird species. In fairly recent years, Costa Rica has tried to cut down its reliance on the income produced by the export of coffee beans, bananas, and beef by becoming _____ producer of _____ microchips. Unfortunately, _____ microchip market has turned out to be as unstable as that for cash crops.

 54.7 ÉCOUTEZ L'ENREGISTREMENT, PUIS COCHEZ LES BONNES RÉPONSES.

Trois personnes discutent de la géographie
de pays qu'elles connaissent bien.

	True	**False**
The ocean is on the eastern border of Chile.	☐	✓

1 Chile contains extremely dry deserts and also lakes made from glaciers. **True** ☐ **False** ☐

2 Most of South Korea's islands are to the east of the country. **True** ☐ **False** ☐

3 The weather in South Korea can be quite dramatic. **True** ☐ **False** ☐

4 Morocco is in the south of Europe, near North Africa. **True** ☐ **False** ☐

5 Morocco is generally drier in the south than the north. **True** ☐ **False** ☐

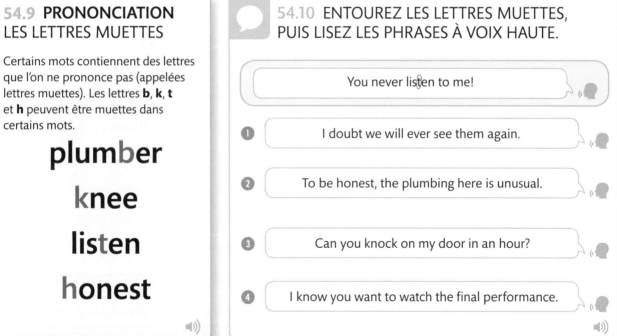

Aa 54.8 LISEZ LES INDICES, PUIS ÉCRIVEZ LES MOTS DE LA LISTE DANS LA GRILLE AU BON ENDROIT.

CONSEIL
Toutes les réponses sont des mots souvent mal orthographiés en anglais.

1 o c c a 5s i o n a l l y

1 Sometimes, but not very often

2 Different from one moment to the next

3 Strange and unusual

4 Person from a country other than your own

5 To divide or keep things apart

6 How tall something is

weird   ~~occasionally~~   height

foreigner   separate   changeable

54.9 PRONONCIATION LES LETTRES MUETTES

Certains mots contiennent des lettres que l'on ne prononce pas (appelées lettres muettes). Les lettres **b**, **k**, **t** et **h** peuvent être muettes dans certains mots.

plum**b**er

knee

lis**t**en

honest

54.10 ENTOUREZ LES LETTRES MUETTES, PUIS LISEZ LES PHRASES À VOIX HAUTE.

You never listen to me!

1 I doubt we will ever see them again.

2 To be honest, the plumbing here is unusual.

3 Can you knock on my door in an hour?

4 I know you want to watch the final performance.

54 ✓ CHECK-LIST

⚙ Les articles ☐ **Aa** Les fautes d'orthographe les plus courantes ☐ 🧩 Prononcer les mots avec des lettres muettes ☐

55 Les idées abstraites

La plupart des noms abstraits sont indénombrables. Toutefois, certains peuvent être à la fois dénombrables et indénombrables, et les deux formes ont souvent un sens légèrement différent.

⚙ **Grammaire** Les noms concrets et abstraits
Aa Vocabulaire Les systèmes éducatifs
🧩 **Compétence** Parler d'idées abstraites

55.1 POINT CLÉ LES NOMS CONCRETS ET ABSTRAITS

Les noms abstraits font référence à des idées, événements, concepts, sentiments et qualités qui n'ont pas d'existence physique. Les noms concrets sont des choses qui ont une existence physique.

He has a lot of books, but not much knowledge.

« Books » est un nom dénombrable, concret.

« Knowledge » est un nom indénombrable, abstrait.

55.2 AUTRES EXEMPLES LES NOMS CONCRETS ET ABSTRAITS

teacher   classroom

NOMS CONCRETS

paper   chair   exam

progress   freedom

NOMS ABSTRAITS

truth   sadness   health

55.3 ÉCRIVEZ LES NOMS DE LA LISTE DANS L'ENCADRÉ CORRESPONDANT.

CONCRETE NOUNS	
computer	

ABSTRACT NOUNS	
relaxation	

building   ~~relaxation~~   professor   pride   misery   hate   sun   clock

beauty   artist   anger   library   photograph   heat   trouble   ~~computer~~

55.4 POINT CLÉ LES NOMS ABSTRAITS DÉNOMBRABLES ET INDÉNOMBRABLES

Certains noms abstraits ont une forme dénombrable et une forme indénombrable.
Les deux formes ont un sens légèrement différent : la forme dénombrable est plus
spécifique et la forme indénombrable plus générale.

DÉNOMBRABLE		INDÉNOMBRABLE

I've been there a few times.

Chaque « fois » (« time ») est
une occasion spécifique.

There's plenty of time left.

« Time » fait référence
au concept en général.

He has had many successes.

« Successes » fait référence aux
accomplissements spécifiques.

Hard work leads to success.

« Success » fait référence
à la réussite en général.

She has some great qualities.

« Qualities » fait référence aux traits
de caractère de cette personne.

It has a reputation for quality.

« Quality » fait référence
à un haut niveau.

We learned several new skills.

Il s'agit des aptitudes
particulières acquises.

It takes skill to do that job.

« Skill » est l'aptitude générale
à faire quelque chose.

55.5 BARREZ LES MOTS INCORRECTS DANS CHAQUE PHRASE.

> The top four racing drivers have very similar average speed / speeds.

1 She was deep in thought / thoughts so we did not disturb her.

2 In college, you can meet people from many different culture / cultures.

3 My father formed many lasting friendship / friendships in college.

4 This house is amazing. There are so many interesting space / spaces.

5 My brother does a lot of work for several local charity / charities.

6 Apparently, this is the worst weather in living memory / memories.

7 In these difficult times it's so important not to give up hope / hopes.

55.6 COMPLÉTEZ LES PHRASES AVEC LES MOTS ABSTRAITS DE LA LISTE.

Australians have a lot of ____pride____ in their system of _____ .
The system in Australia is quite hard to describe because it is largely controlled
by the states or territories, rather than the federal _____ .
Depending on where they live, students must go to school from five years old
until 16 or 17 _____ old. There is also nursery level education, but
this is not compulsory. After secondary school, students have a number of
options to develop their _____ . They can choose to undertake
vocational education and training (VET) by taking a _____ in a
subject such as computer programming, engineering, or tourism, where they
also learn key workplace _____ . Alternatively, young people can
apply to go into higher education or, of course, look for work. Generally, the
system in Australia is recognized as being a _____ .

skills   ~~pride~~   education   success   course   abilities   years   government

55.7 ÉCOUTEZ LE REPORTAGE, PUIS RÉPONDEZ AUX QUESTIONS.

Deux personnes discutent des différents
systèmes éducatifs dans le monde.

The female speaker comes from England.	True ✓	False ☐	Not given ☐
❶ The English system is similar to the Australian system.	True ☐	False ☐	Not given ☐
❷ In the UK, education is compulsory until the age of 19.	True ☐	False ☐	Not given ☐
❸ The male speaker comes from Finland.	True ☐	False ☐	Not given ☐
❹ Students in Finland take lots of exams.	True ☐	False ☐	Not given ☐
❺ Finnish schools are inspected every year.	True ☐	False ☐	Not given ☐

55.8 RÉCRIVEZ LES PHRASES EN CORRIGEANT LES ERREURS.

There's really no need to rush. We have plenty of times left.
There's really no need to rush. We have plenty of time left.

① We had a training day to help us develop our customer service skill.

② These products don't have any redeeming quality. They are so cheaply built!

③ Your plan is not very sensible. It needs a bit more thoughts.

④ There are time when I wonder if I should have become a teacher.

⑤ Some of the applicants don't have enough experiences for the job.

---

55 ✓ CHECK-LIST

⚙ Les noms concrets et abstraits ☐   **Aa** Les systèmes éducatifs ☐   🧩 Parler d'idées abstraites ☐

🔄 **BILAN** L'ANGLAIS QUE VOUS AVEZ APPRIS DANS LES CHAPITRES 52-55

NOUVEAU POINT LINGUISTIQUE	EXEMPLE TYPE	☑	CHAPITRE
UTILISER DES ADJECTIFS COMME NOMS	The Chinese **have invented many things.** All the houses here are owned by the rich.	☐	52.1, 52.4
« BE USED TO » ET « GET USED TO »	**It took me weeks to** get used to **getting up** early. Now, I am used to **it.**	☐	53.1
LES ARTICLES	The Pope **is visiting another country.** **We are trying to choose** a vacation.	☐	54.1, 54.2, 54.4
LES NOMS CONCRETS ET ABSTRAITS	**He has a lot of** books, **but not much** knowledge.	☐	55.1
LES NOMS ABSTRAITS DÉNOMBRABLES ET INDÉNOMBRABLES	**I've been there a few** times. **There's plenty of** time **left.**	☐	55.4

56.1 LA TECHNOLOGIE ET L'AVENIR

We must make arrangements **for childcare this weekend.**

make arrangements
[plan ahead so that something can happen]

Every December I make a prediction **about what will happen next year.**

make predictions
[say what you think might happen in the future]

There's no point having good intentions **if you don't do anything.**

have good intentions
[have good or positive plans]

He worked hard to realize his dream **of being a tennis player.**

realize a dream
[make a dream or hope real]

I didn't study for the exam, but I'll hope for the best**!**

hope for the best
[hope for a successful or positive outcome]

My parents had a big influence on **the type of food I enjoy.**

have an influence on something
[change or affect something]

The internet has had an impact on **how we communicate globally.**

have an impact on something
[affect something powerfully]

Being able to meet my favorite singer was a dream come true**.**

a dream come true
[something that has been wished for and has now happened]

It's only a matter of time **before someone buys one of my paintings.**

only a matter of time
[something that will happen, but it is not possible to say when]

We will have to wait and see what the future holds **for us.**

what the future holds
[what will happen in the future]

This electric car will save us money in the long run.

in the long run
[eventually, after a long time]

I really hope this isn't the shape of things to come.

the shape of things to come
[the way things are likely to develop in the future]

Having an internet connection is vital in this digital age.

digital age
[an era based on digital information, when technology is dominant]

Have you seen the latest model **of their smartphone? It's amazing!**

the latest model
[the most recent version of a product]

Her design won an award for technical innovation.

innovation
[a new invention or idea]

The team made an important medical breakthrough.

breakthrough
[an important discovery or achievement]

The internet has seen a revolution **in communication.**

revolution
[a huge change in ideas or methods]

She has a new kitchen filled with state-of-the-art **appliances.**

state-of-the-art
[the most modern and up-to-date]

We need to future-proof **the design, not just look at today's market.**

future-proof
[design something to work in the future, even if technology changes]

That company is famous for its cutting-edge **design.**

cutting-edge
[extremely modern and innovative]

57 Les espoirs pour l'avenir

Pour parler de souhaits, souvent lorsque vous voulez que quelque chose change, utilisez les modaux « would » et « could » au passé.

⚙ **Grammaire** « Wish » avec « would » ou « could »
Aa Vocabulaire Les espoirs pour l'avenir
🧩 **Compétence** Parler de souhaits et d'espoirs pour l'avenir

---

57.1 POINT CLÉ « WISH » POUR LES ESPOIRS

Utilisez « wish » avec « could » pour parler d'espoirs personnels.

I wish I could move somewhere warm.
[I would like to be able to move somewhere warmer.]

Utilisez « wish » avec « would » lorsque quelqu'un fait quelque chose que vous n'aimez pas et lorsque vous voulez que cette personne change.

She wishes her teacher would give her less work.
[She wants her teacher to give out less homework in future.]

57.2 AUTRES EXEMPLES « WISH » POUR LES ESPOIRS

I wish I could get a new job in a different department.

I wish I could go to the concert with my friends this evening.

Colin is always talking about cars. I wish he would stop.

I wish they wouldn't make it so hard to buy tickets online.

57.3 RÉCRIVEZ LES PHRASES EN CORRIGEANT LES ERREURS.

> This homework is so boring! I wish I would do something else.
> *This homework is so boring! I wish I could do something else.*

① That college seems really great. I could wish I go there.

_____

② We can't change their development plans, but we wish we can.

_____

③ Sarah wishes her husband would to buy her flowers more often.

_____

④ My favorite band is coming to our city. I wish can go!

_____

57.4 COMPLÉTEZ LES PHRASES AVEC « COULD », « WOULD » OU « WOULDN'T ».

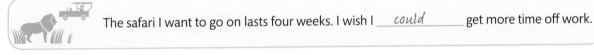

The safari I want to go on lasts four weeks. I wish I ___could___ get more time off work.

① I wish you _____ criticize my clothes. I think I look fabulous!

② My neighbor plays the trumpet all the time. I wish he _____ be a little quieter.

③ Mike's car always breaks down. He wishes he _____ afford a new one.

④ We work far too hard. I wish we _____ do this more often!

58 Le futur continu

Vous pouvez utiliser le futur continu avec « will »
pour faire des prédictions et pour faire des hypothèses
sur ce qui peut se passer au moment où l'on parle.

⚙ **Grammaire** Le futur continu avec « will »
Aa Vocabulaire Les demandes polies
🧩 **Compétence** Planifier votre carrière

58.1 POINT CLÉ LE FUTUR CONTINU AVEC « WILL »

Le futur continu décrit un événement qui sera en cours à un moment donné du futur.
L'événement commencera avant le moment en question et pourra continuer après.

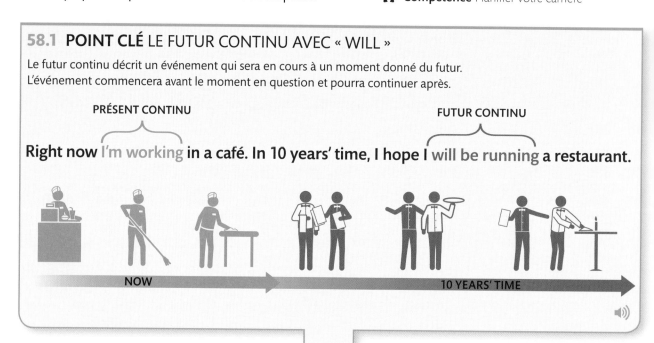

PRÉSENT CONTINU   FUTUR CONTINU

Right now I'm working in a café. In 10 years' time, I hope I will be running a restaurant.

NOW   10 YEARS' TIME

58.2 AUTRES EXEMPLES LE FUTUR CONTINU AVEC « WILL »

This time next week,
I'll be relaxing on a beach.

This time tomorrow,
she'll be taking her last exam.

58.3 CONSTRUCTION LE FUTUR CONTINU AVEC « WILL »

SUJET	« WILL »	« BE »	PARTICIPE PRÉSENT	OBJET
I	will	be	running	a restaurant.

58.4 COMPLÉTEZ LES PHRASES EN CONJUGUANT LES VERBES AU FUTUR CONTINU AVEC « WILL ».

By this time next year, I think I _____*will be living*_____ (live) in a different country.

1 In a few years' time, I think you _____ (run) this place.

2 I suppose you _____ (feel) too tired to go out after work this evening.

3 Tomorrow evening, Jorge's band _____ (perform) at a concert.

4 I guess she _____ (not come) to the office party if she doesn't like the boss.

5 Jane bought two tickets so I think she _____ (bring) a friend to the exhibition.

6 Meilin has already told me that she _____ (not check) her emails today.

58.5 UTILISEZ LE FUTUR CONTINU AVEC « WILL » POUR DÉCRIRE LES ÉVÉNEMENTS DE LA LIGNE CHRONOLOGIQUE À VOIX HAUTE.

WORKING IN THE SAME OFFICE	WORKING IN A NEW DEPARTMENT	WORKING AT HEADQUARTERS	MANAGING HEAD OFFICE	ENJOYING MY RETIREMENT
NEXT WEEK	1 YEAR'S TIME	5 YEARS' TIME	10 YEARS' TIME	20 YEARS' TIME

This time next week, _*I will still be working in the same office.*_

1 In a year's time, _____.

2 In 5 years' time, _____.

3 In 10 years' time, _____.

4 In 20 years' time, _____.

221

58.6 **POINT CLÉ** LE FUTUR CONTINU AVEC « ANYWAY »

Le futur continu peut aussi être utilisé pour parler d'événements qui vont se produire naturellement ou « anyway ».

Oh no, I've run out of milk.

I can get some for you later.

No, please don't worry!

It's okay, I'll be driving **past the store anyway.**

58.7 **POINT CLÉ** LES QUESTIONS NEUTRES

Le futur continu est aussi utilisé pour poser des questions neutres. Il s'agit de questions posées pour obtenir une information et non pour faire une demande.

QUESTION NEUTRE

Futur continu.

Will you be coming into work tomorrow?

Yes, I will.

OK, let's talk about the report then.

DEMANDE

Futur avec « will ».

Will you come into work tomorrow, please?

Sure, no problem.

58.8 RÉCRIVEZ LES QUESTIONS AU LE FUTUR CONTINU AVEC « WILL ».

Are all of your family coming?
Will all of your family be coming?

❶ Are you leaving soon?
_____

❷ Are you going to watch all of those DVDs?
_____

❸ Are the children coming too?
_____

❹ Will you eat all of those cakes?
_____

❺ Are you going to the store?
_____

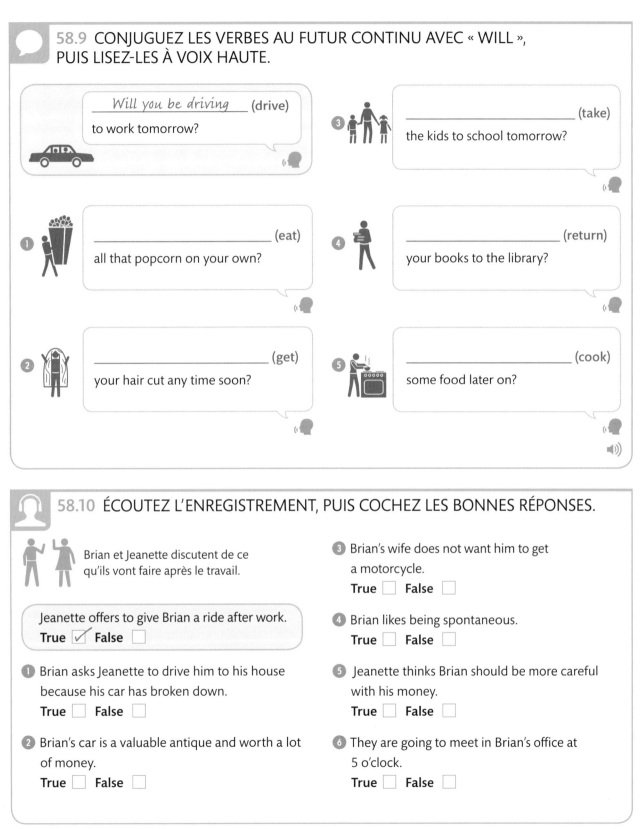

58.9 CONJUGUEZ LES VERBES AU FUTUR CONTINU AVEC « WILL », PUIS LISEZ-LES À VOIX HAUTE.

Will you be driving (drive) to work tomorrow?

3 _____ (take) the kids to school tomorrow?

1 _____ (eat) all that popcorn on your own?

4 _____ (return) your books to the library?

2 _____ (get) your hair cut any time soon?

5 _____ (cook) some food later on?

58.10 ÉCOUTEZ L'ENREGISTREMENT, PUIS COCHEZ LES BONNES RÉPONSES.

Brian et Jeanette discutent de ce qu'ils vont faire après le travail.

Jeanette offers to give Brian a ride after work.
True ✓ False ☐

1 Brian asks Jeanette to drive him to his house because his car has broken down.
True ☐ False ☐

2 Brian's car is a valuable antique and worth a lot of money.
True ☐ False ☐

3 Brian's wife does not want him to get a motorcycle.
True ☐ False ☐

4 Brian likes being spontaneous.
True ☐ False ☐

5 Jeanette thinks Brian should be more careful with his money.
True ☐ False ☐

6 They are going to meet in Brian's office at 5 o'clock.
True ☐ False ☐

58.11 POINT CLÉ LE FUTUR CONTINU POUR PARLER DU PRÉSENT

Vous pouvez également utiliser le futur continu pour faire des hypothèses
sur quelque chose qui pourrait avoir lieu au moment où l'on parle.

 Have you noticed that Andrew isn't at work today?

 He'll be working on his presentation at home.

 It's more likely that he'll be watching the golf on TV!

58.12 ÉCOUTEZ L'ENREGISTREMENT, PUIS COCHEZ LA BONNE RÉPONSE.

Darren et Kate discutent de la raison
qui pourrait expliquer pourquoi Jonas
n'est pas venu au travail aujourd'hui.

He'll be playing basketball with his nephew.
Darren ☐ **Kate** ✓ **Nobody** ☐

❶ His nephew will be studying for his big exam.
Darren ☐ **Kate** ☐ **Nobody** ☐

❷ He'll be playing football with his brother.
Darren ☐ **Kate** ☐ **Nobody** ☐

❸ I imagine he'll be doing something fun though.
Darren ☐ **Kate** ☐ **Nobody** ☐

❹ He'll be preparing for tomorrow's big meeting.
Darren ☐ **Kate** ☐ **Nobody** ☐

❺ He'll be practicing his presentation.
Darren ☐ **Kate** ☐ **Nobody** ☐

❻ He'll be panicking about the annual accounts.
Darren ☐ **Kate** ☐ **Nobody** ☐

58.13 COMPLÉTEZ LES PHRASES AU FUTUR CONTINU AVEC « WILL », PUIS LISEZ-LES À VOIX HAUTE.

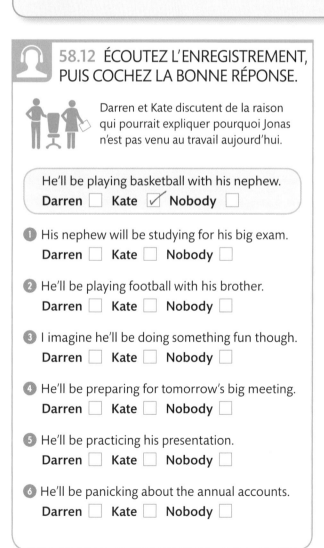

She'll be doing the gardening.

❶ _____ a book at home.

❷ _____ with her friend.

❸ _____ on the treadmill.

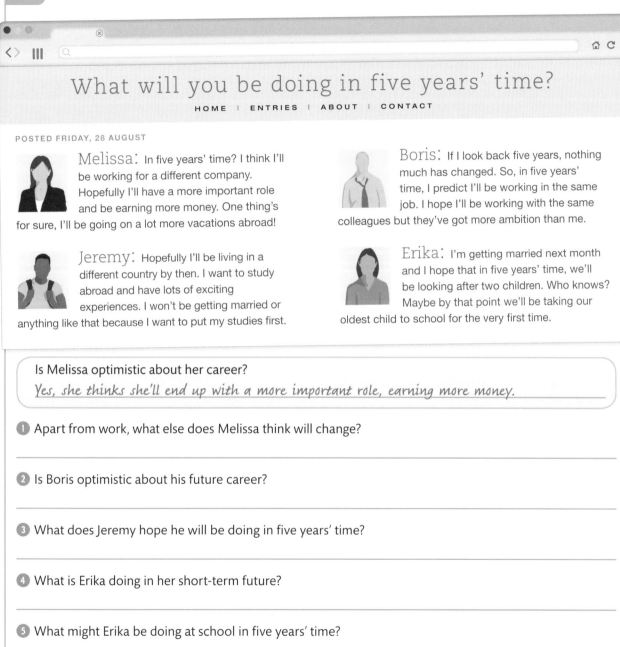

What will you be doing in five years' time?

HOME | ENTRIES | ABOUT | CONTACT

POSTED FRIDAY, 28 AUGUST

Melissa: In five years' time? I think I'll be working for a different company. Hopefully I'll have a more important role and be earning more money. One thing's for sure, I'll be going on a lot more vacations abroad!

Boris: If I look back five years, nothing much has changed. So, in five years' time, I predict I'll be working in the same job. I hope I'll be working with the same colleagues but they've got more ambition than me.

Jeremy: Hopefully I'll be living in a different country by then. I want to study abroad and have lots of exciting experiences. I won't be getting married or anything like that because I want to put my studies first.

Erika: I'm getting married next month and I hope that in five years' time, we'll be looking after two children. Who knows? Maybe by that point we'll be taking our oldest child to school for the very first time.

Is Melissa optimistic about her career?

Yes, she thinks she'll end up with a more important role, earning more money.

❶ Apart from work, what else does Melissa think will change?

_____

❷ Is Boris optimistic about his future career?

_____

❸ What does Jeremy hope he will be doing in five years' time?

_____

❹ What is Erika doing in her short-term future?

_____

❺ What might Erika be doing at school in five years' time?

_____

---

58 ✓ CHECK-LIST

⚙ Le futur continu avec « will » ☐   **Aa** Les demandes polies ☐   🧩 Planifier votre carrière ☐

Le futur perfect

Vous pouvez utiliser le « futur perfect » pour parler d'événements qui vont chevaucher, ou finir avant, un autre événement du futur.

⚙ **Grammaire** Le futur perfect
Aa Vocabulaire Les projets de vie
🧩 **Compétence** Faire des projets et des prédictions

59.1 POINT CLÉ LE FUTUR PERFECT

Vous pouvez utiliser le futur perfect pour dire si une action ou un événement sera terminé avant un certain moment du futur.

They will have built the skyscraper by next year.

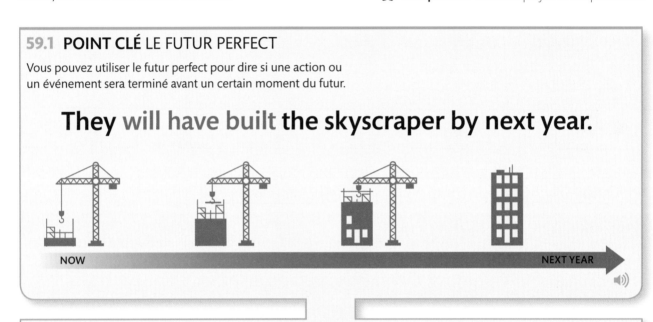

NOW   NEXT YEAR

59.2 AUTRES EXEMPLES LE FUTUR PERFECT

 Cai will have read all his course books by next week.

 **Sam will have finished the laundry by this afternoon.**

59.3 CONSTRUCTION LE FUTUR PERFECT

SUJET	« WILL »	« HAVE »	PARTICIPE PASSÉ	OBJET	RÉFÉRENCE TEMPORELLE
They	will	have	built	the skyscraper	by next year.

59.4 COMPLÉTEZ LES PHRASES EN CONJUGUANT LES VERBES AU FUTUR PERFECT.

By next March, I _____will have bought_____ (buy) my own house.

❶ By the end of the night, I _____ (watch) all the films in the series.

❷ You _____ (experience) so many different things by the time you return.

❸ Dimitri _____ (cycle) around the world by this time next year.

❹ By next year, she _____ (see) all of her favorite bands live.

❺ I hope he _____ (clean) the car by the time he goes to the wedding.

❻ Before I leave tonight, I _____ (finish) all my work.

◀))

59.5 ÉCRIVEZ DES PHRASES AU FUTUR PERFECT POUR DÉCRIRE LES ÉVÉNEMENTS DE LA LIGNE CHRONOLOGIQUE.

GRADUATE	MOVE ABROAD	START A BUSINESS	MARRY SOMEONE	RETIRE
23 YEARS OLD	25 YEARS OLD	30 YEARS OLD	35 YEARS OLD	60 YEARS OLD

By the time I'm 23, _I will have graduated from college._

❶ By the time I'm 25, _____

❷ By the time I'm 30, _____

❸ By the time I'm 35, _____

❹ By the time I'm 60, _____

◀))

59.6 POINT CLÉ LE FUTUR PERFECT CONTINU

Vous pouvez utiliser le futur perfect continu pour prédire la durée d'une activité.
Ce temps permet de regarder en arrière à partir du moment imaginé rdans le futur.

By July, I will have been working here for a year.

LAST JULY → NOW → JULY

59.7 AUTRES EXEMPLES LE FUTUR PERFECT CONTINU

By the time this is all ready, I will have been cooking all day!

By the time I arrive home, I will have been driving for 6 hours.

By this time next month, I will have been learning English for a year!

59.8 CONSTRUCTION LE FUTUR PERFECT CONTINU

RÉFÉRENCE TEMPORELLE	SUJET	« WILL »	« HAVE »	« BEEN »	PARTICIPE PRÉSENT	RESTE DE LA PHRASE
By July,	I	will	have	been	working	here for a year.

59.9 LISEZ LA LETTRE, PUIS BARREZ LES OPTIONS INCORRECTES.

Dear Graham,

By now you will have returned / been returning from your honeymoon. I hope you had a great time! Don't forget that we're having a party for Jane on Saturday. She will have been working / worked here for 20 years on Friday! I hope Frank will have sent / been sending you an email with all the details by the time you get this. I'll see you at the party. I hope you'll have caught / been catching up with all your work by then!

Sian

59.10 ÉCOUTEZ L'ENREGISTREMENT, PUIS COCHEZ LES BONNES RÉPONSES.

C'est le dernier jour de lycée de Jon et Eva. Ils parlent de leurs projets.

Jon and Eva took the same exams at school.
True ☐ **False** ☐ **Not given** ☑

1 Jon will finish his college course before Eva.
True ☐ **False** ☐ **Not given** ☐

2 Jon wants to work for a big marketing agency.
True ☐ **False** ☐ **Not given** ☐

3 Eva hopes to work in a big accountancy firm.
True ☐ **False** ☐ **Not given** ☐

4 Jon says that they could do work for each other.
True ☐ **False** ☐ **Not given** ☐

59.11 ÉCOUTEZ À NOUVEAU, PUIS COCHEZ LE BON RÉSUMÉ.

1 Jon is taking a course in accountancy while Eva is going to study marketing. He wants to run his own business, but she does not. ☐

2 Jon is going to start working now while Eva is going to study accountancy. He wants to run his own business, but she does not. ☐

3 Jon is taking a course in marketing while Eva is going to study accountancy. He wants to run his own business, but she does not. ☐

4 Jon is taking a course in marketing while Eva is going to study accountancy. She wants to run her own business, but he does not. ☐

59 ✓ CHECK-LIST

⚙ Le futur perfect ☐   **Aa** Les projets de vie ☐   🧩 Faire des projets et des prédictions ☐

60 Le futur dans le passé

En anglais, vous pouvez utiliser plusieurs constructions pour décrire les pensées concernant l'avenir qu'une personne a eues à un certain moment du passé.

⚙️ **Grammaire** « Would » et « was going to »
Aa Vocabulaire Changer ses plans
🧩 **Compétence** Dire ce que vous pensiez

60.1 POINT CLÉ LE FUTUR DANS LE PASSÉ AVEC « WOULD »

Là où vous utiliseriez « will » pour parler d'un événement futur à partir du présent, vous utilisez « would » pour parler de votre point de vue passé sur cet événement.

EARLIER   NOW

I think I will finish the gardening today. It shouldn't take too long.

I thought I would finish today, but there is still a lot left to do. 🔊

 60.2 BARREZ LES MOTS INCORRECTS DANS CHAQUE PHRASE.

I thought I ~~will~~ / would go to France last summer, but I didn't. I will / ~~would~~ go next year instead.

1 David said that he will / would try to get me a ticket to the game, but he doesn't / didn't manage to.

2 I would / will buy the movie on DVD. I thought I will / would see it at the movie theater, but I didn't.

3 Last year she thought she will / would be promoted, but she wasn't. Maybe next year she would / will be.

4 I bring / brought all the food for the picnic because I knew that Tom won't / wouldn't remember.

5 We knew that the concert will / would be amazing, so we buy / bought really good tickets.

6 My brother promised that he won't / wouldn't show anyone pictures of me when I was / were little.

60.3 POINT CLÉ LE FUTUR DANS LE PASSÉ AVEC « WAS GOING TO »

Là où vous utiliseriez « going to » pour parler d'un événement futur à partir du présent, vous utilisez « was/were going to » pour parler de votre point de vue passé sur cet événement.

EARLIER   NOW

This traffic is awful! I think I'm going to be late for work.

I thought I was going to be late, but I'm right on time.

60.4 COCHEZ LES PHRASES CORRECTES.

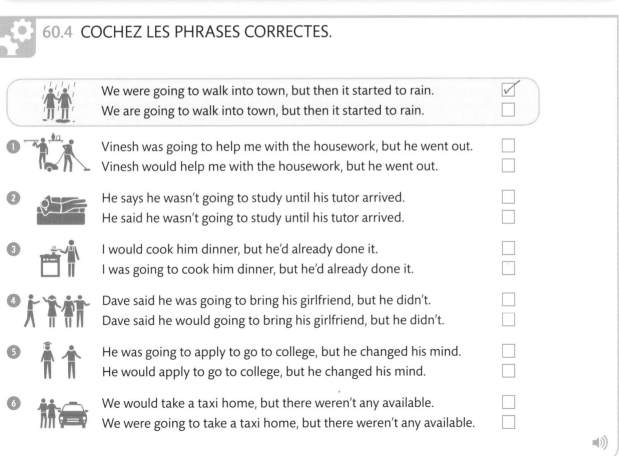

We were going to walk into town, but then it started to rain.	☑
We are going to walk into town, but then it started to rain.	☐

① Vinesh was going to help me with the housework, but he went out. ☐
Vinesh would help me with the housework, but he went out. ☐

② He says he wasn't going to study until his tutor arrived. ☐
He said he wasn't going to study until his tutor arrived. ☐

③ I would cook him dinner, but he'd already done it. ☐
I was going to cook him dinner, but he'd already done it. ☐

④ Dave said he was going to bring his girlfriend, but he didn't. ☐
Dave said he would going to bring his girlfriend, but he didn't. ☐

⑤ He was going to apply to go to college, but he changed his mind. ☐
He would apply to go to college, but he changed his mind. ☐

⑥ We would take a taxi home, but there weren't any available. ☐
We were going to take a taxi home, but there weren't any available. ☐

231

60.5 POINT CLÉ LE FUTUR DANS LE PASSÉ AVEC LE PASSÉ CONTINU

Vous pouvez aussi utiliser le passé continu pour parler
d'un événement futur organisé à un moment du passé.

LAST MONDAY MORNING   LAST MONDAY AFTERNOON   NOW

**Jenny was extremely nervous on Monday morning.
She was taking her driving test that afternoon.**

60.6 METTEZ LES PHRASES AU PASSÉ, PUIS LISEZ-LES À VOIX HAUTE.

They are thinking of telling him the good news about his job.

They were thinking of telling him the good news about his job.

① Sarah is planning to take her children to the park on Tuesday.

② Peter's nervous because he's meeting his girlfriend's parents.

③ I am planning to go out that evening because my parents are having guests over.

④ We can't make it to the party on Friday because we're visiting some friends that day.

⑤ I'm planning to book a vacation just after the New Year.

60.7 ÉCOUTEZ L'ENREGISTREMENT, PUIS INDIQUEZ CE QUI S'EST RÉELLEMENT PASSÉ.

60 ✓ CHECK-LIST

⚙️ « Would » et « was going to » ☐   **Aa** Changer ses plans ☐   🧩 Dire ce que vous pensiez ☐

🔄 BILAN L'ANGLAIS QUE VOUS AVEZ APPRIS DANS LES CHAPITRES 57-60

NOUVEAU POINT LINGUISTIQUE	EXEMPLE TYPE	☑	CHAPITRE
« WISH » POUR LES ESPOIRS	I wish I could move somewhere warm. She wishes her teacher would give her less work.	☐	57.1
LE FUTUR CONTINU AVEC « WILL »	In five years' time I will be working in a restaurant.	☐	58.1
LE FUTUR CONTINU COMME INCIDENCE NATURELLE	I'll be driving past the store anyway. Will you be coming into work tomorrow?	☐	58.6 58.7
LE FUTUR CONTINU POUR PARLER DU PRÉSENT	He'll be working on his presentation by now.	☐	58.11
LE FUTUR PERFECT	Cai will have read all his course books by next week.	☐	59.1
LE FUTUR PERFECT CONTINU	In September, I will have been working here for a year.	☐	59.6
LE FUTUR DANS LE PASSÉ	I thought I would finish the gardening today. I thought I was going to be late.	☐	60.1, 60.3, 60.5

61.1 L'ART ET LA CULTURE

Reviews can have a big **influence** on a film's success.

influence
[the effect someone or something has]

The documentary **inspired** me to start painting.

inspire
[give somebody the enthusiasm to do something they may not have done otherwise]

Mary was **strongly influenced by** his speech.

strongly influenced by something
[greatly affected by something or somebody]

I can **highly recommend** the new restaurant.

highly recommend
[say that something is very good and tell others about it]

The reviewers always **heap praise on** him.

heap praise / criticism on something
[say that something is extremely good / bad]

I was so **engrossed in** the book that I didn't hear the phone.

be engrossed in something
[be extremely absorbed in something]

Make up your mind, do you prefer the red or black one?

make up your mind
[finally make a decision]

I chose the red one, but then I **changed my mind**.

change your mind
[alter or change a decision or feeling about something]

I know you're a vegetarian and will **bear it in mind** when I cook.

bear something in mind
[hold something in consideration when doing or thinking about something else]

Don't be afraid to **speak your mind**.

speak your mind
[say what you feel, even if it is controversial]

We have candles to help create a romantic atmosphere.

create an atmosphere
[to set a particular mood or tone]

This opera is a bit too highbrow for me. I prefer movies.

highbrow / lowbrow
[complicated / simple artistic or cultural ideas]

The movie's plot was too complicated to understand.

plot
[the series of events that makes up the story in a book, film, or play]

My favorite character was the funny best friend.

characters
[the fictional people in a book, film, or play]

I really enjoyed the opening scene of the play.

opening / closing scenes
[the first / last moments of a book, film, or play]

The dramatic chain of events was almost unbelievable.

chain of events
[a sequence of causes and effects]

Have you seen the latest TV drama about firefighters?

drama
[a play, movie, television show, or radio show about a serious subject]

I like to relax by reading romance novels.

novels
[long, written stories that are fictional]

The book left a lasting impression on me. It was incredible.

lasting impression
[a feeling or effect that lasts a long time]

The new film has had glowing reviews from all the critics.

glowing reviews
[very positive reviews]

62 Omettre des mots

Il peut être utile d'éviter les répétitions, lorsque vous voulez communiquer clairement. Pour cela, vous pouvez supprimer tous les mots inutiles.

⚙ **Grammaire** L'ellipse
Aa Vocabulaire Les divertissements
🧩 **Compétence** Omettre les mots inutiles

62.1 POINT CLÉ L'ELLIPSE

Si le sens d'une phrase est clair à partir de son contexte, vous pouvez utiliser l'ellipse (omettre certains mots) pour éviter les répétitions.
Ce procédé est plus courant après « and », « but » et « or ».
Vous pouvez parfois omettre un verbe répété à une forme différente.

He bought tickets, but [he] didn't go.

Un sujet répété est souvent omis après « and », « but » et « or ».

She loved the original and [she loved] the sequel.

Si le sens reste clair, un sujet et un verbe répétés peuvent être omis.

I'm happy to go out or [I'm happy to] stay home.

De manière générale, vous pouvez omettre les mots qui ont déjà été mentionnés et qui ne nécessitent pas de répétition.

🔊

 62.2 COMPLÉTEZ LES PHRASES AVEC LES MOTS QUI ONT ÉTÉ OMIS.

I told him I would book the tickets, but I haven't [_booked the tickets_] yet.

1 They wanted to see the band perform live, but now they can't [_____].

2 He was fantastic in the television series and [_____] the movie adaptation.

3 If you want to see a movie we could go to the multiplex or [_____] the art house.

4 The reviews said that the acting was bad and [_____] the soundtrack was terrible.

5 The two lead actors did all the stunts and [_____] sang all the songs themselves.

6 I am quitting my job this week. I will call you later to explain why [_____].

🔊

62.3 LISEZ L'ARTICLE, PUIS COCHEZ LES BONNES RÉPONSES.

> *Marine Blue* was directed by Fay Little.
> **True** ☐ **False** ☑

1. The reviewer thinks the film will be a success.
   True ☐ **False** ☐

2. The plot in the film was unusual and exciting to follow.
   True ☐ **False** ☐

3. The special effects in *Marine Blue* were not very good.
   True ☐ **False** ☐

4. The plot of *Death Reviewed* was not very exciting.
   True ☐ **False** ☐

5. *Death Reviewed* was emotional and extremely moving.
   True ☐ **False** ☐

THIS WEEK'S NEW OPENINGS

Find out what to see (and what to avoid) this week.

The new film starring Fay Little will surely be another box office hit for director Lee Jones. Thriller *Marine Blue* is released on Thursday and brings back characters Max and Alice. The plot was original and surprising, although some elements may prove highly controversial. *Marine Blue* was heavily subsidised, but the money was incredibly well spent as the visual effects and soundtrack are stunning. A must see!

The new play *Death Reviewed* is supposed to be a tragedy. It is just tragic. Terrible acting, painfully slow dialogue, and a completely predictable plot make it a disaster. The play did leave me deeply moved, but only because the ticket prices were so astronomically high! Bitterly disappointed.

Aa **62.4 COMPLÉTEZ LES PHRASES AVEC LES MOTS DE LA LISTE.**

The film was very dull and the plot was [painfully *slow*].

1. I knew that the family would turn out to be aliens. It was [completely].

2. I was so [deeply] by the sad scenes that I cried for hours!

3. We loved the last film, but were [bitterly] by this one.

4. We waited too long! The ticket prices are now [astronomically].

5. The plot is shocking and the theme is [controversial].

6. The government helped pay for the film. It was [subsidized].

| predictable | moved | ~~slow~~ | heavily | highly | high | disappointed |

62.5 BARREZ LES MOTS QUI PEUVENT ÊTRE SUPPRIMÉS DE LA PHRASE.

He might have been in the original film or ~~he might have been in~~ the remake.

1. I was planning to buy tickets for the show, but now I can't buy tickets for the show.

2. The film had great special effects and the film had a wonderful soundtrack.

3. He was chosen for the orchestra and he played brilliantly.

4. This evening I'm going to have dinner and then I'm going to watch a play.

5. They said that they would come to the launch party, but they haven't come to the launch party.

6. They should join in or they should not bother coming.

62.6 RELIEZ LE DÉBUT DE CHAQUE PHRASE À LA FIN QUI LUI CORRESPOND.

He has always made thrillers and	doesn't have very good acoustics.
1. The actors were good, but	ends just after midnight.
2. The performance starts at 8 and	full of young children!
3. You could buy a season ticket or	he always will.
4. The building is beautiful, but	very satisfied with the performance.
5. The cast are all exhausted, but	sign up for membership.
6. The audience was very loud and	seemed uncomfortable on screen.

62.7 POINT CLÉ L'ELLIPSE CONVERSATIONNELLE

Vous pouvez également omettre des mots dans les phrases qui n'incluent pas « and », « but » ou « or », si le sens peut être déduit du contexte. Ce type d'ellipse n'a pas de règles strictes, et est très courant dans le discours informel, notamment dans les réponses.

What time does the movie start?

Eight.

[It starts at eight o'clock.]

What kind of popcorn would you like?

Salted, please.

[I would like salted popcorn, please.]

What did you think of the film?

Complete nonsense.

[I thought the film was complete nonsense.]

62.8 ÉCOUTEZ L'ENREGISTREMENT, PUIS NUMÉROTEZ LES PHRASES DANS L'ORDRE DANS LEQUEL VOUS ENTENDEZ LEUR FORME COURTE.

Ⓐ "Good evening." ☐

Ⓑ "No, it's a horror film." ☐

Ⓒ "I think that it's better than the book version." ☐

Ⓓ "I'd like two seats, please." ☐

Ⓔ "Is this film a drama?" ☐ 1

Ⓕ "So, what did you think of the film?" ☐

Ⓖ "Are you sure about that?" ☐

---

62 ✓ CHECK-LIST

⚙ L'ellipse ☐   **Aa** Les divertissements ☐   🧩 Omettre les mots inutiles ☐

63 Substituer des mots

De même qu'avec les ellipses (omission de mots), vous pouvez éviter de vous répéter en remplaçant certaines phrases par des phrases plus courtes. On appelle ce procédé la substitution.

⚙ **Grammaire** La substitution
Aa Vocabulaire Les livres et la lecture
🧩 **Compétence** Remplacer des phrases

63.1 POINT CLÉ SUBSTITUER AVEC « ONE/ONES » ET « SOME »

On peut utiliser « one » et « ones » pour remplacer des noms dénombrables singuliers et pluriels. Pour employer « ones », vous devez faire référence à un groupe spécifique. Utilisez « some » lorsque le groupe n'est pas défini.

NOMS DÉNOMBRABLES SINGULIERS

Does anyone have a copy of the book?

Yes, I have one.

« One » remplace « a copy of the book ».

NOMS DÉNOMBRABLES PLURIEL

Are there any bookstores near here?

Yes, there are some on Main Street.

There are a few great ones across town.

« Ones » ne peut être utilisé que si vous le modifiez pour définir les choses spécifiques dont vous parlez.

63.2 BARREZ LES MOTS INCORRECTS DANS CHAQUE PHRASE.

 He's such a great writer. I think his best novels are the later ~~one~~ / ones / ~~some~~.

 ❶ The book with the long title is the one / ones / some I wanted.

 ❷ The buildings in New York were taller than the one / ones / some in Paris.

 ❸ If you still want a copy of that book, there are one / ones / some over here.

 ❹ If you need an umbrella, I can lend you one / ones / some.

 ❺ Have you seen her new sunglasses? The one / ones / some with the silver frames?

63.3 RELIEZ LE DÉBUT DE CHAQUE PHRASE À LA FIN QUI LUI CORRESPOND.

I have a few recommendations

1. They bought me a signed copy,
2. I think the most engrossing novels
3. If you want to join a book club,
4. I know you want to buy a new car,
5. If you need a plastic bag,

are the ones about spies.

there are some in the box over there.

make sure it's one with regular meetings.

if you want some.

but the one we have is only a year old.

but I already had one.

🔊

63.4 COMPLÉTEZ LES PHRASES AVEC « ONE », « ONES » OU « SOME ».

BookCon review notes

Black Glasses is Martin Owens' fourth book in this series. Like the third book, this ___one___ is all about the brilliant detective Amanda Brook. Unlike the other _____ in the series though, this time her personal life starts falling apart. Excellent plot as usual.

I have read some boring books in my time, but Sara Umborne's Pink Tree is the dullest _____ ever. Sadly, I can't tell you much about the book as I gave up after 20 pages.

Little Water Princess is a fabulous book for little children, or even older _____ ! There are few words, but the illustrations are beautiful. Lots of the pictures pop up, but _____ are 2D. A lovely gift idea.

There are endless books about cooking pasta, but How to Cook Pasta by Daniela Capril is the best _____ on the market today.

63.5 POINT CLÉ SUBSTITUER AVEC « DO »

Pour éviter des répétitions, vous pouvez aussi remplacer des verbes et leur(s) complément(s) par des mots. On utilise souvent « do » et « did » pour remplacer les verbes au présent et au prétérite par exemple.

Des formes différentes de « do » remplacant « think ».

I think this homework is really difficult.

I did too, so I asked for help.

I don't. It's easy.

63.6 COCHEZ LES PHRASES CORRECTES.

I don't read much, but my dad does read. ☐
I don't read much, but my dad does. ☑

1 I didn't like it, but my friend did. ☐
I didn't like it, but my friend liked. ☐

2 Did you go to the show? We did go. ☐
Did you go to the show? We did, too. ☐

3 You read a lot last month. I did, too. ☐
You read a lot last month. I do, too. ☐

4 Do I recycle? Yes, I do. ☐
Do I recycle? Yes, I did. ☐

5 He works hard, but she doesn't. ☐
He works hard, but she isn't. ☐

63.7 ÉCOUTEZ L'ENREGISTREMENT, PUIS COCHEZ LES BONNES RÉPONSES.

Deux amis, Deborah et Clive, sont dans une librairie.
Écoutez-les discuter des livres disponibles.

Deborah has Nadine Hussein's new cookbook. **True** ☐ **False** ☑

1 Clive thinks more cookbooks should be written. **True** ☐ **False** ☐

2 Clive thinks Deborah does not bake at home. **True** ☐ **False** ☐

3 Clive is going to Rome the following weekend. **True** ☐ **False** ☐

4 Clive prefers guidebooks with lots of pictures. **True** ☐ **False** ☐

5 Deborah is going to help Clive choose some novels. **True** ☐ **False** ☐

6 Clive believes that Deborah is going to bake later. **True** ☐ **False** ☐

63.8 POINT CLÉ SUBSTITUER AVEC « SO » ET « NOT »

Vous pouvez utiliser « so »
pour éviter une répétition
dans les phrases affirmatives
après les verbes de la pensée.
Utilisez « not » ou « not... so »
dans les phrases négatives.

Will she be signing copies of her book?

No, I don't think so.

I'm afraid not.

I hope so!

63.9 AUTRES EXEMPLES SUBSTITUER LES PHRASES NÉGATIVES
AVEC « NOT... SO » ET « NOT »

Utilisez « not... so » avec « think »,
« believe », « expect » et « imagine ».

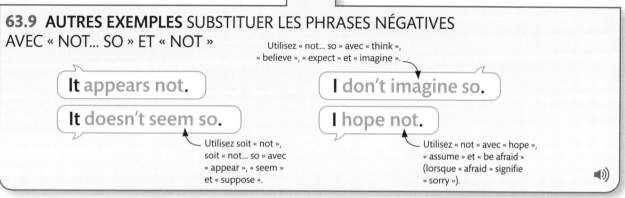

It appears not.

It doesn't seem so.

I don't imagine so.

I hope not.

Utilisez soit « not »,
soit « not... so » avec
« appear », « seem »
et « suppose ».

Utilisez « not » avec « hope »,
« assume » et « be afraid »
(lorsque « afraid » signifie
« sorry »).

63.10 RÉPONDEZ AUX QUESTIONS DE L'ENREGISTREMENT EN UTILISANT DES SUBSTITUTIONS, PUIS LISEZ LES PHRASES À VOIX HAUTE.

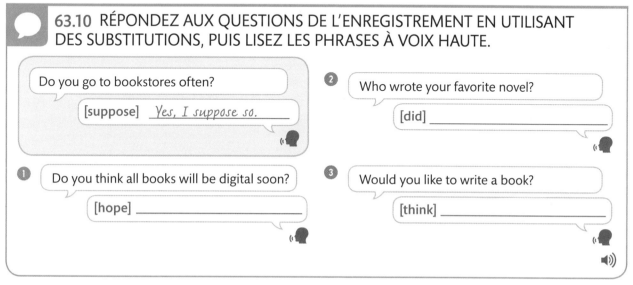

Do you go to bookstores often?

[suppose] _Yes, I suppose so._

2 Who wrote your favorite novel?

[did] _____

1 Do you think all books will be digital soon?

[hope] _____

3 Would you like to write a book?

[think] _____

64 Réduire les propositions infinitives

En plus de l'ellipse et de la substitution, vous pouvez réduire les propositions infinitives pour éviter des répétitions. Ce procédé vous permettra de parler anglais de façon plus naturelle.

⚙ Grammaire Réduire les propositions infinitives
Aa Vocabulaire La musique et le monde du spectacle
🧩 Compétence Éviter les répétitions

64.1 POINT CLÉ RÉDUIRE LES PROPOSITIONS INFINITIVES

Vous pouvez utiliser « to » seul plutôt que de répéter l'intégralité de la proposition infinitive. Vous ne pouvez employer ce procédé que si le sens de la phrase reste clair.

Let's go to see that new DJ tonight.

I don't really want to [go to see the new DJ].

Si la phrase ou proposition précédente contient le verbe « be », vous devez alors utiliser « be » dans la phrase ou proposition suivante.

She was really critical of the new album.

It's difficult not to be [critical of it]. The singing is awful!

🔊

 64.2 BARREZ TOUS LES MOTS QUE VOUS POUVEZ SUPPRIMER.

> I want to get the best tickets for the show, but can't afford to ~~get them~~.

1 I tried to contact Max about the concert tickets, but wasn't able to contact him.

2 My brother often forgets our dad's birthday, but this year he's promised not to forget.

3 Georgia was enjoying the performance. At least, she seemed to be enjoying it.

4 Ian is going to the new nightclub, but I don't really want to go to there.

5 The festival tickets cost a lot more than they used to cost.

6 I want to come with you, but I won't be able to come with you.

🔊

64.3 POINT CLÉ OMETTRE L'INTÉGRALITÉ DE LA PROPOSITION INFINITIVE

Vous pouvez omettre l'intégralité de la proposition infinitive,
ou ne conserver que « to » après certains verbes, tels que « agree »,
« ask », « forget », « promise », « start » et « try ».

Chris is going to come to the show. He $\begin{cases} \text{promised [to come]} \\ \text{promised to [come]} \end{cases}$ **.**

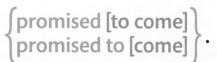

Vous pouvez aussi omettre l'intégralité de la proposition infinitive
ou n'utiliser que « to » après certains noms comme « chance »,
« plans », « promise », « idea » et « opportunity ».

I haven't seen this band before. I'd love the $\begin{cases} \text{chance [to see them]} \\ \text{chance to [see them]} \end{cases}$ **.**

C'est aussi possible après certains adjectifs tels que
« delighted », « afraid », « willing » et « determined ».

I want to perform on stage, but I'm $\begin{cases} \text{afraid [to perform on stage]} \\ \text{afraid to [perform on stage]} \end{cases}$ **.**

🔊

64.4 ÉCOUTEZ L'ENREGISTREMENT, PUIS COCHEZ LES BONNES RÉPONSES.

Deux étudiants discutent de l'apprentissage d'instruments de musique.

Luca has a double bass in his case.
True ☐ **False** ☑

1 Luca says the cello is harder to play than the guitar.
True ☐ **False** ☐

2 Tanya plays the trumpet now.
True ☐ **False** ☐

3 Luca will be joining a new orchestra next week.
True ☐ **False** ☐

4 Luca was confident about his orchestra audition.
True ☐ **False** ☐

5 Tanya is a member of the college orchestra.
True ☐ **False** ☐

6 Tanya cannot audition again.
True ☐ **False** ☐

7 Tanya and Luca have played together before.
True ☐ **False** ☐

64.5 POINT CLÉ LES VERBES AVEC COMPLÉMENTS

Vous ne pouvez pas omettre l'intégralité d'une proposition infinitive après les verbes qui nécessitent des compléments (des éléments qui complètent leur sens) tels que : « advise », « afford », « be able », « choose », « decide », « expect », « hate », « hope », « love », « need » et « prefer ». Après ceux-ci, vous devez conserver le « to ».

We want to see a band tonight, but we really can't afford to.

64.6 AUTRES EXEMPLES LES VERBES AVEC COMPLÉMENTS

 I tried to get to the front of the crowd, but I wasn't able to.

 I had piano lessons as a child, but I didn't choose to.

 You could bring some snacks along, but you don't need to.

 I have never been to the opera, but I would love to.

64.7 COMPLÉTEZ LES PHRASES AVEC LES MOTS DE LA LISTE.

I asked my sister to sing with me and she said she'd be _____*delighted*_____ .

1 I would like to read music, but it will be a long time until I'm _____ to.

2 Don't forget that it's supposed to rain tonight. Try to leave before it _____ .

3 Some people aren't nervous about performing, but I'm too _____ to.

4 Some artists don't like to have family in the audience on the first night, but I _____ to.

5 It's such a shame. I would absolutely love to see him sing, but cannot _____ to.

6 I've seen other artists who love talking to the audience, but I _____ to.

7 You don't need to worry. I will come along to all of your recitals. I _____ .

| afford | starts | ~~delighted~~ | promise | afraid | prefer | hate | able |

64.8 POINT CLÉ « WANT » ET « WOULD LIKE »

On conserve habituellement le « to » plutôt que d'omettre l'intégralité de l'infinitif après « want » ou « would like ».

He asked if I wanted to go, and I said I would like to.

Toutefois, dans les propositions avec « if », vous pouvez souvent utiliser « to » seul ou omettre l'intégralité de l'infinitif après « want » ou « would like ».

You can come with us if you { want / want to } **.**

Il faut conserver le « to » si la proposition est négative.

Don't go to the concert if you don't want to.

64.9 COCHEZ LES PHRASES CORRECTES.

Thanks for the offer! I would really like to. ☑
Thanks for the offer! I would really like. ☐

1. I asked him to come, but he didn't want. ☐
   I asked him to come, but he didn't want to. ☐

2. You can have one if you want. ☐
   You can have one if you do. ☐

3. You can stay, but I don't really want to. ☐
   You can stay, but I don't really want. ☐

4. If you're free to meet, I would still like to. ☐
   If you're free to meet, I would still like. ☐

5. You can call me "Sam" if you want to call. ☐
   You can call me "Sam" if you want. ☐

64.10 RÉPONDEZ AUX QUESTIONS DE L'ENREGISTREMENT, PUIS LISEZ LES PHRASES À VOIX HAUTE.

Will you record my performance tonight?

Yes, _I promise._ (promise)

1. Are you going to sell your CD collection?

   No, _____ (decide)

2. Will you practice every day?

   Yes, _____ (try)

3. Would you like to come to the concert?

   Yes, but _____ (afford)

---

64 ✓ CHECK-LIST

⚙ Réduire les propositions infinitives ☐   **Aa** La musique et le monde du spectacle ☐   🧩 Éviter les répétitions ☐

65 Décrire des réactions

Bien que les marqueurs rhétoriques n'aient pas souvent de contenu sémantique, ils peuvent rendre la conversation plus fluide et apporter un complément d'information concernant l'opinion du locuteur.

⚙ **Grammaire** Les marqueurs rhétoriques informels
Aa Vocabulaire Les préfixes niveau avancé
🧩 **Compétence** Structurer une conversation

65.1 POINT CLÉ LES MARQUEURS RHÉTORIQUES INFORMELS COURANTS

CONSEIL
N'oubliez pas de tenir compte du langage du corps, qui peut communiquer des messages supplémentaires lorsque vous parlez à quelqu'un face à face.

Utilisez « actually » pour corriger un malentendu ou une attente erronée.

I don't think this painting is worth that much.

Actually, it sold at auction for $2 million.

Wow! Do you like it?

I don't, actually. It's not very impressive.

Utilisez « by the way » pour indiquer que vous changez de sujet.

I think this one is fantastic, too.
Oh, by the way, did you read the article about the painter in *The Times*?

Utilisez « as I was saying » pour revenir à un sujet abordé précédemment, après un changement de sujet ou une interruption.

As I was saying, this is a fantastic painting. I really like the way the sea is painted.

Utilisez « anyway » pour revenir à un sujet après une interruption, un changement de sujet, ou pour clore un sujet ou une conversation.

Anyway, I should say goodbye. I want to visit the gallery shop before it closes.

65.2 BARREZ LES MOTS QUI CONVIENNENT LE MOINS DANS CHAQUE PHRASE.

 I know you say he's talentless, but actually / ~~by the way~~ this is a very impressive sculpture.

1 These gardens are fabulous. Did you bring your camera, as I was saying / by the way ?

2 Yes, but by the way / as I was saying before, I really think I could paint that myself.

3 No, I don't hate all modern art. I actually / as I was saying really like some street art.

4 Anyway / Actually, to get back to my question, would you pay two million dollars for that?

5 These paintings aren't the reason I come here. I anyway / actually prefer the architecture.

65.3 RÉPONDEZ AUX QUESTIONS DE L'ENREGISTREMENT EN UTILISANT LES MARQUEURS RHÉTORIQUES QUI CONVIENNENT LE MIEUX, PUIS LISEZ LES PHRASES À VOIX HAUTE.

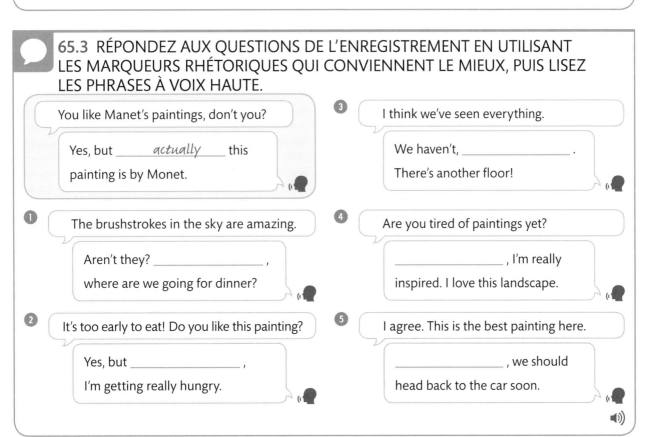

You like Manet's paintings, don't you?

Yes, but ___*actually*___ this painting is by Monet.

1 The brushstrokes in the sky are amazing.

Aren't they? _____, where are we going for dinner?

2 It's too early to eat! Do you like this painting?

Yes, but _____, I'm getting really hungry.

3 I think we've seen everything.

We haven't, _____. There's another floor!

4 Are you tired of paintings yet?

_____, I'm really inspired. I love this landscape.

5 I agree. This is the best painting here.

_____, we should head back to the car soon.

65.4 LISEZ L'ARTICLE, PUIS COCHEZ LES BONNES RÉPONSES.

The show is by well-known established artists.
True ☐ **False** ☑

1 The first room in the show contained paintings.
True ☐ **False** ☐

2 There is a small room before the second room.
True ☐ **False** ☐

3 There were many artists in the second room.
True ☐ **False** ☐

4 The young performer will make you happy.
True ☐ **False** ☐

5 The final room makes you feel very relaxed.
True ☐ **False** ☐

6 The reviewer recommends the exhibition.
True ☐ **False** ☐

ART SCENE

Dean Hill Art School Exhibition

The opening of the Dean Hill Art Exhibition highlighted the mix of influences on these creative final-year students. The paintings in the first room were clearly inspired by classical artists and the more modern neoclassical movement.

From this more traditional first room, you are led to a small anteroom to wait for the next "performance." You are then taken to a dark room with lots of

ropes hanging from the ceiling. Without giving too much away for future visitors to the show, you will see a young boy dressed in blue and red and you will laugh and probably be reminded of a certain superhero.

The next room was another complete change. This time an angry antisocial woman made us all feel very uncomfortable with the idea of progress in a modern world. It was a typical postmodern performance.

A hugely varied exhibition by talented, proactive artists. Well worth a visit.

Aa 65.5 RELIEZ LE DÉBUT DE CHAQUE PHRASE À LA FIN QUI LUI CORRESPOND.

"Ante-" and "pre-" as in "anteroom" and "preschool"

1 "Super-" as in "superhero" and "supernatural"

2 "Anti-" as in "antisocial" and "antibiotics"

3 "Pro-" as in "proactive" and "proceed"

4 "Neo-" as in "neoclassical" and "neoliberal"

5 "Post-" as in "postmodern" and "postwar"

means "beyond."

means "for."

means "after."

mean "before."

means "against."

means "new."

◀))

65.6 COMPLÉTEZ LES PHRASES AVEC LES PRÉFIXES DE LA LISTE.

To find a career in your field, you need to be very ___pro_active.

1 Many children go to _____school before they are five years old.

2 My husband is 40 years old, but he still loves _____hero comics and films.

3 A lot of the architecture here is _____classical and looks Roman.

4 I think that dropping litter in public is extremely _____social.

5 Before the ceremony began, we were told to wait in a small _____room.

6 Many 20th-century art movements have been called _____modern.

| post | pre | anti | neo | super | ante | ~~pro~~ |

◀))

---

65 ✓ CHECK-LIST

⚙ Les marqueurs rhétoriques informels ☐   **Aa** Les préfixes niveau avancé ☐   🧩 Structurer une conversation ☐

↻ BILAN L'ANGLAIS QUE VOUS AVEZ APPRIS DANS LES CHAPITRES 62-65

NOUVEAU POINT LINGUISTIQUE	EXEMPLE TYPE	☑	CHAPITRE
L'ELLIPSE	She went to see the play and loved it. Seen the film?	☐	62.1, 62.5
SUBSTITUER AVEC « ONE/ONES » ET « SOME »	Do you need a pencil? I have one. Would you like a cookie? There are some left.	☐	63.1, 63.3
SUBSTITUER AVEC « DO » ET « SO »	You read a lot last month. I did, too. Is Mary going to come? I hope so.	☐	63.5, 63.7
RÉDUIRE LES PROPOSITIONS INFINITIVES OU LES OMETTRE	I don't really want to. I asked her to buy me tickets and she agreed.	☐	64.1, 64.3
LES VERBES AVEC COMPLÉMENTS	We want to see our friend's band play, but can't afford to.	☐	64.5
LES MARQUEURS RHÉTORIQUES INFORMELS	Actually, it sold at auction for $2 million.	☐	65.1

66 Réaliser ses projets

Vous voudrez parfois parler de personnes qui font des choses pour vous. Pour cela, vous devrez utiliser une construction différente.

⚙ **Grammaire** « Have/get something done »
Aa Vocabulaire Les services et les réparations
🧩 **Compétence** Décrire ce que d'autres personnes font pour vous

66.1 POINT CLÉ « HAVE/GET SOMETHING DONE »

Utilisez « have » ou « get » suivi d'un nom et un participe passé pour parler de quelque chose que quelqu'un fait pour vous. « Get » est moins formel que « have ».

Did you get your computer updated?

[Did somebody update your computer for you?]

Yes, the company has the computers updated regularly.

[Yes, somebody regularly updates them for the company.]

🔊

66.2 AUTRES EXEMPLES « HAVE/GET SOMETHING DONE »

Utilisez la construction avec « should » pour donner un conseil.

You should get your connection checked.

[I think you should arrange for someone to check your connection.]

Will you get the oven fixed soon?

[Will somebody fix the oven for you soon?]

They haven't had the locks changed yet.

[They haven't arranged for somebody to change the locks for them.]

The store has its produce checked daily.

[Somebody checks the store's produce each day.]

🔊

66.3 CONSTRUCTION « HAVE/GET SOMETHING DONE »

Modifiez la forme de « have » et de « get » pour utiliser les différents temps des formes simples et continues. Modifiez ces verbes pour changer de temps. L'action porte sur l'objet.

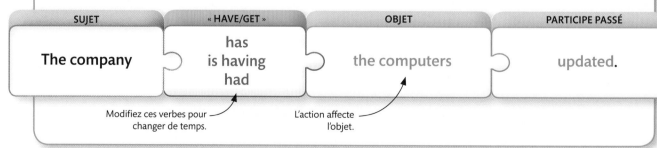

SUJET	« HAVE/GET »	OBJET	PARTICIPE PASSÉ
The company	has is having had	the computers	updated.

Modifiez ces verbes pour changer de temps.

L'action affecte l'objet.

Jane is repairing her car. ☑
Jane is getting her car repaired. ☐

Ahmed has been fixing his oven. ☐
Ahmed is getting his oven fixed. ☐

Sally's having her nails painted. ☐
Sally's painting her own nails. ☐

Natasha got her photograph taken. ☐
Natasha took a photograph. ☐

Gavin is getting his hair cut. ☐
Gavin is cutting his hair. ☐

Joe did the ironing at home. ☐
Joe had the ironing done at the mall. ☐

Annie is delivering some flowers. ☐
Annie had some flowers delivered. ☐

They're having their house painted. ☐
They're painting their own house. ☐

66.5 RELIEZ LE DÉBUT DE CHAQUE PHRASE À LA FIN QUI LUI CORRESPOND.

We're getting our furniture — replaced at the moment.

① I'm taking the car to — the garage to get it fixed.

② You should go to a salon — and have your hair cut.

③ I don't want to cook. Should we — get a pizza delivered?

④ They've just had their staff — trained to deal with malware.

⑤ I'm going to have my computer — checked for malware. It's so slow.

⑥ I took my daughter to the dentist — to get her teeth checked.

⑦ They bought a dog and had — a deluxe kennel built for him.

Fins de phrases disponibles :
- and have your hair cut.
- to get her teeth checked.
- trained to deal with malware.
- replaced at the moment.
- checked for malware. It's so slow.
- the garage to get it fixed.
- a deluxe kennel built for him.
- get a pizza delivered?

🔊

66.6 RÉCRIVEZ LES PHRASES EN CORRIGEANT LES ERREURS.

When are we going to get repaired the TV?
When are we going to get the TV repaired?

① Remember, today we're have the bedroom carpets fitted.

_____

② Your coat is really filthy. It should get you dry-cleaned.

_____

③ My eyes hurt when I read. I should had them tested soon.

_____

④ My friend has his wallet stolen when he was in Barcelona.

_____

⑤ I get to have my birth certificate translated into Spanish for my application.

_____

🔊

66.7 RÉPONDEZ AUX QUESTIONS DE L'ENREGISTREMENT AVEC « HAVE/GET », PUIS LISEZ LES PHRASES À VOIX HAUTE.

Is that Maria over there in the salon?

Yes, _she's getting her hair cut_ (she / her hair / cut).

❶ Does Jacob clean the house himself?

No, _____ (he / it / clean) by someone else.

❷ Why is Anneke putting on make-up?

The photographer's here. _____ (she / her picture / take).

❸ Is your oven still broken?

Yes, but _____ (I / it / fix) on Monday.

❹ Why is all your furniture covered?

The painter's coming. _____ (we / the house / paint).

❺ Are you going to make dinner tonight?

No, _____ (I / a pizza / deliver).

❻ Do you go to the dentist regularly?

Yes, _____ (I / my teeth / check) twice a year.

❼ Do you go to the store for your newspaper?

No, _____ (we / it / deliver) to the house.

---

66 ✓ CHECK-LIST

✿ « Have/get something done » ☐ **Aa** Les services et les réparations ☐ ⟆ Décrire ce que d'autres personnes font pour vous ☐

67 Les accords complexes

L'un des principes fondamentaux de la langue anglaise est que les sujets et les verbes doivent s'accorder. Néanmoins, certains sujets peuvent se comporter comme des noms singuliers ou pluriels en fonction du contexte.

⚙ Grammaire Les accords complexes
Aa Vocabulaire Les noms collectifs
🧩 Compétence Utiliser l'accord correct

67.1 POINT CLÉ LES NOMS COLLECTIFS

Les noms collectifs sont au singulier mais font référence à un groupe de personnes ou d'objets. En anglais américain, ils ont généralement un verbe au singulier. En anglais britannique, ils peuvent souvent être utilisés soit avec un verbe au singulier, soit avec un verbe au pluriel.

Si le sujet décrit une entité unique, le verbe doit être au singulier.

The team is getting a new manager next year.

[The team as a whole is getting a new manager.]

The team are feeling excited about the news.

[Each individual member of the team is feeling excited.]

Si le sujet décrit un ensemble d'individus, le verbe peut alors être au pluriel en anglais britannique.

67.2 COMPLÉTEZ LES PHRASES AVEC LES NOMS COLLECTIFS DE LA LISTE.

Some of my wife's _____ *family* _____ are coming to visit.

1 The legal _____ in my office is the largest in the company.

2 Members of the _____ are rehearsing in different rooms in the building.

3 The _____ is having an emergency meeting in New York.

4 The soccer _____ is arriving later this evening.

5 The entire _____ was delighted by the guest performer last night.

| ~~family~~ | team | orchestra | government | department | audience |

67.3 POINT CLÉ LES NOMS INDÉNOMBRABLES AVEC ACCORD AU SINGULIER

Les noms ou titres de livres et autres œuvres d'art qui se terminent par un nom au pluriel sont considérés comme singuliers en termes d'accord.

Bien que « tales » soit pluriel, *The Canterbury Tales* est une œuvre littéraire au singulier.

The Canterbury Tales was **first published in the 1400s.**

D'autres noms indénombrables semblent être au pluriel parce qu'ils se terminent par un « -s » mais ont, en fait, un accord au singulier. Ces noms comprennent les noms de lieux et les matières scolaires.

Mathematics is **becoming a more popular subject.**

67.4 AUTRES EXEMPLES LES NOMS INDÉNOMBRABLES AVEC ACCORD AU SINGULIER

 Little Women is **a novel by Louisa May Alcott.**

 Athletics was **an important part of the ancient Olympic Games.**

 The Netherlands is **known for its tulip industry.**

 Politics has **long been a topic for academic debate.**

67.5 COCHEZ LES PHRASES CORRECTES.

The news starts at 10 tonight. ☑
The news start at 10 tonight. ☐

❶ I want to study economic. ☐
I want to study economics. ☐

❷ Is athletics popular in your country? ☐
Are athletics popular in your country? ☐

❸ *Cats* are a successful musical. ☐
Cats is a successful musical. ☐

❹ The Philippines are an island country. ☐
The Philippines is an island country. ☐

❺ Physics are my favorite subjects. ☐
Physics is my favorite subject. ☐

❻ *Hard Times* was written by Dickens. ☐
Hard Times were written by Dickens. ☐

❼ The United States has nine time zones. ☐
The United States have nine time zones. ☐

67.6 POINT CLÉ L'ACCORD APRÈS « EITHER... OR » ET « NEITHER... NOR »

Lorsque vous utilisez « either... or » ou « neither... nor » pour lier deux noms, le verbe s'accorde avec le second. Toutefois, si le dernier nom est au singulier et le premier est au pluriel, vous pouvez mettre le verbe soit au singulier, soit au pluriel.

Le verbe s'accorde avec le second nom au singulier.

  Either a tablet or a laptop **is needed for the course.**

Le verbe s'accorde avec le second nom au pluriel.

 Neither the teacher nor the children were **happy.**

 Neither the classrooms **nor the** office **internet access.**

$$\left\{ \begin{array}{c} \text{has} \\ \text{have} \end{array} \right\}$$

Le verbe peut s'accorder au singulier ou au pluriel.

 67.7 RELIEZ LE DÉBUT DE CHAQUE PHRASE À LA FIN QUI LUI CORRESPOND.

I think either an email or a letter → is fine for sending this kind of news.

❶ Neither her mother nor her father — is a great pet for a family.

❷ Either a cat or a dog — is safe to drive anymore.

❸ Either the diner or the coffee shop — are happy with the announcement.

❹ Neither the boss nor the workers — has worked hard enough at school.

❺ We think that neither Tom nor Katya — was there to pick her up from school.

❻ Either the giraffes or the elephant — are the most popular animals in the park.

❼ Neither my car nor my motorbike — is fine for our meeting.

67.8 ÉCOUTEZ L'ENREGISTREMENT, PUIS COCHEZ LES BONNES RÉPONSES.

Deux amis, Gavin et Nadiya,
parlent de nouveaux gadgets.

Gavin's new watch is six months old.
True ☐ **False** ☐ **Not given** ☑

❶ The new watch is available in different colors.
True ☐ **False** ☐ **Not given** ☐

❷ Nadiya is impressed by the watch's battery life.
True ☐ **False** ☐ **Not given** ☐

❸ Gavin thinks all his old gadgets look great.
True ☐ **False** ☐ **Not given** ☐

❹ Nadiya was initially impressed by smartphones.
True ☐ **False** ☐ **Not given** ☐

❺ "R&D" stands for "Research and Development."
True ☐ **False** ☐ **Not given** ☐

❻ Gavin sells his old gadgets on the internet.
True ☐ **False** ☐ **Not given** ☐

❼ Gavin will give Nadiya his "old" watch.
True ☐ **False** ☐ **Not given** ☐

67.9 CHOISISSEZ LE MOT CORRECT, PUIS EN LISEZ LA PHRASE À VOIX HAUTE.

Neither writing nor speaking to people in English **is** / ~~are~~ difficult any more.

❶ The school **is** / **are** getting new equipment for its technology department.

❷ Computer studies **is** / **are** my favorite subject at college at the moment.

❸ Neither the cable nor the batteries **is** / **are** included with the new digital radio.

❹ The Bahamas **has** / **have** many beaches, including some with pink sand.

❺ I don't know what's wrong with it! Either the engine or the fan **is** / **are** broken.

67 ✓ CHECK-LIST

⚙ Les accords complexes ☐   **Aa** Les noms collectifs ☐   🧩 Utiliser l'accord correct ☐

259

68 « So » et « such »

Vous pouvez utiliser « so » et « such » avec certains mots pour ajouter de l'emphase. Les deux ont une signification similaire mais sont employés différemment.

🔧 **Grammaire** « So » et « such » emphatiques
Aa Vocabulaire La science médicale
🧩 **Compétence** Accentuer des descriptions

68.1 POINT CLÉ « SO » ET « SUCH »

On peut placer « such » devant un nom pour ajouter de l'emphase. On peut aussi l'ajouter devant une combinaison adjectif et nom. « Such » se place devant « a /an ».

« SUCH » + « A/AN » + NOM

The trial was such a success.

« SUCH » + « A/AN » + ADJECTIF + NOM

It was such an important experiment.

> **CONSEIL**
> « Such » + « a/an » + nom est plus courant avec des noms relativement extrêmes plutôt qu'avec des noms neutres.

On peut placer « so » devant un adjectif ou un adverbe pour ajouter de l'emphase.

« SO » + ADJECTIF

The reaction is so dangerous.

« SO » + ADVERBE

The surgery went so well!

 ## 68.2 BARREZ LES MOTS INCORRECTS DANS CHAQUE PHRASE.

> The disease spread so / ~~such~~ slowly that he didn't notice it for many years.

1. Even at the start of her career, she was so / such a well-respected scientist.

2. My brother fell off his bike this morning. The injury was so / such bad that we called a doctor.

3. Colds spread so / such fast between children, particularly in large groups.

4. I was hoping to get some positive news, but the test results were so / such a disappointment.

5. I'm pleased that he's so / such an experienced surgeon. It's very reassuring!

68.3 POINT CLÉ « SO » ET « SUCH » AVEC « THAT »

Vous pouvez utiliser « that » avec « so » et « such » pour mettre l'accent sur un mot en particulier que vous souhaitez mettre en exergue.

« SUCH » + « A/AN » + NOM + « THAT »

The disease is such a mystery that it doesn't even have a name yet.

« SUCH » + « A/AN » + ADJECTIF + NOM + « THAT »

This is such a strange injury that it is hard to diagnose.

« SO » + ADJECTIF + « THAT »

Medical research is so expensive that drugs are often costly.

« SO » + ADVERBE + « THAT »

He recovered so quickly that he was able to go home the next day.

 68.4 RELIEZ LE DÉBUT DE CHAQUE PHRASE À LA FIN QUI LUI CORRESPOND.

The doctor was so tired that → he nearly fell asleep!

you have to train for many years.

1. Dentistry is such a difficult job that

only a few patients have had it.

2. He recovered so rapidly that

he was soon able to walk again.

3. She had such steady hands that

4. The medicine tasted so bad that

she could perform delicate operations.

5. It is such a new treatment that

I nearly spat it all out!

68.5 POINT CLÉ « SO » ET LES QUANTIFICATEURS

On utilise aussi « so » devant des quantificateurs tels que « few », « little », « many » et « much ».

CONSEIL
N'utilisez pas « so » et « such » seuls devant un adjectif comparatif.

Utilisez « so much » devant les comparatifs.

She had so little experience that I was really nervous.

These treatments are so much better than the old ones.

68.6 AUTRES EXEMPLES « SO » ET LES QUANTIFICATEURS

So many lives have been saved by advances in science.

So few people have survived this illness. I'm very lucky.

This hospital is so much cleaner than the other one.

Diseases can spread so much faster as a result of air travel.

68.7 RÉCRIVEZ LES PHRASES EN CORRIGEANT LES ERREURS.

So much young doctors have to work very long hours.
So many young doctors have to work very long hours.

❶ Surgeons train hard, which is why they make such few mistakes.

_____

❷ I think these tablets work such much better than the others.

_____

❸ Doctors have to pass so much exams during their training.

_____

❹ Thank you, doctor. I feel such better than I did last week.

_____

68.8 LISEZ LE TEXTE, PUIS COMPLÉTEZ LES PHRASES AVEC LES MOTS DE LA LISTE.

68 MEDICINE TODAY

RATS TRAINED TO DETECT DISEASE

An incredible breakthrough

People from all over the world fear and dislike rats, believing them to be dirty, diseased, and generally dangerous. But a little-known fact is that rats are so intelligent that they can be trained to do many things for humans that we cannot do ourselves. In Mozambique, rats are even being used to sniff out tuberculosis (TB).

Rats have a sense of smell that is _____*so*_____ well developed that they can _____ traces of TB in test _____ given by humans. They signify when they smell TB by rubbing their legs together and are then given a treat through a syringe. There are a number of reasons why this is _____ an important breakthrough. First, the rats are able spot the _____ in its early stages, which is so much better than testing later because then treatment can be started right away on any patients who have tested positive. TB is _____ if it is detected in its early stages. If left undetected, it can be _____ . Second, rats only take 30 minutes to test nearly 100 samples. This is so _____ more efficient than human laboratory _____ , which can take up to four days to do the same number. Finally, using rats is so much cheaper than buying expensive devices and paying a lot of money per test. This is important because TB is still a global concern. The situation in Mozambique was so bad _____ TB was declared a national emergency in 2006. By 2014, 60,000 people were said, by the ministry of health, to be _____ .

testing	~~so~~	that	detect	treatable	disease
deadly	much	such	samples	infected	

---

68 ✓ **CHECK-LIST**

⚙️ « So » et « such » emphatiques ☐   **Aa** La science médicale ☐   🧩 Accentuer des descriptions ☐

« The » est le mot le plus couramment usité dans la langue anglaise. Il peut être employé dans de nombreuses situations, tout comme l'article indéfini « a » et l'article zéro.

⚙ **Grammaire** Le « the » générique
Aa Vocabulaire Les explorations et les inventions
🧩 **Compétence** Utiliser les articles de niveau avancé

69.1 POINT CLÉ LE « THE » GÉNÉRIQUE

Vous pouvez utiliser « the » avec un nom dénombrable singulier pour parler de catégories en général : inventions, instruments de musique et espèces animales sont souvent décrits de cette façon.

 The telescope changed the way we see the night sky.

On parle de l'invention, et non pas de l'objet.

 The violin is often the key instrument in an orchestra.

On parle du type d'instrument de musique, et non pas de l'objet individuel.

 The cheetah can run faster than any other land animal.

On parle de l'espèce animale, et non d'un animal.

69.2 BARREZ LES MOTS INCORRECTS DANS CHAQUE PHRASE.

 Look over there! There's a / ~~an~~ / ~~the~~ lion and her cub.

1 Apparently, a / an / the French horn is the most difficult instrument to play.

2 Alexander Graham Bell is often credited with inventing a / an / the telephone.

3 My sister has a / an / the saxophone that she plays in her school orchestra.

4 A / An / The blue whale is the largest animal that has ever lived on Earth.

69.3 DIRE AUTREMENT PARLER DE CATÉGORIES

Vous pouvez aussi utiliser un nom dénombrable
pluriel sans article pour parler de catégories.

Telescopes **changed the way we see the night sky.**

On parle de l'invention, et non pas
d'un groupe particulier de télescopes.

Violins **are often the key instruments in an orchestra.**

On parle du type d'instrument de musique,
et non pas d'un groupe particulier de violons.

Cheetahs **can run faster than any other land animal.**

On parle d'une espèce animale, et non pas
d'un groupe particulier de guépards.

69.4 RÉCRIVEZ LES PHRASES EN CORRIGEANT LES ERREURS.

Thomas Edison is widely acknowledged as the inventor of a moving picture.
Thomas Edison is widely acknowledged as the inventor of the moving picture.

1 I enjoy playing a piano, but I hated having lessons as a child.

2 Mountain gorilla are one of the most endangered species on Earth.

3 In 2007, a Russian lawyer paid nearly $4 million for the violin.

4 Sloth is a slow animal, but the Galápagos tortoise is even slower.

5 Steve Wozniak designed and built a 1976 Apple I computer.

6 This concert is incredible. I love the sound of trumpet.

69.5 POINT CLÉ LES ARTICLES DÉFINIS ET INDÉFINIS AVEC DES NOMS

On utilise généralement l'article zéro devant le nom d'une personne.

This is my uncle, Neil Armstrong.

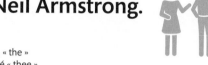

Dans ce cas, « the » est prononcé « thee ».

Vous pouvez utiliser l'article défini devant un nom de personne pour différencier cette personne d'une autre qui porte le même nom.

He's not the Neil Armstrong, is he?

[He isn't the famous person with that name, is he?]

Vous pouvez utiliser l'article indéfini quand l'accent est mis sur un nom particulier plutôt que sur une personne.

I'm afraid there isn't a "Joseph Bloggs" on the list.

[The particular name given is not on the list.]

 69.6 COMPLÉTEZ LES PHRASES AVEC L'ARTICLE APPROPRIÉ EN LAISSANT UN BLANC POUR L'ARTICLE ZÉRO.

The Space Race produced two truly iconic moments in _the_ history of humankind. The first happened on April 12, 1961, when Yuri Gagarin became _____ first human in space. The entire Vostok 1 mission, including one orbit around Earth, lasted only 1 hour 29 minutes. Gagarin's voyage changed how people all over _____ world thought about _____ space.

Just over eight years later in July 1969, _____ Neil Armstrong, "Buzz" Aldrin, and Michael Collins traveled to space in _____ Apollo 11 space craft. On July 20, 1969, Armstrong stepped onto _____ Moon's dusty surface. What he actually said next is _____ interesting story in itself. For many years he argued that he had said, "That's one small step for a man, one giant leap for mankind." After listening to repeated transmission recordings, however, he admitted that he may have dropped the indefinite article "_____ ." Either way, it was _____ huge step for mankind.

69.7 ÉCOUTEZ L'ENREGISTREMENT, PUIS COCHEZ LES BONNES RÉPONSES.

Un animateur radio passe en revue une exposition sur les femmes dans l'espace.

The reviewer states that only women will like this exhibition.	True ☐	False ☑
❶ The exhibition is being held in the City Museum.	True ☐	False ☐
❷ All of the exhibits in "There's Space for Women" are replicas.	True ☐	False ☐
❸ Valentina Tereshkova was the first female cosmonaut in 1992.	True ☐	False ☐
❹ Jan Davis and Mark Lee flew in space when they were married.	True ☐	False ☐
❺ The first person in space from South Korea was a woman.	True ☐	False ☐
❻ An astronaut is definitely visiting the exhibition this month.	True ☐	False ☐
❼ You can book tickets for the exhibition online.	True ☐	False ☐

69 ✔ CHECK-LIST

⚙ Le « the » générique ☐   **Aa** Les explorations et les inventions ☐   🧩 Utiliser les articles de niveau avancé ☐

↻ BILAN L'ANGLAIS QUE VOUS AVEZ APPRIS DANS LES CHAPITRES 66-69

NOUVEAU POINT LINGUISTIQUE	EXEMPLE TYPE	☑	CHAPITRE
« HAVE/GET SOMETHING DONE »	Did you get your software updated?	☐	66.1
ACCORD SUJET-VERBE COMPLEXE	The team is getting a new manager next year. The team are feeling excited about the news.	☐	67.1, 67.3, 67.6
« SO » ET « SUCH »	The trial was such a success. The reaction is so dangerous.	☐	68.1, 68.3, 68.5
LE « THE » GÉNÉRIQUE	The telescope changed the way we see the night sky.	☐	69.1
LES ARTICLES AVEC DES NOMS	He's not the Neil Armstrong, is he? I'm afraid there isn't a Joseph Bloggs on the list.	☐	69.5

Réponses

1.2

Hi José,
Today **is** my first day in my new job, so **I am leaving** the house early.
I'm a bit nervous, but **I'm also** very excited!
Anyway, **I'm already running** late, and **I need** to leave to catch the bus. **Don't forget** to pick up some milk on your way home from work tonight!
See you later!

1.4 ◀))

❶ I **have been reading** for hours. My eyes **have started hurting**.
❷ Has the mail **arrived** yet? I **have been expecting** a letter all week.
❸ My leg **has been hurting** all day, but I **haven't seen** a doctor yet.
❹ Have you **seen** my keys? I **have been looking** for them for ages.
❺ Have you **heard** about Carl? He **has decided** to move.
❻ I **have finished**! I **have been writing** this essay for ages.
❼ Have you ever **visited France**? We **have been looking** at brochures.
❽ I **have been trying** to reach Tao all day, but he **has not answered** yet.

1.6 ◀))

❶ They aren't very welcoming, **are they**?
❷ He should try harder to be friendly, **shouldn't he**?
❸ She hasn't made many friends here, **has she**?
❹ He doesn't like going to new places, **does he**?
❺ They're so happy to be here, **aren't they**?
❻ They would be here if they could, **wouldn't they**?

1.8

❶ Answer required
❷ Answer not required
❸ Answer not required
❹ Answer required
❺ Answer not required
❻ Answer not required

1.9 ◀))

❶ People don't have their own office space here, **do they**?

❷ You have been introduced to Mr. Thomas, **haven't you**?
❸ You'd like to come to dinner with us all tonight, **wouldn't you**?
❹ Oscar and Kate aren't here yet, **are they**?

2.3 ◀))

❶ She has long, wavy hair.
❷ Sorry, I don't believe you.
❸ That jacket fits you very well.
❹ I rarely think about the past.
❺ Jess is having a great time at the party.
❻ That milk smells dreadful.
❼ I'm thinking about going home soon.
❽ I'm slowly realizing the problem here.
❾ You seem unhappy. Can I help?

2.4

Hi Sara,
I'm writing about Gavin. I **think** there's something wrong. I'm not **suggesting** that it's anything serious, but he doesn't **seem** to be his usual happy self. Maybe he's not **fitting** in well in his new job. I was going to **suggest** that the three of us go out for a drink, or perhaps you would **prefer** a meal. Let me know what you think.
Tina

3.2 ◀))

❶ She doesn't have any **close** family left, only an uncle.
❷ Sometimes the only solution is to **do** your best and hope.
❸ All their lives they appeared to be **happily** married.
❹ Unfortunately, the financial crisis ruined his **career**.
❺ He first **went** into business when he was only 17.
❻ Looking at old photographs can stir up **memories**.
❼ I can distinctly **remember** meeting him 20 years ago.
❽ Looking at them, the difference in age is **clearly** visible.

3.3

❶ False ❷ False ❸ True ❹ False
❺ False ❻ True ❼ False

3.4 ◀))

❶ poles apart ❷ a popular belief
❸ opinions are divided ❹ firmly believe

3.5 Réponses modèles

❶ Mariam is from northern France.
❷ She studied architecture in college.
❸ She met her husband on a photography field trip.
❹ The turning point was when a wildlife magazine published her photos.
❺ Yes, Mariam and Julian have two children.
❻ They are planning to travel to Japan and Korea next year.

3.6

❶ 25 years ago ❷ 23 years ago
❸ 3 years ago ❹ 1 month ago

3.7 ◀))

❶ Lisa **went** to Thailand 25 years **ago**.
❷ Bill **was teaching** when Lisa arrived in Thailand.
❸ Lisa and Bill **got married** 23 years ago, **in** March.
❹ Lisa **had been traveling** for 25 years before she returned.
❺ Barbara **graduated** from college **last** month.

3.8 ◀))

❶ I got married **while I was living in China.**
❷ I was **living in China when** I had a baby.
❸ I wrote my thesis **while I was studying part-time.**
❹ I was **studying part-time when** I started a small business.

4.4 ◀))

GÉNÉRAL : **awful, terrible, awesome**
SPÉCIFIQUE : **cruel, expensive, tasty**
TAILLE : **enormous, huge, tiny**
FORME : **round, oval, square**
ÂGE : **elderly, modern, ancient**
COULEUR : **green, red, orange**
MATÉRIAU : **silk, leather, metal**

4.5 ◀))

❶ I don't like him at all. He's a **terrible, rude** man. Let's not invite him to the party.
❷ My mother thinks he's a **nice, intelligent young** boy.
❸ Dad, look at this **sweet, friendly brown** puppy! Can we take him for a walk?

④ Should we buy this **wonderful**, **comfortable** sofa for the living room? We really need a new one.

4.6
① True ② Not given ③ False ④ True
⑤ False

4.7
②

4.8 ◀))
① His last employer said he was **un**trustworthy.
② She doesn't realize how **in**sensitive she is.
③ He's 25 now, but he's rather **im**mature at work.
④ I'm afraid she's quite an **in**efficient worker.
⑤ He gossips and is **un**kind to his co-workers.
⑥ Her office desk and her work are **dis**organized.
⑦ He makes mistakes because he's **im**patient.
⑧ She's **dis**loyal to the company.

4.9 ◀))
POSITIVE ADJECTIVES: **helpful**, **excellent**, **popular**, **proactive**, **mature**
NEGATIVE ADJECTIVES: **disloyal**, **unkind**, **frustrating**, **impatient**, **arrogant**

05

5.3 ◀))
① With busy work and social lives, it's **true that** most people have little time to study.
② Languages are so useful. It is **a shame that** so few people learn a second language.
③ Learning doesn't have to be expensive. It is not **essential to** spend a lot of money.
④ Try internet study groups. It is **easy to** meet other language learners online.
⑤ Don't worry if you need time. It's **unlikely that** you'll be able to speak fluently quickly.

5.5 ◀))
① Remember, it's important **to** be relaxed about making mistakes.
② With so many options, it's no longer difficult **to** find language courses online.
③ **To** take the exam now would be a waste of time. She hasn't studied at all.
④ **It** is unlikely that he will finish the class before the end of the year.
⑤ Don't give up! It's true **that** the more you study, the better you will become.

5.6
① Dave ② Mei ③ Sam ④ Mei ⑤ Alice

5.7 ◀))
① I am surprised that my son **has** an aptitude for copying accents.
② Unfortunately, I have a **complete** inability to remember vocabulary.
③ Some people appear to have a natural **ability** to speak a number of languages.
④ My father had a remarkable **capacity** to memorize lists of words.

5.8 ◀)) Réponses modèles
① It is important to be able to communicate with people across the world.
② It's best to be patient with yourself and take things slowly.
③ It is difficult to make sure that you practice every day when you are busy.

07

7.2 ◀))
① Be careful, it's absolutely **pouring down** with rain.
② He's behind on his work, so he needs to **catch up**.
③ They are **taking down** the offensive posters today.
④ She'll have a backup. She always **backs up** her files.
⑤ They **split up** every time they have an argument.

7.4 ◀))
① I'll **pick** your shopping **up** for you.
② They're **putting** posters **up** outside again.
③ Have you **checked** the restaurant menu **out**?
④ He hasn't **set** the computer **up** yet.

7.5 ◀))
① He should ask **her** out if he wants to.
② Remember to take **it** out later.
③ You should send **it** back if it's broken.
④ Could you turn **them** off when you leave?

7.7 ◀))
① My big brother is a CEO. I have a lot to **live up to**.
② Slow down! I can't **keep up with** you any more, I'm tired.
③ His parents aren't very strict. He **gets away with** everything!

7.8
① B ② F ③ C ④ D ⑤ A ⑥ E

7.9
① Komodo dragons ② Tour guide
③ Blog ④ Travel guides ⑤ Good pay

7.10 ◀))
① cut off
② stop off
③ take off
④ set off

7.11 ◀))
① Our plane was due to **take off** an hour ago.
② We have to **set off** really early for our vacation.
③ He went with her to the train station to **see her off**.
④ They missed the ferry, so they were **cut off** from the mainland.

08

8.2 ◀))
① I **was walking** down the road when someone **asked** me to take their photo.
② Someone **was talking** during the tour until we **told** them to be quiet.
③ I **stopped** twice to take photos while I **was driving** through the country.
④ We **decided** to order some champagne while we **were eating** lunch.
⑤ We were lost and our feet **were aching** before we finally **found** a map shop.

8.3 ◀))
① My feet really ached by the end of the day because **we had walked all around the city**.
② The trip was perfect because **we had spent a long time planning it**.
③ We got completely lost because **we had crossed over the wrong bridge**.
④ We went to see a great show because **our tour guide had recommended it**.

8.6 ◀))
① We **had been waiting** for at least an hour when the taxi finally arrived.
② I eventually went to the pharmacy because I **had not been feeling** well for days.
③ We went to see the movie because they **had been promoting** it for months.
④ The streets were beautiful and white because it **had been snowing** all night.

8.7
❶ False ❷ True ❸ True ❹ True

8.8
❸

8.9
❶ bright and early
❷ off the beaten track
❸ travel light

09

9.2 🔊
❶ It's such a sunny day! You could go to the park later if you have time.
❷ You really must try the new Italian restaurant on Main Street.
❸ You ought to have a big party with all your friends. It would be great!

9.3 🔊
❶ Everything about this hotel from the dark interior to the hard stares of the grumpy staff was unwelcoming. **They ought to hire a new receptionist!**
❷ The hotel's employees are wonderful. They did everything to make our honeymoon perfect. **You should tell them if it's a special occasion.**
❸ Not bad although the furniture in the hotel was falling apart. The walls were very thin and it was quite noisy. **You might want to bring earplugs.**
❹ I paid for a room with a view of the ski slopes, but all I could see was the wall of the building across from us. **You could ask to change rooms if this happens.**
❺ Outstanding! I can understand the rave reviews for this great place. Our balcony overlooked the ocean. **You must ask for a room with an ocean view!**

9.4
❶ Like ❷ Like ❸ Dislike ❹ Like
❺ Dislike

9.7 🔊
❶ That snake is poisonous. You **must** go to the doctor about that bite or it'll get worse.
❷ We **had better** go back to the boat. It's leaving soon and we don't want to miss it.
❸ Perhaps you **could** go to France this summer. That would be nice.
❹ Everyone says the castle is stunning and that we **must** see the view from the tower.

9.8
❶ Like ❷ Like ❸ Dislike ❹ Like ❺ Like
❻ Dislike

9.9 Réponses modèles
Hi **Jake**,
I'm traveling back tonight. I can't believe my trip is over already! I really enjoyed **relaxing on the beach and swimming in the ocean.** The town was **beautiful and the restaurants were amazing. We ate out every night.** You really should **visit. You must ask if they have any vacancies at the Hotel Del Mar. The food was so fresh and the hotel's employees were wonderful.**
Lots of love,
Sara

10

10.2 🔊
❶ I don't have much money. **I definitely won't go on vacation this year.**
❷ He's worked so hard for his exams. **He'll pass them all, no problem.**
❸ She's a talented young pianist. **She might be famous one day.**
❹ Look at the line outside the stadium. **We probably won't get tickets.**
❺ You don't have a very good voice. **You definitely won't ever be in an opera.**
❻ My sister loves to travel. **She'll probably go to Australia one day.**
❼ Joe goes running every day. **He might be running a marathon soon.**

10.3
❶ likely to happen
❷ definitely will happen
❸ probably won't happen
❹ unlikely to happen

10.4
❶ funda**men**tally ❷ es**sen**tially
❸ sur**pri**singly ❹ pre**dic**tably
❺ **for**tunately ❻ **in**terestingly
❼ **luck**ily ❽ un**for**tunately

10.5 Réponses modèles
❶ They're buying them as short-term investments or as places to live part-time.
❷ They can't afford to buy a house because of rising house prices.
❸ There are fewer people there as it's empty most of the year.
❹ They're reserving a certain percentage of new buildings for local people and they're introducing higher fees for overseas buyers.

10.6 🔊
❶ This is only a **short-term** solution. We'll have to fix the fence properly soon.
❷ OK, we'll order pizza tonight, but **in the long run** we need to sort out a meal plan.
❸ I don't understand this new digital system, but I know it's **the shape of things to come**.
❹ It was **only a matter of time** before the company hit its targets.

12

12.2 🔊
❶ All my siblings love playing football, especially my brother.
❷ We are all quite interested in our family history, so we've made a family tree.
❸ I love talking to my aunt, because she has lots of interesting stories from her travels abroad.
❹ My grandmother thinks I should get married, but I am not as traditional as she is.
❺ We don't have family gatherings very often, since my grandparents live abroad.

12.3
❶ D ❷ A ❸ C

12.5 🔊
❶ Elizabeth had two children, **whereas / yet** Mary had none.
❷ The two elderly sisters were **equally / similarly** wealthy.
❸ The father left the army **due to / owing to** a serious arm injury.
❹ James and Tom were identical twins. **Therefore / Hence**, they looked alike.

12.6 🔊
❶ You have failed to respond to our messages. **Hence**, your subscription has been canceled.
❷ My friends say I take after my dad, **because** we both like mountain biking.
❸ After a successful book tour, the professor's lectures were **equally** well-received.
❹ I love my aunts, **especially** Meera, because she's so funny.

12.7
❶ False ❷ True ❸ True ❹ False

13

13.5 🔊
1. My mother **used to walk** five miles to school and back.
2. I **didn't use to like** using the internet, but now I think it's great!
3. **Did** you **use to eat** your lunch at school?
4. My grandmother's house **didn't use to have** electricity.
5. Whenever I had a toothache, my dad **would take** me to a scary dentist.

13.6
1. used to complain 2. would walk
3. used to get upset 4. didn't use to do
5. used to write 6. would

13.7
1. They go to the movies together
2. Documentaries and news archives
3. Older family members
4. It's very important to them
5. Understanding other people's values

13.8 🔊
1. acceptance 2. honesty 3. values
4. greedy 5. character 6. interrupt

13.9 Réponses modèles
1. They started talking because they were both researching their family history.
2. They both had a brother they hadn't seen for 50 years and they had both been teachers after leaving the army.
3. It was surprising because they lived very close to each other for 50 years.
4. Last week, the two brothers met for the first time in half a century.

14

14.3 🔊
1. The giraffe is **just as** tall **as** the house.
2. The flower is **not as / nowhere near as** large **as** the tree.
3. The phone is **not as / half as** expensive **as** the laptop.
4. The baby is **not as / nowhere near as** old **as** the man.
5. The pizza is **not as / almost as / not quite as** wide **as** the plate.

14.5
1. The old video 2. The car 3. The new house 4. Andrew 5. Less often

14.6
1. a lawyer 2. Jon 3. 40 minutes 4. rainy
5. with her family 6. good

14.7 🔊
1. Thankfully, our baby is a **heavy** sleeper and only wakes once a night.
2. The commute to work takes ages, even when there is **light** traffic.
3. Feeling sick every day is a **high** price to pay for going on a cruise.
4. I only really wake up in the morning after a **strong** coffee.
5. My mother has a **low** opinion of anyone who doesn't work hard.

14.8
Alex and Sue are both chefs. She owns a café and he works in a famous restaurant. Her cooking is **just as** good **as** his, maybe even better, although his cooking is mostly savory and she has a sweet tooth. Unfortunately, just because her food costs **half as** much **as** his, some people do not have as **high** an opinion of her skills. Her café is seen as somewhere with **low** prices to grab a bite to eat, not somewhere to wine and dine. Sue says this is a small price to pay for owning her own business. Some people just like to go out of their way to pay **twice as** much **as** they should for a three-course meal in Alex's restaurant, rather than enjoy a delicious piece of cake or pastry in Sue's café.

14.9 🔊
1. sweet tooth 2. grab a bite to eat
3. wine and dine 4. savory 5. go out of your way

15

15.4 🔊
1. The longer the film went on, the more bored I became.
2. The more it rained, the quicker the vegetables grew.
3. The more she told me not to laugh, the more I laughed.
4. The more sugar a dessert contains, the worse it is for you.

15.5 🔊
1. The louder my music is, the **angrier** my mother gets.
2. The **younger** the skier is, the less frightened they are of falling.
3. The **more annoyed** my teacher gets, the more I giggle nervously.

4. **The faster** the car went, **the louder** the passengers screamed.

15.7 🔊
1. The more the merrier.
2. The bigger the better.
3. The stronger the better.

15.9
1. Not given 2. True 3. False 4. True

15.10 Réponses modèles
1. Older people require more financial support in their old age.
2. In the first suggested solution, people are responsible for their own care in old age.
3. In the second suggested solution, the government is responsible for people's care in old age.
4. The final suggested solution is to increase the official retirement age.

17

17.2 🔊
SEQUENCING: **first**, **second**
ADDING: **additionally**, **furthermore**
EXAMPLES: **such as**, **for example**
CONCLUDING: **overall**, **to sum up**

17.3 🔊
1. Others, **such as** Sydney University and Toronto, are renowned for their stunning historical buildings.
2. **Moreover**, there are newer universities like Moscow and Xiamen that have equally impressive buildings.
3. **For instance**, Moscow State University is incredibly impressive at night.
4. **Additionally**, a number of modern university buildings in Australia are spectacular.
5. **Overall**, there are some amazing educational buildings around the world.
6. **To sum up**, it can be worth your time to look at educational buildings, even if you are visiting as a tourist.

17.4
1. False 2. True 3. Not given 4. Not given 5. False

17.7 🔊
1. You must pay to play tennis **unless you join the club.**
2. If you are a history student, **you can join the historical society.**

3 If you join the water sports club, **you can learn how to sail.**

4 You can join today **unless you need more time to think.**

17.8 🔊

1 If you hear **discourse** markers, use them to help organize your notes.

2 When you take notes, **use** a simple shorthand with symbols and abbreviations.

3 If your handwriting is messy, try to **make** sure it is readable.

4 Unless you record every lecture, try to **review** your notes soon after.

17.9

2

17.10 Réponses modèles

Active note-taking examples:
Think about expected content before lecture.
Use own words for notes (paraphrase).
Find relationships between parts of lecture.
Write down follow-up questions.

18

18.3

1 B **2** C **3** D **4** A

18.5 🔊

1 The vast **majority** of the lecture halls have wireless internet access.

2 **Just** over a quarter of classes are recorded for students to listen to online.

3 After one week, **most** people know their way around campus.

4 Only a **tiny** minority of our students do not have smartphones.

5 Well **over** half of our students eat a hot meal on campus.

6 Just **over** two-thirds of our professors can speak two languages.

18.7

1 True **2** False **3** True **4** True **5** False

18.9 🔊 Réponses modèles

1 Really? **I heard that there are 40 different clubs.**

2 Is that so? **I read that most students prefer to live on campus.**

3 Are you sure? **I was told that they have a dedicated team to help with future career decisions.**

19

19.4

2

19.5 🔊

1 English is **spoken** by millions of people across the world.

2 Online courses **are being studied** by a variety of students.

3 The courses **are being paid for** by a number of universities.

4 Certificates **can be printed out** at home by participants.

5 Some exams can **be taken** in several different languages.

19.6 🔊

1 Eighty percent **of the courses are written in English.**

2 Credits **are offered for MOOC courses (by some universities).**

3 Technical help **is provided for the participants (by some people).**

4 Next year, MOOCs **will be taken by millions of students.**

19.8 🔊

1 downfall **2** crackdown **3** backup
4 login **5** input **6** leftovers **7** check-in
8 outset

19.9

1 Not given **2** True **3** Not given

19.10 🔊

1 The things we learn are **tested** in a weekly online exam.

2 The face-to-face lessons expand on the online course **input**.

3 From the **outset**, I knew this course would be successful.

4 Lack of motivation has always been my **downfall** in online learning.

5 The course is **written** by language-learning experts.

6 They have made changes to make it easier to **log in** to your account.

7 There has also been a **crackdown** on security to prevent cheating.

20

20.3 🔊

1 I'm going to take a water bottle **in case the exam room is hot.**

---

2 Suppose you cannot afford to study. **Maybe you could apply for funding.**

3 I am studying really hard tonight **in case we have a test tomorrow.**

4 What if I forget to bring a calculator? **Maybe they will have spares.**

20.6

1 Likely **2** Unlikely **3** Likely
4 Unlikely **5** Likely **6** Unlikely
7 Likely **8** Unlikely

20.8

1 False **2** False **3** False **4** True

20.9

1 Unlikely **2** Likely **3** Likely
4 Unlikely

20.10 🔊 Réponses modèles

1 I'd like to meet Abraham Lincoln.

2 I would make fruit and vegetables free for everybody.

3 I'll apply for a place at college.

22

22.3 🔊

1 **Before** seeing that job listing, I thought I would never find my perfect job.

2 After **qualifying** as an engineer, I volunteered in Cambodia.

3 **Instead of** working in a low-paid job, I decided to train as an accountant.

4 Without **passing** my exams, it would be difficult to have a decent career.

22.4

1 False **2** True **3** Not given **4** True
5 False **6** Not given

22.5 🔊

1 keen **2** have an eye for detail
3 post **4** in the near future
5 take the position

22.6

1 True **2** Not given **3** False **4** True
5 False

22.7

1 Work experience and skills

2 Say what you were doing

3 Less than two sides of paper

22.8 🔊

1 The job was quite challenging in terms of improving the consumer experience.

② I traveled to Vietnam where I volunteered for a number of educational projects.
③ I am a qualified fire warden and am trained in writing risk assessments.
④ I have an in-depth knowledge of real estate due to having eight years' experience.

23

23.2 ◄))
① I was wondering **when you are available**.
② I'd like to know **why you have applied for this job**.
③ Do you have any idea **what our best-selling product is**?
④ I'm curious to know **who your last manager was**.

23.4 ◄))
① We were wondering **if / whether you like working with animals?**
② Would you mind telling us **if / whether you've applied for any other jobs?**
③ Could you tell me **if / whether you have any computer skills?**
④ We'd like to know **if / whether you have relevant experience.**

23.5 ◄))
① We were wondering why you left your last job.
② Could you tell us about your future career ambitions?
③ I'd like to know whether you like taking risks.

23.6
① False **②** True **③** False **④** True

23.8
① He has learned new techniques and skills
② She had already read about them
③ He used to be very critical of himself
④ It was part of his second-year project

23.9 ◄)) **Réponses modèles**
① Well, my last role required a lot of teamwork.
② Actually, quite a lot. I have researched your company online.
③ Let's see, I hope to be directing a large company.
④ Good question. I think I have exactly what you're looking for.

24

24.2 ◄))
① The new product launch caused **the profits to rise**, which was excellent news.
② I recently lost my job, but I **managed** to find a new one quite quickly.
③ The employees were furious, so they **threatened** to not work yesterday.
④ I always get scared when my boss **invites me to** her office. It's never good news.
⑤ Sometimes it can be good to **volunteer** to do extra work. It'll impress your boss.
⑥ On Fridays, my manager sometimes **allows me** to leave early to enjoy the weekend.

24.4 ◄))
① Over the years we have enjoyed **leading** the market when it comes to the environment.
② An auditor has advised us **to change** some of our policies in order to improve further.
③ One change we would like **to make** is to no longer supply disposable cups.
④ We're sure that you will approve of us **trying** to become more environmentally friendly.
⑤ The change will prevent our company **throwing away** up to 25,000 cups each year.
⑥ Bringing your own mug will enable us **to stick** to this new initiative.
⑦ We hope that you approve of the company **making** a change like this. It's for a great cause.
⑧ I'll send another quick memo on Friday **to remind** you to bring your own mug to work.

24.7 ◄))
① He appealed **to** the audience, asking them to stop booing the actors in the play.
② She always shouts **at** him when he doesn't take the dog for a walk.
③ You should wait **for** Jane to arrive before talking to Max about this important issue.
④ I'm sure that I can count **on** you to support your boss at this difficult time.
⑤ I've arranged **for** the doctor to see you tomorrow morning at 10am.
⑥ My children never listen **to** me when I tell them what to do.

24.8 **Réponses modèles**
① They used to design the business cards, but they don't anymore.
② They focused on providing the quality materials and printing.

③ YouToPrint passed on the savings to the customers by lowering their prices.
④ You can tap them on a smartphone and they take you straight to a website.

25

25.3 ◄))
① Barbara gave it **to** me.
② We gave **them** some candy. / We gave some candy to them.
③ James passed **me** the documents. / James passed the documents to me.

25.5 ◄))
① The teacher gave homework **to** the students.
② He made a speech **for** the business.
③ He gave advice **to** them.
④ He's collecting money **for** the charity.

25.6
① Not given **②** True **③** False

25.7 **Réponses modèles**
① The business will start trading next month.
② Starting a business is expensive, and Colin doesn't have much money.
③ Not many companies have made walking map apps.
④ If it fails, he will be happy that he tried.

25.8
I've been planning to start my own map shop for years, and finally I've done all the paperwork and all the **red tape** is out of the way. We don't formally open until next month, but I'm getting everything ready now so we can really **hit the ground running**. It hasn't been cheap though. Starting a business is very expensive and I don't have a **blank check** to buy thousands of maps. The walking map app is the **ace up my sleeve** though. Not many people do those yet and I hope to have **cornered the market** by the end of next year. Of course, it might all go horribly wrong, but **nothing ventured, nothing gained**, eh?

25.9
① For all **your** map needs.
② We **have** 20 years' experience.
③ we are **ahead** of the times.
④ will be **launching**
⑤ will be **available**
⑥ once **you've** returned
⑦ **an** enormous stock

27.3 🔊
1 We had to run the meeting **ourselves**.
2 Do you ever send meeting reminders to **yourself**?
3 I taught **myself** how to play the guitar.
4 Do you and Priya see **yourselves** as team players?
5 He put **himself** forward for a big promotion.
6 The company promotes **itself** online.

27.5 🔊
1 I'm very impressed that they planned this conference **themselves**!
2 I spent all evening doing research for this presentation **myself**.
3 The area is traditional, but the city **itself** is full of modern offices.
4 Nobody helped us. We won this contract **ourselves**.
5 I couldn't believe it! The Queen **herself** presented the award.
6 Marta writes summaries for her boss. He can't write them **himself**.
7 It's very important that you fix these problems **yourself**, Jacob.
8 The company founders **themselves** will be making the final decision.

27.8
Steven Strange, CEO of AngloEuroCorp, left the company in unusual circumstances last week. Acting CEO Don Black was called into the CEO's office by Strange, who said, "You should **familiarize yourself** with this office and **make yourself** at home." Another employee commented on Strange's odd behavior: "He usually **absented himself** from our meetings because he didn't **concern himself** with day-to-day matters. Last Friday was different. Mr. Strange **tore himself** away from his office and attended the weekly meeting. He even thanked us for our hard work!" As he left, Strange supposedly announced: "Go home early and **enjoy yourselves**!"

27.9
1 catch up 2 take on 3 sort out
4 knock off 5 stay behind

27.10 🔊
1 If you have caught up with your work, you can knock **off** early today.
2 We should be proud of our sales results and congratulate **ourselves**.

3 These two women have worked **themselves** into positions for promotions.
4 I can't leave early today. I'm snowed **under** with work at the moment.

28.2 🔊
1 He was fired because he continued **to ignore his duties.**
2 How would you propose **to raise the money?**
3 I was so late that I began **to run for the bus.**
4 Let's go inside. I really can't stand **being cold and wet.**
5 I have to say that I prefer **writing to people by hand.**

28.5 🔊
1 I hope you remembered **to put** the advertisement for the grand reopening in the newspaper?
2 Unfortunately, when the hotel reopened, they had forgotten **to advertise**, so it was empty.
3 I'll never forget **seeing** the manager's face when there were no guests at the party.
4 Do you remember **planning** the grand opening party with Ceri last year?
5 Do you regret **asking** Tim to promote the reopening?
6 After the initial failure, the refurbished hotel went on **to be** a huge success.
7 Now it's famous and successful, the hotel will probably go on **being** popular for many years.

28.6 🔊
1 I need to **stop** spending so much money on food at work.
2 My dad says he could never **forget** meeting Elvis, even though it was a long time ago.
3 If I'm not busy tonight, I'd absolutely **love** to go to dinner with you.
4 My boss **prefers** talking on the phone to video calls.
5 Thanks for the offer. If you don't mind, I'd like to **continue** to do my work instead.
6 After the book was published, he **went on** to write an award-winning screenplay.
7 I **regret** to inform you that the meeting has been postponed.
8 It looks like it will be expensive to get catering. I **propose** making the food ourselves.

28.7
1 Yes 2 No 3 Yes 4 No 5 No
6 No 7 Yes

29.2 🔊
EXTREME: **awful, enormous, superb, tiny, disgusting**
ABSOLUTE: **unique, unknown, dead, right, wrong**
CLASSIFYING: **organic, digital, chemical, industrial, electronic**

29.3 🔊
1 Have you seen this amazing designer watch?
2 This new software is so slow. It's awful.
3 Because it runs on solar power, it's extremely cheap.
4 The instructions for this product are impossible.
5 The numbers on the watch are tiny!
6 I need to replace my computer. It's broken.

29.6 🔊
1 It is **incredibly** important to know a lot about the product you are trying to sell.
2 Did you see that **completely** digital presentation by the marketing team?
3 Don't you think that this kind of product is extremely **useful** for teenagers?
4 To copy and then sell someone else's invention as your own is **utterly** wrong.
5 From the initial product design to marketing is a **rather** long process.
6 The new designer in my department is **absolutely** fantastic.
7 I think the food at the conference was bad. I felt extremely **sick** this morning.
8 I have to say that I think it was an absolutely **superb** presentation.

29.8
1 Liked it a lot 2 Not very good
3 Liked it a lot 4 Didn't like it very much
5 Hated it

29.10
1 False 2 False 3 True 4 True 5 False

29.11 🔊
1 The coffee capsules are **wholly recyclable**.
2 The Blingtech3000 is an **utterly stylish** timepiece.

③ The Blingtech3000's software is **absolutely state-of-the-art**.
④ Most air freshener refills are **extremely expensive**.
⑤ Coz-E-Slip slippers have a **totally automatic** thermostat.
⑥ The slippers are supposed to be **incredibly comfortable**.

30

30.3 ◀))
① She searched for the company online **so as to find its email address.**
② They gave her a refund **so as to keep her business.**
③ The goods were packed carefully **to protect them.**
④ They paid for express delivery **in order to get the goods on time.**
⑤ I booked an expensive hotel **so as to be able to relax on my trip.**

30.6
① False ② True ③ True ④ False
⑤ True ⑥ Not given ⑦ False

30.7 ◀))
① Last year we had to complain in order to get a bigger room.
② I usually go to the same resort so that I can stay in the same hotel.
③ He bought the latest model to impress his friends.
④ I pack very carefully so as not to forget anything.
⑤ I went to the top of the highest mountain so that I could race down.
⑥ I went to a hospital in order to get an X-ray of my leg.

30.9 ◀))
① Special "outlet" stores are known **for** selling excess goods at reduced prices.
② This process is for customers who want **to** complain about the products they have received.
③ People are employed **to** check the quality of the goods before they are sent to stores.
④ These notes are here **to** help you complete the form and submit your complaint.
⑤ There is a telephone number **for** unhappy customers who wish to make further complaints.
⑥ I think a large number of people only complain **to** get refunds.
⑦ This new product is **for** busy people who want to make their lives simpler.

32

32.4 ◀))
① If I **had chosen** the trip, we **would have gone** to Spain.
② If we **had arrived** earlier, we **would not have missed** the show.
③ I **could have helped** them if they **had called** me earlier.
④ If we **had stopped** eating earlier, we **might not have felt** so sick.
⑤ She **would have passed** her exam if she **had worked** a bit harder.
⑥ If you **had shut** the door, we **might not have been** so cold.

32.6
① B ② A ③ A ④ A ⑤ B

32.8 ◀))
① I might've worked harder if I'd been paid more.
② If more people had voted for him, he would've won.
③ If you'd left earlier, we would've arrived on time.
④ She might've finished on time if she'd started sooner.

32.9 ◀))
① If **you'd** kept the fire alight, we wouldn't have been so cold.
② You **might have** slept better if you had brought a sleeping bag!
③ If she'd **worn** her boots, she wouldn't have had such wet feet.
④ If they'd **kept** the river clean, the fish might not have died.

32.10
① False ② True ③ True ④ False
⑤ False ⑥ False

32.11
②

32.14 ◀))
① I wish we **weren't** outdoors right now.
② I think about the trip a lot. I wish I **had taken** more photos.
③ I feel sick. If only I **had eaten** fewer of those berries.
④ The bus has broken down! If only the driver **knew** how to fix it.
⑤ I'm so exhausted! If only I**'d slept** a little more.

32.15 ◀))
① I missed the bus again. I wish **I'd set an alarm.**
② I caught a huge fish yesterday. If only **I'd taken a photo.**
③ I can't afford those boots. If only **I hadn't spent all my money.**
④ I was so cold this winter. I wish **I had bought a coat**.

32.16 ◀))
① He wished he'd **stopped** the fishermen from killing the seal.
② He thought, if only he'd **done** something to protect the seals.
③ If I hadn't helped, I know I would've **felt** guilty forever.
④ If he'd seen me become a campaigner, he'd have **been** very proud.

33

33.3 ◀))
① People **shouldn't have** thrown things in the river. The fish population has declined dramatically.
② Factories **should have** reduced pollution in accordance with environmental agreements.
③ Companies **should have** used fewer vehicles in order to lower their carbon footprint.
④ Factories **shouldn't have** released pollution into the water. It has poisoned the ecosystem.

33.4 ◀))
① I **ought to** have gone to bed earlier last night. I'm feeling really exhausted now.
② We really **shouldn't have** eaten so much at lunchtime. I'm feeling sleepy now.
③ You **should have driven** more carefully on the wet road. You could have had an accident.
④ **Should I have** bought this desktop computer, or would the laptop have been better?

33.5
① False ② True ③ True ④ True ⑤ False

33.7
Ⓐ 2 Ⓑ 1 Ⓒ 3 Ⓓ 5 Ⓔ 4

33.8 🔊
① **Following** the rise of a new civilization, the islanders built statues to honor their ancestors.
② **Throughout** this time, the islanders were cutting down lots of trees.
③ **During** his visit, the first European explorer noticed that there weren't many trees.
④ The ship HMS Blossom visited in 1825, and **by that time**, the statues had been toppled over.
⑤ An airport was built in 1987 and **since then**, lots of tourists have visited Easter Island.

33.9
① Not given ② False ③ True ④ True

34

34.2 🔊
① Please make sure you **ask for** help if you need it.
② Who is giving the lecture? I have never **heard of** him.
③ My brother and I are always **arguing about** current affairs.
④ The global **decline in** natural resources is worrying.
⑤ Thank you so much! I am so **grateful for** all you have done.
⑥ When you're stressed, it is good to **talk about** problems.
⑦ The **effect of** the economic crisis is enormous.
⑧ Most of the population **knows about** climate change.
⑨ All of the scientific evidence **points in** one direction.

34.3 🔊
① Why do they always argue **about** everything?
② There was a decline **in** the number of birds.
③ There's a lot to be grateful **for**.
④ This demonstrates a real lack **of** talent.
⑤ How do I ask **for** directions in Greek?
⑥ I don't think we'll ever agree **about** this.
⑦ I really don't want to be late **for** work.
⑧ My mother is very afraid **of** heights.
⑨ What is the long-term effect **of** this?

34.5 🔊
① I'm so **bored with** their constant fighting about policies.
② They've **made** a new app **for** children to learn about the Earth.

③ Do you have any **objection to** this environmental policy?
④ I often **worry about** the future of our planet.
⑤ You need to **apologize to** them **for** the things you said.
⑥ Do you think a policy like this is **suitable for** a country like ours?

34.7 🔊
① What do **you** think of the new statistics in this report?
② These carbon emissions **are** extremely harmful to the environment.
③ It is very important that we think of our children's **futures**.
④ We **need** to find solutions sooner rather than later.

34.8
What are the environmental **consequences** of urbanization on such a massive scale? One major effect of urbanization is the creation of "urban heat islands." Rural areas can remain cooler **due to** the sun evaporating the moisture from the vegetation and the soil. However, in the cities there is much less soil and vegetation. **Consequently**, the sun beating on the buildings and roads **leads** to an increase in temperatures. Additional heat from vehicles, factories, and cooling units also increases temperatures. This heat then **causes** changes in local weather patterns.
Not only is there increased air pollution, but also higher levels of rainfall, **resulting** in flooding within the cities themselves and also downstream. Another **consequence** of urbanization is the increased consumption of food, energy, and durable goods. This has a far-reaching **impact** on levels of natural resources.

35

35.4 🔊
① I'm afraid we have **little** time to catch the train. We must hurry.
② That cake is delicious. I'll have **a little** bit more.
③ Sadly, there are **few** examples of this quality craftmanship left.
④ Great! We have **a little** spare money. Should we go out for dinner?
⑤ Wow! Look at all these monkeys! I think there are **a few** different species here.
⑥ Unfortunately, I have **few** friends. It's quite lonely here.

35.5 🔊
① Great! There are **a few** magazines to choose from.
② Sadly, there are **few** fish in my aquarium.
③ There is very **little** cake left, I'm afraid.
④ It should be OK. We have **a little** time left.
⑤ The café is closing soon. There are so **few** customers.

35.7
Ninety-year-old Ken Wilson has finally decided to have **a little** time off after volunteering at his local wildlife park for 30 years. Ken started volunteering **a few** years after he retired from teaching. He says, "I started making coffee for people in the little visitor center, but I've had quite **a few** different roles since then."
Ken has been a guide, he's surveyed butterflies, and he even managed to get his hands dirty quite **a few** times clearing litter. What does he like so much about the park? "Well, there are **few** green places left like this in big cities. For **little** or no money, a family can explore all day and learn **a little** about local wildlife. It's **a little** bit of calm in a busy world."
What will he do now? "I'd like quite **a few** days sitting in the park doing nothing." After three decades looking after the wildlife, it's time for Ken to take **a little** break.

35.10 🔊
① Protesters have demanded fewer **harmful emissions by 2025.**
② The charity has fewer **volunteers than last year.**
③ The new light bulbs use far less **electricity than the old ones.**
④ Unsurprisingly, there is much less **wildlife near big factory sites.**
⑤ Since the new traffic laws, there is a lot less **pollution in the capital city.**

35.13
① False ② True ③ False ④ False
⑤ True ⑥ False

35.14 🔊
① Rachel also had the help of **a few** friends during her campaign.
② Rachel knew that **quite a few** people held the same opinion as her.
③ The area is home to **more than** 500 plant and animal species.
④ The photography exhibition raised $25,000 in **less than** a week.
⑤ **Quite a few** people sent messages of support via social media sites.
⑥ Making Lake Lucid a popular tourist site will only take **a few** years.

37.2 🔊
1 It was raining, so I **could not** have gone sunbathing even if I had wanted to.
2 Look at him! Do you think he **might have** won the lottery?
3 If I had left the house a little earlier, I **might not** have missed the bus.
4 I don't know where she is. She **could have** gone for a run. She loves exercise.

37.3 Réponses modèles
1 At first she believed it, but now she thinks it couldn't have happened.
2 They were celebrating because they had just won a tournament.
3 They dressed it up in one of their golf jackets.
4 The kangaroo hit one of the golfers on the nose.
5 They couldn't continue driving home because the car keys were in the jacket the kangaroo was wearing.

37.5 🔊
1 Amal mentioned **that she was reading a scary story.**
2 Amal told me **that she had finished the book.**
3 I asked her **if / whether she was going to the movies.**
4 I asked her **what kind of movie she was going to see.**
5 I asked her **if / whether she enjoyed it.**

37.6
1 True 2 False 3 True 4 Not given
5 False

37.7 🔊
1 I was so angry that I just **saw red** and shouted.
2 The poor dog had been left in the cold and was a very **sorry sight**.
3 The watch looked genuine **at first sight**, but it wasn't.
4 I'll just have to **wait and see** about my English test results.

38.2 🔊
1 He's walking with crutches. **He must have hurt his legs.**
2 Those teenagers look very tired today. **They may have had a party last night.**
3 The plants are all dry and dead. **It can't have rained all week.**
4 Someone's left the gate open again. **It could have been the delivery man.**
5 The girl next door looks really happy. **She might have passed her exam.**

38.3 🔊
1 The ground is dry so it **can't have** rained last night.
2 She ate two more slices of cake, so it **must have** tasted nice.
3 A police car just drove past. There **might have been** a robbery.
4 He doesn't have any money. He **can't have** bought that car himself.
5 They were in the same store as us. They **might have bought** the same coat.

38.4 🔊
1 I missed a call. It **may** have been Diego, he said he might call.
2 I haven't checked my emails yet, so she **might** have replied already, I'm not sure.
3 After the run, he drank a whole bottle of water. He **must** have been really thirsty.
4 She loved both dresses, but she **can't** have bought both, as they were too expensive.
5 She hadn't slept for two days. She **must** have been exhausted.

38.5 🔊
1 She must have **passed her driving test.**
2 He must have **slept through his alarm.**
3 They must have **failed their exams.**
4 She must have **eaten too much candy.**
5 He must have **won the lottery**.

38.6
3

38.7 🔊
1 Every month my company **sends out** a newsletter to all its customers.
2 Every time my sister sees a spider, she **freaks out** and starts screaming.
3 Should we go to the movie theater and **check out** what's showing?
4 He isn't like anyone else. He really **stands out** from the crowd.

5 I can't **work out** what this guy's written. His handwriting is awful.

38.8
1 False 2 False 3 True 4 True

39.3 🔊
1 You wouldn't be such a success today **if you hadn't worked so hard at school.**
2 If my alarm had gone off, **I wouldn't be in trouble for being late.**
3 She might not be such a celebrity **if she hadn't had famous parents.**
4 He would be playing today **if he hadn't broken his leg yesterday.**
5 If you had spent less money, **you wouldn't have such great tickets.**
6 If I had given up trying, **I wouldn't be managing the business today.**
7 If we had eaten breakfast, **we might not be so hungry now.**

39.4 🔊
1 If Clara **had not stayed** up so late, she might not be so tired now.
2 She might not be a famous actress today if she **had not gone** to that first audition.
3 If he **had kept playing** the guitar, he would be in a famous band by now.
4 If Juan **had listened** to all his critics, he would not be a world-famous chef today.
5 He would not be playing for a premier team if he **had not trained** every day.
6 If she **had said** "yes" to your proposal, you could be married by now.
7 They would not be so confident if they **had seen** their team training yesterday.

39.5
1 False 2 True 3 True 4 False 5 False

39.6 🔊
1 You need **reliable** staff who turn up on time and do their work.
2 He's so **courageous**. He just jumped into the fire to save the kitten.
3 My husband is really **sensitive**. He even cries during romantic films.
4 If he hadn't been so violent and **quick-tempered**, he would not be in jail today.
5 If she hadn't been so **determined**, she might not be such a successful singer.
6 Jane is very **practical**. She can fix the car and put up shelves.

39.7 Réponses modèles

1. Diane would definitely change her plans because of her horoscope's advice.
2. Diane thinks she's a typical Scorpio because she's quite passionate about things.
3. Richard thinks that the things a horoscope says will happen to most people on most days.
4. He says it's not surprising that people who believe in horoscopes often think they're correct.

40

40.2 ◄))

1. Buy red or green peppers, **whichever** is the cheapest.
2. She moves every few years to **wherever** her company asks her to go.
3. I love going to concerts and watching live music, **whoever** is playing.
4. My mother never likes my brother's girlfriends, **however** nice they are.
5. The company director visits our office **whenever** she's in town.
6. The competition winner deserves praise, **whoever** they are.
7. The company is in a difficult situation, **whichever** way you look at it.

40.3 ◄))

1. She's an excellent cook. I'm sure **whichever** cake I choose will be delicious.
2. Sometimes I just can't start my car **whatever** I do. It's really frustrating.
3. I don't think I'll ever be a good long-distance runner, **however** hard I try.
4. During the winter months, we can visit the castle for free **whenever** we want.
5. I will give my full support to the next head chef, **whoever** it is.

40.4 Réponses modèles

1. It was a surprise because Matt had forgotten he'd even entered the competition.
2. His sister wasn't happy because she's always trying to steal Matt's thunder.
3. She said that she couldn't do it because she had the flu.
4. He did the bungee jump off a canal bridge.
5. He's planning to do a sky dive next year.

40.5 ◄))

1. She seems to be on cloud nine this morning.
2. Go on. Throw caution to the wind.
3. Perhaps you should take a rain check.
4. You're constantly trying to steal my thunder.
5. Wow! That's a bolt from the blue.
6. The party's happening come rain or shine.

42

42.2 ◄))

1. There are thought to be more than **6000 languages in the world.**
2. Maria Callas is believed by many **to have been the most talented singer ever.**
3. The escaped criminal is not thought **to be a dangerous threat to society.**
4. It is hoped **that many new jobs will be created.**
5. The damage is expected **to cost more than $50,000 to repair.**

42.5 ◄))

1. I'm so sorry! You should **have been** introduced to each other earlier this evening.
2. Thirty people are expected to **be** awarded top prizes at the ceremony later.
3. It would help if the school children could **be given** different instruments to try.
4. It's been a strange tournament, and there **are** thought to be more surprises to come.

42.6 ◄))

1. The hosts **should have been thanked (by somebody) before we left.**
2. It has **been reported that 20 people were injured in the stampede.**
3. Pelé is **thought to be the best soccer player ever (by many people).**

42.7 ◄))

1. It has been announced that the Cup **has been won by the youth team.**
2. Many homes are said **to have been destroyed by the tornado.**
3. This celebrity couple are reported **to have married in Paris.**

42.8

Bank robber Mark Thomas is **spending** the night in jail before going to court to be **sentenced** tomorrow.
Last June, Mr. Thomas, dressed in a mask and hat and armed with a knife, demanded $10,000 from the cashier of a local bank. He was **given** the money, but at this point Mr. Thomas' planning skills must be **questioned**. Instead of escaping the area, Mr. Thomas took off his hat and mask and walked into the bank next door. He tried to deposit the money and gave the cashiers his full name, address, and bank details. Fortunately, the police had been **called** by the original bank and Mr. Thomas was quickly **arrested**.
He is understood to have been **planning** the robbery for many months. He stated that he had been **saving** for a vacation, but it was taking too long to raise enough money. It is **predicted** that he will given a lengthy sentence, so he will have to wait even longer for his trip abroad.

43

43.2 ◄))

1. There are **approximately** five hundred employees in this factory.
2. These new figures **indicate** a downward trend in sales.
3. The director **allegedly** took all of the money from the company.
4. This kind of market behavior **suggests** an underlying problem.
5. **It has been said** by some that her opinions are controversial.
6. **It looks like** they are not enjoying the film very much.
7. Academics **tend** to use hedging language if something is not proven.

43.4 ◄))

1. It **appears** that two prisoners have escaped from the police station.
2. I don't trust her. I think it **looks like** she is guilty of both crimes.
3. They **seem** to have found more important evidence to support their case.
4. I **believe** that the police have made a mistake and arrested the wrong man.
5. I don't know, but it would **appear** that he stole the car when the owner was inside.
6. With a huge number of hit records, the Beatles are **arguably** the best band ever.
7. After a difficult year, all our figures **indicate** that sales are finally improving.
8. It's too soon to judge. He **probably** committed the crime, but we're not sure.
9. We used to go to Spain a lot. Sometimes we drove there, but we **often** flew.

43.5 ◄))

ADVERBS: **arguably, apparently, approximately, often, probably**
VERBS: **suggest, tend, assume, believe, indicate**
PHRASES: **it looks like, it seems that, it could be said that, to some extent, it would appear that**

43.6
1 False 2 True 3 True 4 True
5 False

43.7 🔊
1 An online video **apparently** shows her pet cat, Mini, protecting her.
2 **It would appear** that the snake was frightened away by Mini.
3 Interviews with neighbors **indicate** that the snake had been seen on other properties.
4 A local animal charity **suggested** that it would be unusual for such a snake to attack.
5 The charity said that these snakes **tend** to be extremely shy.
6 They also stated that **often** these kinds of snakes are pets that have escaped.

44

44.3 🔊
1 Little **did he** know that someone had already invented the same thing.
2 Only after living there for two weeks **did they** notice the smell.
3 Not **until** we spoke to the manager did the company admit their mistake.
4 Not since the children were little **had we** been on such a fun day out.
5 Only **when** she won the award did people start taking her writing seriously.

44.4 🔊
1 **Only** if the company invests more money can the project be completed.
2 **Not** until the wedding day did the groom see the bride's dress.
3 Little did they **realize** that the weather would be absolutely terrible for the festival.
4 Not **until** the final encore did the audience begin to leave their seats at the concert.
5 Only **when** she was paying for the album did she realize she already owned it.
6 Not **only** will you be famous, but you will also be rich beyond your wildest dreams.
7 Only **after** she got home from the party did she notice how late it was.

44.7 🔊
1 Only when he was at home did he feel safe.
2 Hardly had he walked on stage when the fans chanted his name.
3 No sooner had they become the number one band than they split up.
4 Never before had anyone seen so many fans in one place.

44.8
1 False 2 True 3 True 4 True

44.9 🔊
1 No sooner had the rain stopped than it began to snow.
2 Only when she heard his voice did she recognize him.
3 Not only is this car fast, but it's also affordable!
4 Only if you help me will I finish on time.

45

45.3 🔊
1 What I would really appreciate is **some legal advice.**
2 What we really need are **more volunteers to help during the week.**
3 What I love about this city is **the nightlife and the culture.**
4 What businesses really hate is **when people leave bad reviews online.**

45.5 🔊
1 The **justification** she gave for being late for work was not good enough.
2 The **period** in history that fascinates me most is the Jurassic period.
3 A **natural wonder** that we'd really love to visit is Ha Long Bay in Vietnam.
4 One **moment** I'll never forget is when my first grandchild was born.
5 The **thing** I don't understand is why the instructions are so complicated.

45.8 🔊
1 Actually, **the place** I most want to visit **is** Istanbul.
2 Actually, **it was** a while ago **that / when** I started.
3 No, **the person** I most admire **is** Albert Einstein.

45.9
1 True 2 True 3 False 4 False
5 True

47

47.2
1 Subject 2 Subject 3 Object
4 Object 5 Subject 6 Subject
7 Object

47.5 🔊
1 Those children are the ones who want to be detectives.
2 That computer is the one that was stolen.
3 This is the officer who arrested the criminal.
4 A cybercriminal is a person who acts illegally online.
5 That is the phone that I use to make video calls.

47.8 🔊
1 The violent criminals were not sent to jail, which surprised the victim.
2 Detective Smith, who arrested the fraudster, works in a special department.
3 Vivian Jones, who had worked for the bank for 10 years, was arrested yesterday.

47.9
1 On a few street corners
2 Help to clear up the trash
3 They ought to spend a night in a police cell.
4 Other places should be built for them.

47.10
1 True 2 False 3 False 4 Not given

48

48.2 🔊
1 Courtrooms are places **where** lawyers argue their cases in front of a judge.
2 Thursday is the night **when** we usually go to the movies.
3 Sentencing is the legal process **whereby** a judge decides the punishment.
4 Morning coffee break is the time **when** we gossip most.
5 A police station is the place **where** most criminals are taken at first.

48.3 🔊
1 The camera's timer let the police know the exact time **when the robbery took place**.
2 They have developed a system **whereby prisoners can prepare** for life outside jail.
3 Do you know the date **when the suspect** goes to court?
4 This is the café **where the prisoners cook** great food for the public.
5 Conveyancing is a process **whereby one person sells property** to another.
6 I remember the day **when my sister decided** to become a lawyer.
7 This cell is the place **where the suspects** are held until a verdict is reached.

48.4
1 True 2 False 3 Not given 4 False
5 True 6 True 7 True

48.7 🔊
1 Rodrigo, **whose training regime is rigorous**, deserves to be successful.
2 My sister, **whose first book was a huge success**, has become very famous.
3 My neighbor Sara, **whose dogs always win competitions**, loves training dogs.
4 That company, **whose employees work very hard**, has excellent trading figures.
5 That school, **whose students always do well in exams**, is very well respected.

48.8 Réponses modèles
1 They saw him on security video footage outside the burgled premises.
2 Hockly couldn't remember his full name or where he lived.
3 They were shown videos of him driving a car.
4 He said someone asked him to help carry them.

49

49.2 🔊
1 Unfortunately, he **won't be able to** pay his parking fines.
2 **Will you be able to** install a security camera in the store?
3 I **won't be able to** understand all these legal regulations.
4 Hopefully, my sister **will be able to** explain it all to me. She's a lawyer.

49.4 🔊
1 You will have to work longer hours soon.
2 Tomorrow, you won't be able to park here.
3 Will the police be able to arrest them?
4 I will have to call the police.
5 Will they be able to enforce the new law?

49.5 Réponses modèles
1 They've already been introduced in shopping malls in Chongqing, Antwerp, and Liverpool.
2 Young shoppers are particularly frustrated by slower shoppers.
3 They are concerned that these shoppers might start shopping online instead.
4 They might find it difficult to enforce the new rules effectively.
5 Some people strayed into the wrong lane because they were distracted by their phones.

49.6
A new law has just been **passed** by the government. This new law **permits** members of the public to walk on farmers' land. Walkers will have to **observe** reasonable rules set by the landowners. If they **break** these rules, they could be **banned** from walking in the area or they could even be **arrested**. Some farmers, however, think that the police will not be able to **enforce** the law.

49.7 🔊
1 pass 2 observe 3 break
4 enforce 5 arrest 6 permit

50

50.2 🔊
1 I appreciate that it's difficult, but I think you **should** talk to him about it.
2 Finally, after months of studying, I **can** read music.
3 I'm sorry, but I'm terribly busy at the moment, Mr. Jones. **Would** tomorrow be okay?
4 I followed the recipe, so it **ought** to taste great, but sometimes it doesn't.
5 I've tried really hard, but I just **can't** make these figures add up.
6 I'm feeling very unwell. **May** I be excused?

50.3 🔊
1 It's very hot in here. **Would** you open a window, please?
2 This coffee has sugar in it! It **must** be yours.
3 I don't know when the movie will finish. It **might** not be until after 10pm.
4 **Shall** I help you carry those dishes to the kitchen?
5 My lawnmower has broken. **Could** I borrow yours, please?
6 I **can't** swim very well at all, but my sister is an excellent swimmer.

50.4 🔊
1 She was was the lead singer in the band because she **could** sing very well.
2 **Would you** pick me up from work this evening, please?
3 The tree looks like it **may fall** down soon.
4 If she doesn't study hard enough, she **might not** get into medical school.

50.5
1 False 2 True 3 False 4 False

50.6
1 Family homes
2 Leave them standing in rice
3 It was really interesting

52

52.3 🔊
1 The Swiss 2 Brazilians 3 The Swedish
4 Indians 5 The French
6 Koreans 7 Kenyans

52.6 🔊
1 The **homeless** are often without a house as a result of some very bad luck.
2 Often, the **young** are described as being addicted to gadgets and phones.
3 The **rich** often give lots of money to charity, but we don't know about it.
4 Many countries have laws to ensure that the **disabled** can access public transportation.
5 After the accident, the **injured** were all taken to a nearby hospital.
6 The **elderly** have often cared for others all their lives and deserve care in return.

52.7
1 False 2 False 3 False 4 True
5 False 6 True 7 True

52.8
1 B 2 F 3 C 4 D 5 A 6 E

52.9 🔊 Réponses modèles
1 The unemployed **are given financial support until they find a new job.**
2 The elderly **are respected and seen as an important part of society.**
3 The young **are often depicted as selfish, which I think is incorrect.**

53

53.3 🔊
1 My parents **are** used to living in an old building, but the creaking floorboards scare me!
2 They **were** used to eating with chopsticks, but it was new to me. I found it hard!

③ My friend said I'd **get** used to eating my dinner later at night after a few weeks.

④ It took a while, but now I **am** used to recycling all my paper and plastic each week.

⑤ His friends found it strange, but he **was** used to doing things without using the computer.

⑥ It was difficult at first, but I **got** used to the new routine after a few months.

⑦ We **were** used to the old system at work, but then it changed completely.

⑧ Eventually I **got** used to answering the phone in English. It almost feels natural now!

53.4 🔊
① I don't think I will ever **get** used to the noise in my street at night.

② I'm so used **to** drinking coffee every morning that I can't function without it.

③ They said that they could not **get** used to the icy weather.

④ Don't worry. After a while you'll **get** used to the cold water.

⑤ Do you think that you'll **get** used to the long hours in your new job?

53.6
When I was living abroad, I used to **go out** a lot so that I could meet people and make friends. Even though I was nervous, I used to **agree** to any offer people made to try something new. Also, I didn't **force** things to fit around my old routines, but got used to **doing** things in line with local customs instead. These were quite unusual at first, but I **am** used to them now. The staff in my local café are used to me **making** mistakes when I talk, but they always appreciate the effort and help me.

53.7 🔊
① Be sure to experiment and try not **to only do things you used to do at home.**

② Visit the country before you move **to start getting used to the culture.**

③ Ask other people from abroad how **they got used to the different culture.**

④ Don't worry if things aren't what **you're used to. That's the adventure!**

⑤ Trying activities in your new country **is a great way to get to know new people.**

53.8
① Her salary and when she will have children

② Lunches lasting a long time

③ She stayed overnight with a friend

④ An old lady helped Julie cross the road

53.9 🔊
① Not any more. I**'m used to** it now.

② It's tradition! We**'re used to** doing it.

③ It was at first, but now I**'m used to** them.

④ No, it took me many years to **get used to** it.

54

54.3 🔊
① I want to visit **a** really modern city like Tokyo.

② I've always wanted to go up **the** Empire State Building.

③ Should we go to **the** restaurant we ate at on Friday?

④ Did you ride on **a** gondola in Venice?

54.5 🔊
① Have you ever been on **a** guided tour of Rio de Janeiro?

② The Christ the Redeemer statue in Rio de Janeiro is **the** largest statue of its type.

③ **Soccer** is a hugely popular sport in Rio and Brazil in general.

④ There is **a** famous lagoon in central Rio called Lagoa Rodrigo de Freitas.

54.6
The Republic of Costa Rica in Central America has **an** estimated population of just under 5 million people and one of **the** highest life expectancy levels in the West. Its incredible beauty and the diverse nature of the flora and fauna in its rainforests make **[-]** Costa Rica a top destination for tourists. Indeed, tourism is **the** country's number one source of foreign exchange. As well as famous cash crops like bananas and coffee, Costa Rica boasts 1,000 species of orchids and **a** huge number of bird species. In fairly recent years, Costa Rica has tried to cut down its reliance on the income produced by the export of coffee beans, bananas, and beef by becoming **a** producer of **[-]** microchips. Unfortunately, **the** microchip market has turned out to be as unstable as that for cash crops.

54.7
① True ② False ③ True ④ False
⑤ True

54.8 🔊
① occasionally ② changeable ③ weird
④ foreigner ⑤ separate ⑥ height

54.10 🔊
① I dou**b**t we will ever see them again.

② To be **h**onest, the plum**b**ing here is unusual.

③ Can you **k**nock on my door in an **h**our?

④ I **k**now you want to watch the final performance.

55

55.3 🔊
CONCRETE NOUNS: **computer**, **building**, **professor**, **sun**, **clock**, **artist**, **library**, **photograph**
ABSTRACT NOUNS: **relaxation**, **pride**, **misery**, **hate**, **beauty**, **anger**, **heat**, **trouble**

55.5 🔊
① She was deep in **thought** so we did not disturb her.

② In college you can meet people from many different **cultures**.

③ My father formed many lasting **friendships** in college.

④ This house is amazing. There are so many interesting **spaces**.

⑤ My brother does a lot of work for several local **charities**.

⑥ Apparently, this is the worst weather in living **memory**.

⑦ In these difficult times it's so important not to give up **hope**.

55.6
Australians have a lot of **pride** in their system of **education**. The system in Australia is quite hard to describe because it is largely controlled by the states or territories, rather than the federal **government**. Depending on where they live, students must go to school from five years old until 16 or 17 **years** old. There is also nursery level education, but this is not compulsory. After secondary school, students have a number of options to develop their **abilities**. They can choose to undertake vocational education and training (VET) by taking a **course** in a subject such as computer programming, engineering, or tourism, where they also learn key workplace **skills**. Alternatively, young people can apply to go into higher education or, of course, look for work. Generally, the system in Australia is recognized as being a **success**.

55.7
① True ② False ③ Not given ④ False
⑤ False

55.8 ◀))

1 We had a training day to help us develop our customer service **skills**.
2 These products don't have any redeeming **qualities**. They are so cheaply built!
3 Your plan is not very sensible. It needs a bit more **thought**.
4 There are **times** when I wonder if I should have become a teacher.
5 Some of the applicants don't have enough **experience** for the job.

57

57.3 ◀))

1 That college seems really great. **I wish I could** go there.
2 We can't change their development plans, but we wish we **could**.
3 Sarah wishes her husband **would buy her** flowers more often.
4 My favorite band is coming to our city. I wish I **could go**!

57.4 ◀))

1 I wish you **wouldn't** criticize my clothes. I think I look fabulous!
2 My neighbor plays the trumpet all the time. I wish he **would** be a little quieter.
3 Mike's car always breaks down. He wishes he **could** afford a new one.
4 We work far too hard. I wish we **could** do this more often!

58

58.4 ◀))

Note : vous pouvez utiliser « won't » au lieu de « will not » dans les réponses suivantes.
1 In a few years' time, I think you **will be running** this place.
2 I suppose you **will be feeling** too tired to go out after work this evening.
3 Tomorrow evening, Jorge's band **will be performing** at a concert.
4 I guess she **will not be coming** to the office party if she doesn't like the boss.
5 Jane bought two tickets so I think she **will be bringing** a friend to the exhibition.
6 Meilin has already told me that she **will not be checking** her emails today.

58.5 ◀))

1 In a year's time, **I will be working in a new department.**

2 In 5 years' time, **I will be working at headquarters.**
3 In 10 years' time, **I will be managing head office.**
4 In 20 years' time, **I will be enjoying my retirement.**

58.8 ◀))

1 **Will you be leaving** soon?
2 **Will you be watching** all of those DVDs?
3 **Will the children be coming** too?
4 **Will you be eating** all of those cakes?
5 **Will you be going** to the store?

58.9 ◀))

1 **Will you be eating** all that popcorn on your own?
2 **Will you be getting** your hair cut any time soon?
3 **Will you be taking** the kids to school tomorrow?
4 **Will you be returning** your books to the library?
5 **Will you be cooking** some food later on?

58.10

1 False   2 False   3 True   4 True
5 True   6 False

58.12

1 Darren   2 Nobody   3 Kate   4 Darren
5 Nobody   6 Kate

58.13 ◀))

1 **She'll be reading** a book at home.
2 **She'll be shopping** with her friend.
3 **She'll be running** on the treadmill.

58.14   Réponses modèles

1 She thinks she'll be going on more holidays abroad.
2 No, he predicts he'll be working in the same job in the same office.
3 In five years' time, he hopes he'll be studying abroad.
4 In her short-term future, she's getting married.
5 She might be taking her oldest child there for the first time.

59

59.4 ◀))

1 By the end of the night, I **will have watched** all the films in the series.
2 You **will have experienced** so many different things by the time you return.

3 Dimitri **will have cycled** around the world by this time next year.
4 By next year, she **will have seen** all of her favorite bands live.
5 I hope he **will have cleaned** the car by the time he goes to the wedding.
6 Before I leave tonight, I **will have finished** all my work.

59.5 ◀))

1 By the time I'm 25, **I will have moved abroad.**
2 By the time I'm 30, **I will have started a business.**
3 By the time I'm 35, **I will have married someone.**
4 By the time I'm 60, **I will have retired.**

59.9

Dear Graham,
By now you will have **returned** from your honeymoon. I hope you had a great time! Don't forget that we're having a party for Jane on Saturday. She will have **been working** here for 20 years on Friday! I hope Frank will have **sent** you an email with all the details by the time you get this. I'll see you at the party. I hope you'll have **caught** up with all your work by then! Sian

59.10 ◀))

1 True   2 False   3 Not given   4 True

59.11

3

60

60.2 ◀))

1 David said that he **would** try to get me a ticket to the game, but he **didn't** manage to.
2 I **will** buy the movie on DVD. I thought I **would** see it at the movie theater, but I didn't.
3 Last year she thought she **would** be promoted, but she wasn't. Maybe next year she **will** be.
4 I **brought** all the food for the picnic because I knew that Tom **wouldn't** remember.
5 We knew that the concert **would** be amazing, so we **bought** really good tickets.
6 My brother promised that he **wouldn't** show anyone pictures of me when I **was** little.

60.4 ◀))

1 Vinesh was going to help me with the housework, but he went out.
2 He said he wasn't going to study until his tutor arrived.

282

③ I was going to cook him dinner, but he'd already done it.
④ Dave said he was going to bring his girlfriend, but he didn't.
⑤ He was going to apply to go to college, but he changed his mind.
⑥ We were going to take a taxi home, but there weren't any available.

60.6 ◄))
① Sarah **was planning** to take her children to the park on Tuesday.
② Peter **was** nervous because he **was meeting** his girlfriend's parents.
③ I **was planning** to go out that evening because my parents **were having** guests over.
④ We **couldn't** make it to the party on Friday because we **were visiting** some friends that day.
⑤ I **was planning** to book a vacation just after the New Year.

60.7
① B ② A ③ B

62

62.2 ◄))
① They wanted to see the band perform live, but now they can't [**see the band perform live**].
② He was fantastic in the television series and [**he was fantastic in**] the movie adaptation.
③ If you want to see a movie, we could go to the multiplex or [**we could go to**] the art house.
④ The reviews said that the acting was bad and [**the reviews said that**] the soundtrack was terrible.
⑤ The two lead actors did all the stunts and [**the two lead actors**] sang all the songs themselves.
⑥ I am quitting my job this week. I will call you later to explain why [**I am quitting my job this week**].

62.3
① True ② True ③ False ④ True ⑤ False

62.4 ◄))
① I knew that the family would turn out to be aliens. It was completely **predictable**.
② I was so deeply **moved** by the sad scenes that I cried for hours!
③ We loved the last film, but were bitterly **disappointed** by this one.
④ We waited too long! The ticket prices are now astronomically **high**.

⑤ The plot is shocking and the theme is **highly** controversial.
⑥ The government helped pay for the film. It was **heavily** subsidized.

62.5 ◄))
① I was planning to buy tickets for the show, but now I can't.
② The film had great special effects and a wonderful soundtrack.
③ He was chosen for the orchestra and played brilliantly.
④ This evening I'm going to have dinner and then watch a play.
⑤ They said that they would come to the launch party, but they haven't.
⑥ They should join in or not bother coming.

62.6 ◄))
① The actors were good, but **seemed uncomfortable on screen.**
② The performance starts at 8 and **ends just after midnight.**
③ You could buy a season ticket or **sign up for membership.**
④ The building is beautiful, but **doesn't have very good acoustics.**
⑤ The cast are all exhausted, but **very satisfied with the performance.**
⑥ The audience was very loud and **full of young children!**

62.8
1 ⓔ 2 ⓑ 3 ⓖ 4 ⓐ 5 ⓓ 6 ⓕ 7 ⓒ

63

63.2 ◄))
① The book with the long title is the **one** I wanted.
② The buildings in New York were taller than the **ones** in Paris.
③ If you still want a copy of that book, there are **some** over here.
④ If you need an umbrella, I can lend you **one**.
⑤ Have you seen her new sunglasses? The **ones** with the silver frames?

63.3 ◄))
① They bought me a signed copy, **but I already had one.**
② I think the most engrossing novels **are the ones about spies.**
③ If you want to join a book club, **make sure it's one with regular meetings.**
④ I know you want to buy a new car, **but the one we have is only a year old.**

⑤ If you need a plastic bag, **there are some in the box over there.**

63.4
Black Glasses is Martin Owens' fourth book in this series. Like the third book, this **one** is all about the brilliant detective Amanda Brook. Unlike the other **ones** in the series though, this time her personal life starts falling apart. Excellent plot as usual.
I have read some boring books in my time, but Sara Umborne's Pink Tree is the dullest **one** ever. Sadly, I can't tell you much about the book as I gave up after 20 pages.
Little Water Princess is a fabulous book for little children, or even older **ones**! There are few words, but the illustrations are beautiful. Lots of the pictures pop up, but **some** are 2D. A lovely gift idea.
There are endless books about cooking pasta, but How to Cook Pasta by Daniela Capril is the best **one** on the market today.

63.6 ◄))
① I didn't like it, but my friend did.
② Did you go to the show? We did, too.
③ You read a lot last month. I did, too.
④ Do I recycle? Yes, I do.
⑤ He works hard, but she doesn't.

63.7
① False ② True ③ False ④ True
⑤ False ⑥ False

63.10 ◄)) Réponses modèles
① I hope not. / I hope so.
② Jane Austen did.
③ I don't think so. / I think so.

64

64.2 ◄))
① I tried to contact Max about the concert tickets, but wasn't able to.
② My brother often forgets our dad's birthday, but this year he's promised not to.
③ Georgia was enjoying the performance. At least, she seemed to be.
④ Ian is going to the new nightclub, but I don't really want to.
⑤ The festival tickets cost a lot more than they used to.
⑥ I want to come with you, but I won't be able to.

64.4
1 True 2 True 3 True 4 False
5 False 6 False 7 True

64.7 🔊
1 I would like to read music, but it will be a long time until I'm **able** to.
2 Don't forget that it's supposed to rain tonight. Try to leave before it **starts**.
3 Some people aren't nervous about performing, but I'm too **afraid** to.
4 Some artists don't like to have family in the audience on the first night, but I **prefer** to.
5 It's such a shame. I would absolutely love to see him sing, but cannot **afford** to.
6 I've seen other artists who love talking to the audience, but I **hate** to.
7 You don't need to worry. I will come along to all of your recitals. I **promise**.

64.9 🔊
1 I asked him to come, but he didn't want to.
2 You can have one if you want.
3 You can stay, but I don't really want to.
4 If you're free to meet, I would still like to.
5 You can call me "Sam" if you want.

64.10 🔊
1 No, I decided not to.
2 Yes, I will try (to).
3 Yes, but I can't afford to.

65

65.2 🔊
1 These gardens are fabulous. Did you bring your camera, **by the way**?
2 Yes, but **as I was saying** before, I really think I could paint that myself.
3 No, I don't hate all modern art. I **actually** really like some street art.
4 **Anyway**, to get back to my question, would you pay two million dollars for that?
5 These paintings aren't the reason I come here. I **actually** prefer the architecture.

65.3 🔊
1 Aren't they? **By the way / Anyway**, where are we going for dinner?
2 Yes, but **as I was saying**, I'm getting really hungry.
3 We haven't, **actually**. There's another floor!
4 **Actually**, I'm really inspired. I love this landscape.
5 **Anyway**, we should head back to the car soon.

65.4
1 True 2 True 3 False 4 True
5 False 6 True

65.5 🔊
1 "Super-" as in "superhero" and "supernatural" **means "beyond."**
2 "Anti-" as in "antisocial" and "antibiotics" **means "against."**
3 "Pro-" as in "proactive" and "proceed" **means "for."**
4 "Neo-" as in "neoclassical" and "neoliberal" **means "new."**
5 "Post-" as in "postmodern" and "postwar" **means "after."**

65.6 🔊
1 Many children go to **pre**school before they are five years old.
2 My husband is 40 years old, but he still loves **super**hero comics and films.
3 A lot of the architecture here is **neo**classical and looks Roman.
4 I think that dropping litter in public is extremely **anti**social.
5 Before the ceremony began, we we told to wait in a small **ante**room.
6 Many 20th-century art movements have been called **post**modern.

66

66.4 🔊
1 Ahmed is getting his oven fixed.
2 Sally's having her nails painted.
3 Natasha got her photograph taken.
4 Gavin is cutting his hair.
5 Joe did the ironing at home.
6 Annie had some flowers delivered.
7 They're having their house painted.

66.5 🔊
1 I'm taking the car to **the garage to get it fixed**.
2 You should go to a salon **and have your hair cut**.
3 I don't want to cook. Should we **get a pizza delivered?**
4 They've just had their staff **trained to deal with malware**.
5 I'm going to have my computer **checked for malware. It's so slow.**
6 I took my daughter to the dentist **to get her teeth checked**.
7 They bought a dog and had **a deluxe kennel built for him**.

66.6 🔊
1 Remember, today we're **having** the bedroom carpets fitted.
2 Your coat is really filthy. **You should get it** dry-cleaned.
3 My eyes hurt when I read. I should **have** them tested soon.
4 My friend **had** his wallet stolen when he was in Barcelona.
5 I **have to get** my birth certificate translated into Spanish for my application.

66.7 🔊
1 No, **he gets / has it cleaned** by someone else.
2 The photographer's here. **She's getting / having her picture taken.**
3 Yes, but **I'm getting / having it fixed** on Monday.
4 The painter's coming. **We're getting / having the house painted.**
5 No, **I'm getting / having a pizza delivered.**
6 Yes, **I get / have my teeth checked** twice a year.
7 No, **we get / have it delivered** to the house.

67

67.2 🔊
1 The legal **department** in my office is the largest in the company.
2 Members of the **orchestra** are rehearsing in different rooms in the building.
3 The **government** is having an emergency meeting in New York.
4 The soccer **team** is arriving later this evening.
5 The entire **audience** was delighted by the guest performer last night.

67.5 🔊
1 I want to study economics.
2 Is athletics popular in your country?
3 *Cats* is a successful musical.
4 The Philippines is an island country.
5 Physics is my favorite subject.
6 *Hard Times* was written by Dickens.
7 The United States has nine time zones.

67.7 🔊
1 Neither her mother nor her father **was there to pick her up from school.**
2 Either a cat or a dog **is a great pet for a family.**
3 Either the diner or the coffee shop **is fine for our meeting.**

4 Neither the boss nor the workers **are happy with the announcement.**
5 We think that neither Tom nor Katya **has worked hard enough at school.**
6 Either the giraffes or the elephant **are the most popular animals in the park.**
7 Neither my car nor my motorbike **is safe to drive anymore.**

67.8
1 Not given
2 False
3 False
4 False
5 True
6 False
7 True

67.9 🔊
1 The school **is** getting new equipment for its technology department.
2 Computer studies **is** my favorite subject at college at the moment.
3 Neither the cable nor the batteries **are** included with the new digital radio.
4 The Bahamas **has** many beaches, including some with pink sand.
5 I don't know what's wrong with it! Either the engine or the fan **is** broken.

68

68.2 🔊
1 Even at the start of her career, she was **such** a well-respected scientist.
2 My brother fell off his bike this morning. The injury was **so** bad that we called a doctor.
3 Colds spread **so** fast between children, particularly in large groups.
4 I was hoping to get some positive news, but the test results were **such** a disappointment.
5 I'm pleased that he's **such** an experienced surgeon. It's very reassuring!

68.4 🔊
1 Dentistry is such a difficult job that **you have to train for many years.**
2 He recovered so rapidly that **he was soon able to walk again.**
3 She had such steady hands that **she could perform delicate operations.**
4 The medicine tasted so bad that **I nearly spat it all out!**
5 It is such a new treatment that **only a few patients have had it.**

68.7 🔊
1 Surgeons train hard, which is why they make **so** few mistakes.
2 I think these tablets work **so** much better than the others.
3 Doctors have to pass so **many** exams during their training.
4 Thank you, doctor. I feel **so much** better than I did last week.

68.8
Rats have a sense of smell that is **so** well developed that they can **detect** traces of TB in test **samples** given by humans. They signify when they smell TB by rubbing their legs together and are then given a treat through a syringe. There are a number of reasons why this is **such** an important breakthrough. First, the rats are able spot the **disease** in its early stages, which is so much better than testing later because then treatment can be started right away on any patients who have tested positive. TB is **treatable** if it is detected in its early stages. If left undetected, it can be **deadly**. Second, rats only take 30 minutes to test nearly 100 samples. This is so **much** more efficient than human laboratory **testing**, which can take up to four days to do the same number. Finally, using rats is so much cheaper than buying expensive devices and paying a lot of money per test. This is important because TB is still a global concern. The situation in Mozambique was so bad **that** TB was declared a national emergency in 2006. By 2014, 60,000 people were said, by the ministry of health, to be **infected**.

69

69.2 🔊
1 Apparently, **the** French horn is the most difficult instrument to play.
2 Alexander Graham Bell is often credited with inventing **the** telephone.
3 My sister has **a** saxophone that she plays in her school orchestra.
4 **The** blue whale is the largest animal that has ever lived on Earth.

69.4 🔊
1 I enjoy playing **the** piano, but I hated having lessons as a child.
2 Mountain **gorillas** are one of the most endangered species on Earth. / **The mountain gorilla is** one of the most endangered species on Earth.

3 In 2007 a Russian lawyer paid nearly $4 million for **a** violin.
4 **The sloth** is a slow animal, but the Galápagos tortoise is even slower.
5 Steve Wozniak designed and built **the** 1976 Apple I computer.
6 This concert is incredible. I love the sound of **the trumpet**. / This concert is incredible. I love the sound of **trumpets**.

69.6
The Space Race produced two truly iconic moments in **the** history of humankind. The first happened on April 12, 1961, when Yuri Gagarin became **the** first human in space. The entire Vostok 1 mission, including one orbit around Earth, lasted only 1 hour 29 minutes. Gagarin's voyage changed how people all over **the** world thought about **[-]** space.
Just over eight years later in July, 1969, **[-]** Neil Armstrong, "Buzz" Aldrin, and Michael Collins traveled to space in **the** Apollo 11 space craft. On July 20 1969, Armstrong stepped onto **the** Moon's dusty surface. What he actually said next is **an** interesting story in itself. For many years he argued that he said, "That's one small step for a man, one giant leap for mankind." After listening to repeated transmission recordings, however, he admitted that he accidentally dropped indefinite article "**a**." Either way, it was **a** huge step for mankind.

69.7
1 True **2** False **3** False **4** True
5 True **6** False **7** True

Index

Toutes les entrées sont indexées par numéro de chapitre.
Les entrées principales sont en **caractères gras**.

Remerciements

L'éditeur aimerait remercier : Jo Kent, Trish Burrow et Emma Watkins pour le texte supplémentaire ; Thomas Booth, Helen Fanthorpe, Helen Leech, Carrie Lewis et Vicky Richards pour leur assistance rédactionnelle ; Stephen Bere, Sarah Hilder, Amy Child et Fiona Macdonald pour le travail de conception supplémentaire ; Peter Chrisp pour la vérification des faits ; Penny Hands, Amanda Learmonth et Carrie Lewis pour la relecture ; Elizabeth Wise pour l'indexation ; Tatiana Boyko, Rory Farrell, Clare Joyce et Viola Wang pour les illustrations complémentaires ; Liz Hammond pour le montage des scripts et la gestion des enregistrements audio ; Hannah Bowen et Scarlett O'Hara pour la compilation des scripts audio ; George Flamouridis pour le mixage et le mastering des enregistrements audio ; Heather Hughes, Tommy Callan, Tom Morse, Gillian Reid et Sonia Charbonnier pour leur soutien créatif et technique ; Vishal Bhatia, Sachin Gupta, Nehal Verma, Jaileen Kaur, Shipra Jain, Roohi Rais, Nisha Shaw et Ankita Yadav pour leur aide technique.

DK tient à remercier les personnes suivantes qui ont aimablement autorisé l'utilisation de leurs photographies : 101 **Fotolia**: Maksym Dykha (en haut à droite). 111 **Alamy**: MBI (en bas à droite). 131 **Dorling Kindersley**: Malcolm Coulson (au centre droite).

Toutes les autres images sont la propriété de DK. Pour plus d'informations, rendez-vous sur **www.dkimages.com**.